The Peop... In Real Life

Melissa Ann Hopely

BRIGHTON PUBLISHING LLC
435 N. HARRIS DRIVE
MESA, ARIZONA 85203

THE PEOPLE YOU MEET IN REAL LIFE

MELISSA ANN HOPELY

BRIGHTON PUBLISHING LLC
435 N. HARRIS DRIVE
MESA, ARIZONA 85203
BRIGHTONPUBLISHING.COM

COPYRIGHT © 2013

ISBN 13: 978-1-62183-101-3
ISBN 10: 1-621-83101-9

PRINTED IN THE UNITED STATES OF AMERICA

First Edition

COVER DESIGN: TOM RODRIGUEZ

Dedication

To anyone who has ever felt alone and judged for being different and to all those who felt like their voices haven't been heard. May you see that you and your story matter and that hope does exist.

To the many people who have helped shape my journey in life:

Mary Beth Vogel, a close friend that become my hero.

Jane Bartsch, FM Station 99.5 WJBR's general manager who gave me a chance to share my story for the first time on radio (may you rest in peace).

Coach Fran Tacconelli, who always taught me to "fight the good fight" (may you rest in peace).

Inspirational speaker Wendi Fox, suicide prevention advocate Sally Spencer-Thomas, and mental health advocate Tracy B who believed in me and helped to guide me through my growth as a speaker and advocate.

Nathaniel Asselin, an inspiring friend (may you rest in peace).

Dr. Aaron T. Beck, founder of Cognitive Therapy who saved many lives through his work.

Dr. Martin Franklin, the doctor who never gave up on me.

Mrs. Koffler, my high school counselor.

Especially to: my family, my friends, and Richard Rice, the love of my life.

Melissa Ann Hopely

Table of Contents

ACKNOWLEDGEMENTS v

ENDORSEMENTS vi

FOREWORD — *Mariel Hemingway* vii

CHAPTER ONE — *We all have a "Something"* 1
Meet Carolyn Hislop; a young brain cancer survivor

CHAPTER TWO — *It Happens* 11
Meet Maggie Cardin; a young suicide prevention advocate

CHAPTER THREE — *How do we go on?* 17
Meet Kimberly Dorwart; a mother fighting for suicide prevention education in schools

CHAPTER FOUR — *Then and Now* 30
Meet speaker, author and advocate; Ross Szabo
Meet my childhood friend; Jessica

CHAPTER FIVE — *Is this the real me?* 39
Meet my; Aunt Judy

CHAPTER SIX — *You're never too young* 44
Meet an; inspiring sixth grader I spoke to
Meet my; grade school classmate

CHAPTER SEVEN — *Will anybody ever understand?* 53
Meet my mom; Diann

CHAPTER EIGHT — *Supposed to be the best years of your life* 61
Meet my high school classmate; Jennifer Cox
Meet; one of my high school's most popular girls

CHAPTER NINE — *Hitting rock bottom is really just landing on solid ground* 73
Meet Lafayette Kanard; a HIV awareness advocate

CHAPTER TEN — *You're not alone* *81*
Meet my friend, public speaker and advocate; Jordan Burnham

CHAPTER ELEVEN — *Does this now define me?* *87*
Meet my close college friend; who lost her younger brother to drug violence

CHAPTER TWELVE — *What would you do?* *91*
Meet my high school classmate Chuck; a bullying victim
Meet Kirk Smalley; an anti-bullying advocate and founder of Stand for the Silent

CHAPTER THIRTEEN — *Recovery and accepting help—"I could use somebody...kind of...maybe"* *100*
Meet my college soccer teammate Casey Kehoe; in recovery with an eating disorder

CHAPTER FOURTEEN — *Be that somebody* *107*
Meet my college friend and mental health advocate; Kristen East
Meet Alison Malmon; suicide prevention and mental health advocate and founder of Active Minds, Inc.
Meet my LA friend; Allison Bickleman; a mental health advocate

CHAPTER FIFTEEN — *Standing up and stepping out of your comfort zone* *119*
Meet my college friend; P-Track who lives with Asperger's Syndrome

CHAPTER SIXTEEN — *We affect one another—so pay it forward* *124*
Meet local musician; Jamall Anthony

CHAPTER SEVENTEEN — *New normal* *131*
Meet my college classmate Ryan Carson; an amputee survivor

CHAPTER EIGHTEEN — *There is no place like home* *142*
Meet Steve O'Neill; my brother's friend, an advocate against domestic abuse

CHAPTER NINETEEN — *Forgiveness* *150*
Meet my college friend Josh Evans; a gay rights activist

CHAPTER TWENTY — *Fear of Failure* *158*
Meet Justin; my musician friend

CHAPTER TWENTY-ONE — *Heroes*................................. *167*
Meet Megan; from Texas
Meet Brandon; a United States Marine

CHAPTER TWENTY-TWO — *Leaving a mark on the world*............. *176*
Meet college student and advocate; Erin Casey
Meet NBC 10 News anchor; Lori Wilson

CHAPTER TWENTY-THREE — *There's got to be a reason*............. *189*
Meet Nathaniel's father, Denis Asselin; a mental health advocate

CHAPTER TWENTY-FOUR — *Believe it or not*................................. *197*
Meet actress; Nicole Ansari

CHAPTER TWENTY-FIVE — *Say what you need to say*.................. *204*

PHOTO ALBUM *216*

ABOUT MELISSA ANN HOPELY...................................... *221*

RESOURCES AND HELP *223*

Acknowledgements

I would like to thank all those who shared their amazing, resilient stories in this book. Meeting you was no accident, it was fate and a chance for us to unite and help others realize they too matter and that hope does exist. I could not have done this without you.

I would like to thank my boyfriend Rich, my family and my friends for their continued love and support throughout my life and with my work and mission to help others.

I would to thank Minding Your Mind Foundation for trusting me to speak with your free speaking program that is saving many young adult lives all across the nation. I would also like to thank all volunteers and non-profits working to make a difference in the lives of others. Kirk Smalley, thank you for sharing Ty's story and allowing me to unite with you and Stand for the Silent in the fight to end bullying.

I would like to thank my literary agent Anita Melograna, her brother radio host Vince Melograna (who introduced us) and Brighton Publishing for making this dream a reality.

I also want to thank all the youth for their continued support and willingness to pay it forward and help their peers.

For all those I have missed, please forgive me, but thank you for your support, because without any of you my work would not be possible.

Stay #hopestrong everyone!

Endorsements

"Thousands of individuals suffer from depression, mental health issues and low self-esteem. As a society, we need to end the stigma around mental health issues and encourage individuals who are struggling to open up, be brave and seek help. The People You Meet in Real Life is a great jumping off point to start a larger conversation on these timely and critical issues."

~ *Mayor Michael A. Nutter, City of Philadelphia*

"Melissa impressed me with her willingness to be completely vulnerable, so that others might know they are not alone, and that there is victory on the other side of tough times."

"Melissa cares about others, and is focused in her resolve to make sure to share her story, so those who have been bullied know they are not alone. Even at a young age, she is determined to teach her peers, that there is hope on the other side."

~ *Lori Wilson, former NBC 10 news anchor and current WISHTV8 Indianapolis new anchor*

"This book is a safe place to heal, and in safety, we grow in understanding of who we are. I simply believe that we all have a similar story, and that they all come with different wrapping paper."

~ *Mariel Hemingway,*
Actress, Author, Health and Wellness Expert, and Mother.

Foreword

by

MARIEL HEMINGWAY

Actress, Author, Health and Wellness Expert, and Mother

For me life is about the connections you make and the people you meet along the way and of course the relationships you create from the people you most admire or that inspire you. There have been so many people in my life that have shown me about me. Sometimes there is someone that simply has the ability to remind me how connected and all knowing I already am.

I have spent a lot of my past trying to define myself through others people's eyes because at that time I couldn't see my own value. I longed for the approval of others and defined myself through their perception of me. It took me time to embrace my true nature.

I know from experience that until we have built confidence in ourselves we look to our friends, our teachers our tribe to steer us towards our authentic selves when we can't find our self-esteem until it is simply a fact we can no longer deny. There is nothing more powerful than our own knowing and that comes from our experience and the real life examples of feeling our own strength. It is our truthful and conscious experience that reveals you to YOU. The gurus teachers guides and in my case diets programs and plans I have followed over the years have ironically lead me right back to myself. And the people that most helped me along the way are the people that served as mirrors to me. They reflected an energy of myself that I was able to comprehend and apply to my philosophy of life.

Melissa is a young woman who came into my life during a speaking engagement; she had a spark of light, she heard me share my experience and was able to reflect back to me the effect that my life is having on some who can hear me. She listened to me and she helped me to see the parts of myself that I had not yet fully embraced: a woman with a strong intuition a universal story and one who knows at a deep level that her (my) experience is meaningful for others. I share my story often in groups and now after my meeting Melissa I can say that my life can more deeply be expressed as a way to open doors hearts and patterns for others to share and heal in their own time. Melissa saw me and in turn I see her.

She has a passion to share her life, her enthusiasm and her own experience as a way to empower uplift and inspire others to see the relationships that we have in life as a way to learn. She knows all of our pasts have huge merit as part of our journeys and that we all need to embrace our "stories" in order to get past them. She uses her story as a teaching tool to inspire others to get beyond their past and live today, in the present moment conscious of one thing alone and that is being here. How one walks into the world as ourselves with integrity honesty and truth is the only path that truly makes sense and Melissa reflects that. She knows how to inspire others to see and ignite their compassion and success.

Melissa tells the story of her life like I tell the story of my family the "Hemingways" a creative, powerful and wrought with mental illness, cancer heart disease and most of all addiction because when I tell it it gives others permission to share their pain. This book is a safe place to heal and in safety, we grow in understanding of who we are. I simply believe that we all have a similar story and that they all come with different wrapping paper.

When others realize as Melissa does that we all share mutual turmoil of some kind then we have compassion for one another and of course, most importantly, we have compassion for ourselves. The greatest gift we can give ourselves is the gift of forgiveness and a day when we can say "I love me." It has taken me many years to be able to honestly make that statement aloud and mean it and it is a gift that rings with joy. I am thrilled to see the spirit of a woman like Melissa so young and yet so solidly on her path of authentic self-acceptance. Because of that, she can help so many with her words her actions and her intent. Thank you Melissa for making space for your peers to be free of their darkness, their shadows by making it okay to talk about their life.

Chapter One

We all have a "Something"

D id you ever take a second to notice the people around you? Maybe wondering what their story is?

Whether it is the man with the huge, contagious smile who picks up trash in his community every Sunday or the student in your class, who always seems so quiet, lonely, and sad, did that thought ever cross your mind?

There are over seven billion people in this world, all different in looks, age, race, experiences, beliefs, and stories. As I look around and question if things are mostly black and white, I can only wonder what it would be like if we were all exactly the same, having the same clothes, the same personality, the same struggles, the same triumphs, the same goals. Would there be less hate? More acceptance? More love? Maybe that's a possibility, but I then quickly realize how boring and one-dimensional our world would be.

There are so many worldly challenges like bullying, stress, divorce, questioning sexuality, cancer, negative coping, STDs, forgiveness, addiction, mental health, and many more. Sometimes it seems like people are afraid to bring these things to light due to fear of embarrassment, judgment, or being alone in their battles. It's like we fear being judged for being unique and different, but then fear being scolded when we follow the leader.

I get that you can't please everyone, but doesn't everyone have a "something" or a story? The truth is, whether you're a homeless man living on the street, a middle-class college student building his or her future, or a celebrity looking completely perfect on the red carpet, we all have a real story and should have the chance to be ourselves without fear of judgment from others.

The fact that we are judged, mistreated, and bullied for

1

uniqueness, which is actually what we all have in common, completely confuses me. The freedom to be different allows our world to be filled with so many diversities, abilities, dreams, triumphs, and most of all inspiration. Uniqueness led to our inventions, creations, world records, and accomplishments, so why is it so frowned upon for someone to be himself or herself at times—just a real, unique, genuine person we have the great pleasure of meeting in this lifetime?

Throughout my life, I've always had these questions cycling in my head: "Am I alone?" "Does my story really matter?" "Am I the only one going through this?" "Will I ever be important in this world?"

As time went on and I started meeting many different people, my eyes opened and I saw the world in a different light. Even though I was still struggling with my own self-worth, I started realizing that every single person I passed in my journey—whether I was on the subway visiting New York City, on a plane headed to a speaking engagement, at a sports field, at the beach, or even shopping in the local market, had a story and a unique purpose in life.

I always look around at people and wonder who they are, what they did or do or will go through, what they like, what their goals are, and what things make them the person they are. Will they ever be famous or homeless or will they invent something? All in all, what's their story? It's not me judging them, but literally trying to open my eyes and say to myself, "How can I make their day just a little bit better and let them know they do matter and are not alone?"

I didn't always think like this, but after finally realizing that my own struggles didn't define me and that I had a gift to share my story to let others know they weren't alone, life made more sense to me. I began to understand that, with each person I met, there was a true opportunity to learn lessons, become inspired, and gain a much better perspective and respect for others. The lessons and inspirations weren't always perfectly clear; every interaction with someone or something wasn't always positive; but for those that were, I knew I had to share them with the world somehow.

Unfortunately, sometimes when we meet strangers we immediately judge them by their looks, demeanor, sexuality, and manners. Without even knowing them, we totally ignore any possibility that the person may have challenges or may have contributed positively to mankind. Without getting all the facts about someone or something, we make assumptions at times and spread information that isn't always accurate.

I can attest to this through my own experiences and the many stories I have heard throughout my journey. There was a girl in my college that was always happy and laughing all the time. I fully respected her upbeat attitude and outgoing ways, especially because that's how I was. I knew sometimes it didn't go well with some other personality types, but that didn't stop me from being me, and it didn't stop her from being her.

I would see this girl around school saying hi to everyone she passed and getting involved in every activity possible, and I figured she couldn't have any hardships because she was so positive. I remember hearing people mention that she might be pulling her hair out because she was missing patches of it, but I never gave it a second thought. I figured some people were just making assumptions and spreading rumors. I never entertained the idea and just got on with my own life. What I didn't realize was that one day, after learning this girl's amazing story, I would be inspired to hold on to my own strength and resiliency and never give up.

~

Meet Carolyn Hislop; a young brain cancer survivor

I grew up in a small town about twelve miles outside of Philadelphia with my mom, dad, and four younger siblings in a middle-class neighborhood. Life was pretty normal until the day I received the most shocking news of my life.

I attended a high school where I was extremely active, playing multiple sports, running after-school clubs, volunteering, taking mission trips to impoverished areas, fostering farm animals, babysitting, and having a great time with friends.

Everything seemed fine until I started to have horrible headaches during my junior year of high school. After about six months of trying to knock the headaches out with medicines, I had an MRI. On the day after my eighteenth birthday, I learned that I had a baseball-sized tumor in the memory and emotion center of my brain.

All of the professionals felt it was not likely to be cancerous, so just a week later—a month before I was to start my senior year of high school—the chief of neurosurgery at the Hospital of the University of

Pennsylvania, Sean Grady, performed an emergency surgery that removed the entire visible tumor but left me unable to read, recognize numbers, or tell time.

Two weeks later, I learned that the tumor was cancerous and that several months of chemotherapy would follow. With that, my life would change completely.

Chemotherapy was no walk in the park, but fortunately my medicines were not the kinds that make you lose your hair. Because of the chemo-induced nausea and the post-surgical fatigue, I started my senior year by attending only art class each day, and eventually added lunch, then a one-on-one reading class, then small-group social studies, and then a self-paced computer-generated math class.

With the overwhelming support of the school and my peers, I was fortunate enough to graduate on time. Based on my SAT scores from the previous spring, I got into all of the colleges to which I had applied; however, I was struggling to read the actual acceptance letters and the scholarship offers. I could see alphabetical letters, but they did not make sense when bunched together. I wondered how I could even find the strength to survive college.

Through a lot of back-and-forth battles with my emotions, I realized that if I had the strength to fight a brain tumor I could find the strength to take on college. I decided to attend Immaculata University, about 25 minutes from my house, to study sociology. The administration at Immaculata was enormously supportive, and I was optimistic that with help from the tutoring center and my academic advisors, I would succeed. The school agreed that taking two academic classes and one lighter course (like art or physical education) each semester would be manageable. And even with the reduced course load, the administration agreed to let me live on campus so I could fully experience the very best that college life had to offer.

With the generous help offered by professors and learning support staff, I did well during my freshman year, but unfortunately, I learned halfway through my second semester that my tumor was growing again. It was time for a second brain surgery.

This time, my surgery was much less dramatic and the recovery time was shorter, but my surgeon and the oncology team at the hospital opted to follow the surgery with the big guns: a one-two punch to the cancer with both chemo and radiation to the brain. I spent part of five days a week for seven weeks during that summer at the hospital, getting radiation treatments.

In conjunction with the chemo, those treatments left me pretty wiped out, and I lost clumps of hair in the particular spots on my scalp that were targeted by the radiation. These clumps would never grow back, but the rest of the hair on my head mostly covered them so it wasn't so bad.

I was fortunate enough to start my second year of college on time and continued to plug through classes and a busy social and spiritual life. Another year of college came and went, and by February of my third year of college, believe it or not, I had more tumor activity.

This time the doctors decided to give me a gamma knife "surgery," which meant I would essentially have one dose of intense and well-targeted radiation done in a half day, start to finish. We followed that with chemo again, and I lived a relatively normal life, including working a summer job I loved at a camp for boys with intellectual disabilities. And as fate struck, a year later, the specialists determined that there was a suspicious area near the original tumor, and a third traditional brain surgery was in order.

Because I had come out of the second surgery so well, nobody was too worked up about my going in for a third one. I went to work on a Thursday in July, pushing wheelchairs and entertaining special-needs kids, and Dr. Grady performed the surgery the next morning. He closed me up at lunchtime, took a follow-up MRI, decided that he could get more tissue out if he were to go back in again, and opened me up for a second brain surgery on the same day.

By bedtime that night, I was conscious and hugging my parents, and I settled in for the night. That night, I dreamed that I was running through a field, but when I woke up early the next morning, I was paralyzed on my left side. Nothing could have prepared me for the sheer terror I felt when I realized I could not move my left side. I could move my head and could talk and blink both eyes normally, but I could not shrug my left shoulder, lift a finger on my left hand, or wiggle a toe on my left foot. I had suffered a stroke during the night.

I was carted off to a reputable rehab hospital, where I spent the next seven weeks scared to death, fighting to regain some movement, and trying to wrestle with all the huge questions in my life: Would I ever walk again? How could I ever make a living? Who would want to marry me in my current state? Could I ever have children? Would I make it back to school? Why did God hate me? What had I done to deserve this?

My insurance company booted me out of the inpatient hospital too soon and I was losing ground emotionally. I desperately wanted to be home. I started outpatient physical, occupational, and cognitive therapies, which I did until my benefits ran out a few months into it. At that point, I was mostly left to my own devices, to rebuild a life that was badly shaken by my stroke and the three-time recurrence of a tumor I thought had vanished out of my life forever.

After a year of therapy, I started back at Immaculata University as a commuter student, with my severely impaired reading and walking, to take just one relatively easy class that I knew would not demand a lot of textbook reading or memorizing.

Currently I am wondering whether I will ever be able to finish my bachelor's degree, but in the meantime, one class at a time, I am finishing up the requirements for a certificate in studio arts. I walk with a cane and have very limited use of my left arm and hand. I got a job as an aide in a preschool classroom one morning a week. I am trying to strengthen my left side and improve my balance by working out at a gym, and I am planning a two-week mission trip to Africa this coming summer. Life is considerably better than it was a year ago, but considerably more challenging than it was two years ago.

I met the challenges of my cancer diagnosis head-on with my relationship and my faith in God. I know I have a great purpose in this life, even if I can't see it clearly and meet with many more challenges.

Don't get me wrong: I was sometimes completely terrified and outraged. For sure, my emotions did not always follow my faith. There has been great darkness during some of the six-plus years since my diagnosis. I sometimes find sleep to be a safe escape, and at times I smoked or drank to entertain myself and cope, which I knew didn't help me in the long run.

I have held on to my belief that God will not give me more than I can handle. This is where the stubbornness I have been "blessed" with as part of my basic personality has come into play: if I believe it, I stick to it. Despite the ups and downs of treatments, frustrations, anger, and roadblocks, I do (most days!) have enough stubbornness to stick with my basic beliefs and realize how I can ride these tides.

The same stubbornness that helps me hold onto my faith also shows itself in persistence in trying to overcome the obstacles cancer has created. I have found laughter to be one of my cures. I like to laugh and don't want to take things too seriously. Finding something to laugh about even in the most horrific moments has been a big help in keeping calm. I think that being able to find humor even in the midst of these difficult situations also makes it easier for everyone involved.

Sometimes people just don't know what to say, or whether they should bring up the subject of cancer at all. When I maintain my sense of humor, it helps to put people at ease and makes it easier for people to talk to me. This seems to work even if the humor isn't about the cancer directly; it's helpful just to show that my ability to laugh is still very much intact. I believe that laughing is a gift we have available to us even in the most difficult situations.

If I had the chance to make my cancer go away, I certainly would do that. I have experienced a lot of pain, loss, and heartbreak in these years. However, having cancer has given me blessings, a perspective, a faith, and a sense of appreciation that I would not have had without the cancer. Facing the possibility of death has worked like nothing else to help me to be thankful for what I have. Before cancer, I didn't realize how great it was to be able to run around the block, how nice it was to be able to style my own hair, and how blessed I was to be able to see well and attend school.

I also didn't realize how much I could relate to others. Even though we weren't battling the same things, we still battled something and needed support and strength to push through it. Although my difficulties weren't easy, I really have been provided with an amazing opportunity to connect with people and build ties that would not have been created without my cancer.

And as cliché as this might sound, today at twenty-four years old, I am thankful to be alive. At the end of the day, whether I beat cancer or not, I know that not only did I do my best here on earth, but also that I use the strength God gave me to "keep keepin' on."

~

After hearing Carolyn's story, how could I not be inspired? She had faced death more than once and was still helping others through her positive attitude. She was planning to go on mission trips to help those less fortunate, even when she was struggling as well. I couldn't help but feel overwhelmed and realize that no matter the hardships we face, we can't stop living, because there is still so much good that can happen in the midst of the bad. Even through the negative, we have the power to turn it into positive.

I remembered that I too mattered and had some purpose in life, even if I couldn't figure it out at that moment. But Carolyn's story also got me thinking about the fact that we sometimes judge others too quickly and miss the inevitable truth that we all have a story, a purpose, a dream or two or three or one hundred—and an amazing ability to touch someone's life. We are ignorant of the power we have to provide hope to one person through a smile, a good deed, or a kind word. Positive action has the possibility to be recycled from one person to another and paid forward. The fact that Carolyn could still provide hope and laughter to others and help out kids with special needs during her hardships proves that we do have that power and strength, no matter what we face.

I started really seeing that lesson about four years ago, when I had my first big speaking gig on stage for the non-profit mental health organization Minding Your Mind's free school speaking program. I was standing in front a one-thousand-seat auditorium full of high school students. As most of them scoped me out, wondering what this redheaded stranger had to say, I couldn't help but wonder what they were thinking. At the same time, I was trying to come to terms with the fact that I was about to share my personal life story with an auditorium full of strangers and risk being judged and living the pain once again. I remembered sitting in assemblies in high school and wishing they would end while letting every possible thought go through my mind to distract myself from the speaker, so I knew getting students to pay attention would be hard. However, in my mind it wasn't about the crowd at all, but about finally having my time to shine. Thinking that way was a big mistake, and I knew it, but it would soon help me learn one of the greatest lessons in my lifetime.

As I started speaking, I was hiding my nerves as best I could, but I also felt this overwhelming sensation—like I belonged right there in that place at that very moment. It was a feeling I had wanted for a long time: to actually feel like I belonged.

As I scanned the room, looking at each individual face, I couldn't help but wonder what their stories were. I kept asking myself, "Do they struggle with the same issues as I do? Do any of them feel they have to be someone they aren't to please others? Do any of them put on a front so others won't see their daily battles whether at home or in school? Do any of them ever feel that they aren't good enough?"

I became so overwhelmed that I had no idea what was happening. I wondered if I was actually living my purpose in life right then, because the feeling I had was so new and overpowering. Everything inside of me wanted to help these kids and do everything in my power to let them know they were not alone. I wasn't sure exactly what was going on, but I knew at that moment I was blessed with a gift and had to use it the best I could. If I could help one person, then that was enough, because at least that one person would know they mattered, had the power to inspire others, and had a hope and great strength inside of them.

After I finished giving my speech, that's when things really started making sense and getting clearer. As I made my way home, my phone kept alerting me to all these new social media messages and I was eager to check them all. I was overwhelmed by responses from so many different students. I felt like a mini-celebrity, receiving all these friend requests and having people just wanting to connect with me. For years I had felt so different and out of place, and now, when I decided to be myself—the one person who scared me most—people were so much more accepting.

It was strange to think and experience this, but I wasn't going to fight it, just enjoy every minute of it. I honestly had this proud feeling knowing I had done something great, but there was another part of me realizing that I was given a gift to help and inspire others. I knew that there was a much bigger picture than I ever cared to see.

When I opened my first email from a student, tears began rolling down my face. I couldn't stop crying as the messages poured in. I had always wanted to be somebody, but at that moment, I literally realized I didn't need fame and fortune for that, because just being me was more than good enough.

One student wrote, "Hi, I just wanted to let you know that you changed my life a lot! Your speech really helped me understand a lot of people and made me think twice about keeping my mouth shut when I see bullying going on. Now I stand up for a lot more people than I did before."

Another student wrote, "I hide behind my make-up and clothes like my life is perfect, and I think it's time I stop and talk to somebody and now I also don't want to judge others for being different because we all are and that's such a cool thing."

Then another student wrote something I'll never forget: "You reminded me of a lot to live for. You just saved my life and gave me hope. Thank you."

The bigger picture was literally hitting me in the face. It wasn't all about me at all; it was all about a chance to use my gifts to pay it forward, help others, and provide some sense of hope and understanding to people and let them know that they matter. It's ironic because I was still struggling with keeping my own hope alive and, although I helped these strangers in their own lives, strangely enough they were helping me too—without even knowing.

Chapter Two

It Happens

"It's not what happens, but how we cope and react that builds character." I remember hearing this quote years ago when I was in a state of hopelessness.

When things happen, we tend to ask, "Why me?" and sometimes pray that our nightmare will end. Over the years, I've come to realize that at times that quote is completely true; yes, how we cope and react builds character, but sometimes it is about what happens or what we are doing.

These days, a lot of people (not all) on reality TV shows don't have great intentions and are making it big because of the things they do or have done. I'm not here to judge or call them out, because that is the path in life they chose, but what is falling face-first, drunk on the beach, having lots of sex, cursing, and easily becoming a model because you made the cut for a teen pregnancy reality show teaching the people watching and our society as a whole? Act out and do things in front of the camera, get your own clothing line right after, and become rich and famous.

I'll be the first to admit I watch some of those shows and understand that our society loves our reality television. However, after getting a casting call about auditioning for a reality television show by reading lines, I wondered, "Is what we are seeing on reality TV *really* reality? Where are those real-life stories the world wants to see?"

I do admit we sometimes get treated with inspiring, heroic stories that leave us with a sense of hope and determination and make us feel like saving the world is possible. However, when that moment passes, do you ever ask yourself, "What have I done that can even compare to them?" or "Will I ever be that important and inspiring in my lifetime?"

It's scary to think that one day you may be gone without any trace of your existence. But as I learned from Maggie, a high school student, it's not about what we can do tomorrow, it's about what we can do right now—regardless of the cards we are dealt.

Meet Maggie Cardin; a young suicide prevention advocate

Hello, my name is Maggie Cardin, and I'm currently a junior at the Pennsylvania State University (PSU). What follows is a blog post that I wrote my first semester of my freshman year in college. It speaks to why I'm so passionate about being a mental health advocate. I hope that by reading it, you realize that depression and mental illness are real and that it's okay to reach out to someone for help.

May 16, 2009: I reluctantly opened my laptop, as today was the day I promised myself I would finally clean up my email account. I was just about to delete all emails when my attention turned to one email message that was titled "Aevidum." I curiously opened it and read what would be the most defining email I had ever received, just four words…

You saved my life.

At that moment, I knew that what I was doing, what I was passionate about, I would be doing for the rest of my life. I found my life's work.

To explain what my life's work is about, you need to look no further than one word, *Aevidum.* Aevidum means, "I got your back," and it is a term that originated at my high school in January of 2004 when I was just a sixth grader. Aevidum the word and Aevidum the organization were created in the aftermath of an active tenth grade student's completed suicide. Aevidum is a depression and suicide awareness initiative that hopes to shine a light on the taboo subject of mental illness.

The reason this issue is so near and dear to my heart is the tenth grade student that completed suicide was my brother Philip, my only sibling. Since its inception, Aevidum has grown immensely due to the fact that it was founded on the principle that students need to use their gifts and talents to spread the message of hope to other students; in essence, students helping students.

That's not to say that Aevidum doesn't seek assistance from many professionals from both the public and private sector, but in the end, it is students empowering students to make a difference in the world. The message that depression is a real and treatable illness seems to be heard more loudly when coming from a peer. The email I received May 16, 2009, was just that...an email from one student to another.

The email I received that day may or may not have meant something to someone else, but for me, it ignited strength in me that I did not know that I possessed. That email was a student's response to the first time I publicly spoke (to an audience of 1,100 high school students) about my experience with suicide and the loss of my brother Phil. That email is what I think about every time I tell someone my story. That email is what I am thinking about right now as I share a glimpse with you into my past and a peek at what my future holds.

Four words are enough to keep me going forever. Four words are enough for me spend each and every blessed day making sure every single education major, every single person working with students, and every single student is aware that depression is an illness...and that it is okay for those suffering to get help.

There is no reason that I should have to stand up on a stage telling people about my brother in the past tense...Phil should still be here today standing next to me. I have worked through my loss and have accepted that my brother is not coming back. What I have not accepted, though, and what I will never accept is needlessly, students are going to die today, tomorrow, and the day after that. People need to embrace the fact that there should be no stigma surrounding mental illness, and we need to educate ourselves about this issue and be advocates for those who are suffering in silence. We need to do it now.

You saved my life...Aevidum

Since Aevidum started, the organization has continued to do amazing things. Immediately following the kick-off assembly at my high school, students' responses were unprecedented. Students started opening their mouths and using their voices and gifts to break the silence surrounding mental illness. Our life-saving mission didn't stop at our own school.

I, as well as many of my Aevidum peers, spoke at an Aevidum press conference held at the base of the Pennsylvania Capitol's rotunda steps on May 26, 2010. To stand in front of all of Pennsylvania's elected officials, both the full House and Senate, was nerve-wracking to say the least, but was also one of those experiences one would go a whole lifetime trying to reproduce. I am certain I had goose bumps on my goose

13

bumps, but who wouldn't when we were standing in such a historically significant building trying to change the course of history for future generations.

That's what Aevidum and the Minding Your Mind Foundation are doing. We are changing the course of history for future generations. For my brother it is too late, but for you, for your friends, for your family, for your brothers…there is still so much hope right now. *Aevidum.*

After hearing Maggie's courageous story, I couldn't stop thinking about the sad fact that sometimes we are hit with things we can't and don't want to imagine. Unfortunately, we can't know everything that will happen and how we will ultimately cope. Everyone in the world will experience both bad and good. It's just so scary not knowing, but every individual thing that we go through doesn't define "the everything" about us; it adds on to the whole person and becomes a part of us.

Fears of the future, jealously, regrets, death, and questioning our self-worth sometimes take over and lead us to missing out on the moments happening right in front of us. Some moments we fear experiencing and some moments we don't let ourselves experience due to fear.

My good friend and mentor Mariel Hemingway once told me, "The magic happens in the unknown." It's the absolute truth. Yes, the unknown is scary—but remember, if you don't take that step, you will never know and never grow from the things you've experienced.

Everyone in existence right now has a something, whether trials and tribulations or triumphs. Although you can't specifically relate to each one, you can relate to going through something or even a similar topic or situation. If you are ever in a place with a lot of people, take a second and look around. Something amazing is going on in front of your eyes. Each person is living in that particular existence with a past, a present, and a future. Each person is different and unique, possibly struggling with something or celebrating something behind his or her impression.

In that moment you are there with those people, those strangers, each with a genuine story that is unknown to our world. Each person including yourself has a sense of self-worth: a worth that doesn't have to be defined by one thing that happened to you or by one thing you have done, and it doesn't have to be captured by television cameras to be important in this world.

I was approached by a reporter from a famous, well-known magazine about my story relating to suicide, and the work I was doing with mental health. They were looking for stories about suicide from young women all across the country. While I was in mid-sentence talking to a reporter, she just stopped me and calmly said, "Your story isn't extreme enough for this article. We actually have people that survived jumping off bridges, and some of the people and their stories are a little more interesting and extreme than what you can offer."

My phone fell to the floor and a burning sensation filled my whole body. It felt as though someone had just shot me in the heart, and all the work I was doing meant nothing because my story was too boring and insignificant for the world to hear. Was she really serious? Not extreme enough? Should I have tried something else? Tried to get attention in a different way? I couldn't breathe and wished I either had a more attractive story or was born to a famous actor or rock star so I could, in that moment, just feel like a somebody. Right after the call, I started comparing myself to others, their lives, their careers, and their stories. Little by little, I wished I were someone or somewhere else.

After a few minutes of being shocked and pissed off, I knew I had to do something about this. It would partially be for me, but also for everyone I spoke to who shared his or her story with me and who, at times, felt insignificant to others. I wasn't born into a famous household, wasn't dying of a terminal disease, and hadn't had a life-altering moment that changed my future; no top news or media outlet would care about me. But I had to do something for the people out there, and having limited support wasn't going to stop me.

I looked up some things on the Internet and learned about sensationalism and how our media exploits certain stories and situations for ratings and sales. I realized this was the magazine's goal and that sensationalism was a lot more common than I had suspected. It started to make me wonder and ask, "Is what I am seeing in newspapers, on TV, and in the media really the whole, true story?" Cutting footage and misquoting by reporters and TV professionals is way too easy on both the moral side and physical side.

My anger turned into determination because I knew every person that existed on this earth had a story. Sometimes their stories were mistaken and exploited, and sometimes people just walked around hiding behind their happy faces so the world wouldn't have a chance to judge and they wouldn't feel insignificant to others. How did our society get like this? How could they just pick and choose what stories were important enough to tell and how to tell them?

After being denied so inconsiderately by the magazine, it was easy for me to get fired up and come up with a million ideas. My favorite one was where I could host a TV show and travel around America or even the world sharing the real stories of everyday heroes—real people living among us. It would be inspiring, true, and fun as well. Maybe I could ride on a camel's back while interviewing a hero who protects wild animals in Arizona, or tightrope walk while interviewing a circus clown who spends his free time making balloon animals and getting kids to laugh at the local children's hospital. Yes, I wanted to be just like Diane Sawyer and Robin Roberts: a girl can dream, can't she?

It seemed like an awesome idea at the time, but I hit a roadblock, having no access to a production company and no network to air the show. The idea had to be put on the back burner, but I wasn't giving up that easily. There had to be a way for America and even the world to hear more of real people's stories of hope—like Caroline's and Maggie's.

After a lot of ups and downs in my journey, it hit me: write a book to share the stories of real people that I met along my journey, and spread the important messages of self-worth, respect, paying it forward, resiliency, strength, and hope.

I knew I was going to hit some dead ends, but I told myself, "If a door closes, I'm not going through the window, I'm breaking down that same stinkin' door and gathering all the support I can on the way!"

Chapter Three

How do we go on?

When we are faced with horrible situations, how do we go on? Ultimately, no one knows what's going to happen, and one tragedy can change your life for good. However, the only thing we literally know is a past that we lived and what's happening right now in this very moment. Sometimes we have the opportunity to change what is happening, but other times we do not. There are always internal and external factors that affect us, but as we look into our past and experiences we have faced, each of us should see that we have a sense of resiliency. That's not always easy, because horrific tragedies tend to rock our core and sometimes leave us struggling to live on.

I met a woman named Kimberly Dorwart at the Delaware County Suicide Prevention Walk in May 2010. Even before meeting her, I knew a significant part of her story because it had made national headlines just months before. I didn't know, however, if the whole story I had read was true, so it made me wonder.

Here is what I knew: On Thursday, February 25, 2010—just three months before the walk—Kim's daughter Vanessa took her own life while hugging her friend Gina until an oncoming Amtrak Acela Train heading from Boston to Washington hit both girls head on. That day had seemed normal to me until news reports of the tragedy started showing up everywhere. Anytime I heard of a suicide I grew upset and wondered, "If I had spoken to that kid, maybe they'd still be alive today." I wasn't blaming myself or saying I could save everyone (although I wish I could), but I was dedicated to helping anyone and everyone out, so sometimes I took things like that personally. I had never met Kim or Vanessa, but something told me I had to talk to Kim that day and share my work with her.

I knew Kim's daughter's suicide had been sensationalized; that really bothered me. The lives of these two beautiful teen girls were taken in a split second, but instead of using this story as a chance to talk about suicide prevention and help people, the news and media focused on any piece of gossip or information they could publish. I remember an article coming out about Kim and her husband's past, basically exploiting their lives and making them look like horrible people. They had just lost their daughter and, without any time to mourn, their personal business was out in the public—like a reality show that wasn't completely accurate.

I was hesitant when approaching Kim, but I wanted to help in some way and let her know there were good people out there, trying to keep this from happening again. I remember making eye contact with her; my body trembled as I said, "I'm really sorry about Vanessa. I just want you to know that I'm a speaker and share my story to try to give other kids hope."

Immediately Kim grasped me and wouldn't let go. It was a hug I'll never forget. She asked if I had survived suicide, and I told her I'd come very close to ending my life at fifteen but was saved by a peer.

She hugged me again with tears and said, "Thank you for the work you're doing and thank you for being alive today."

I knew this woman was facing the worst tragedy any parent could imagine. Any media outlet that could get close to Kim and her family continuously hassled them for any piece of information they could get. After denying famous talk shows, world-renowned news stations, and most Philadelphia news outlets, Kim shared her full story for the first time with me, so I could share it honestly with the world and offer some sense of truth, understanding, and hope for others.

∾

Meet Kimberly Dorwart; a mother fighting for suicide prevention education in schools

Just three months after my daughter's suicide made national television, radio, and newspaper headlines, I decided to go the Delaware County Suicide Prevention Walk because I felt like I had to do something. I don't know why my daughter did what she did, but I wasn't going to let it be for nothing—it would be for something. That's where I met Melissa and grew to know that she was a survivor of suicide ideation and someone working to help youth understand there is hope and help. I felt comfortable right away working for the cause, because my daughter's death didn't hit me in the immediate months after it.

However, I am convinced I got help way too soon, because over time things got a lot harder and more real.

My daughter Vanessa was one of the most giving and loving people I knew. We called her "little helper," and at times we had to give her something to do because she occasionally wanted to help a little too much, but that's what we loved about her. Every time she walked down the steps ready to go out, she would say, "I look hotter than you, *Mamacita!*"

I miss the sound of her voice and the smell of her hair. There is no bigger pain than losing a child, especially to suicide, but to have news cameras in your face, reporters and every media outlet calling you to get their five-second sensationalized story—well, that made everything even harder for me. I lost a child, and my family and I didn't have time to grieve because, before I even found out about her death, I had news cameras in my face trying to get their ratings up.

People don't see my brokenness or a cast hiding my pain. Some people think suicide is contagious, because I can't count how many people avoided me or backed away and treated me like a two year old. A lot of people didn't know what to say, and I know they were trying to help, but sometimes saying nothing was better than something forced. This was the definition of hell—and I was living in it.

On Thursday, February 25, 2010, Vanessa stayed home from school and was at her dad's house. A few days prior, I noticed she wasn't acting herself and asked her if she wanted her "take five," which I gave my kids to say anything they needed to say without judging or punishing them. But she didn't want it and promised me she would talk to the counselor at school.

I called the school counselor on Monday and left a message about Vanessa's odd mood but heard nothing back. When things didn't change, I was getting worried. I asked Vanessa if something was wrong again, and she just said, "I'll be okay, Mom."

I called the counselor back again Wednesday and still heard nothing. I was hoping Vanessa would talk to her, because she wasn't talking to me, and it wasn't like her at all.

That Thursday I was at work as a homecare nurse, taking care of one of my patients. I was running an errand for my patient when I got a call saying that something was wrong with Vanessa and to rush to the high school.

My daughter Francine called me and said, "Mom, I think Vanessa has been killed. There was a train accident, and I think it was Vanessa and Gina." There were status updates and comments on social media outlets trending that Vanessa got hit by a train and was dead. I just had this instinct to go straight to the train tracks and not look back.

My boss called me on my way to the train tracks and asked why I had left my patient. I was literally in the store and dropped all the food and items in my hand and ran out the door. I told him that I thought a train had hit my daughter, and he told me to go to her.

When I got to the tracks, there were cops and news reporters everywhere. Before I could even talk to anyone, a reporter had a camera in my face. "How did they get there before me?" I wondered, but I was so eager to know what was going on that I didn't acknowledge it.

I saw my husband next to the coroner and remember shaking a nearby police officer, begging him to tell me what had happened. "Tell me my daughter is okay?" I wept.

As tears poured down the officer's face, he said, "I'm sorry, I wish I could."

While I was being notified of my daughter's death, there was a camera in my face. That news reporter took a private moment from me and videoed it for the whole world to see. I remember my brother picking the news reporter up and moving him across the street, advising him never to come near me again. I was a mess—crying, trembling, and so confused. This was the beginning of my living hell.

There was never a minute that my house wasn't filled in the weeks after the tragedy. It was nice to have so many people care. My patient with MS came to support me. He just sat there with his daughter, but it was a comforting feeling because I know it wasn't easy for them to get to my house. However, I was also feeling trapped and like I had to hide from the media. They were camped out across the street, just wanting any piece of information and gossip to up their ratings.

My daughter's death by suicide was becoming more sensationalized every second that went by. We were constantly getting calls from national magazines, news outlets, talk shows, and newspapers, but I denied every outlet.

Somehow, a famous TV doctor's staff member got hold of my ten-year-old daughter Paige's cell phone number and was talking to her about the tragedy. When I found out, I couldn't believe it, and I told Paige to stop talking to her.

I remember at one point talking to a staff member of that same TV doctor's show, who requested that my family come to LA for a taping, and they would pay for the whole trip. This was only two weeks after the tragedy, and they wanted to fly us out Sunday to Monday, even though the memorial services were that Thursday and Friday. I asked the staff member for one thing, which they couldn't give me. I just wanted help and therapy for my family, not a fully paid roundtrip to and from LA, but the staff said they couldn't. I had no problem hanging up the phone right then, and I totally shut myself off to any news or media outlet.

The Philadelphia newspapers were some of the news outlets bugging me for a story and any word they could get. I decided to give them what they wanted on one condition: that they stayed away from my daughter's funeral so my family and I could mourn properly and say goodbye to a loving daughter and sister.

There were so many stories about my daughter's death; I tried not to read them, but I'll never forget what happened after giving an interview to the biggest Philadelphia newspaper. I was overly exhausted. My family and I were at Vanessa's viewing from 3 p.m. to 1 a.m. because so many people came to pay their respects. I can't recall much of that day. The emotional distress from losing my daughter was the hardest thing I ever faced.

At the funeral, my daughters shared their last words to their sister, and my family tried to gain closure and mourn as best they could. The day she was buried was my birthday, so I'll never, ever forget that day. Vanessa was born on March 3rd, just two days before my birthday. I always joked that she stole my big day and, unfortunately at this point, Vanessa's burial made that joke a reality.

The next day on the front page of that newspaper was my baby girl's casket being carried out by my brother and others. I couldn't believe what I was seeing. The reporter from the newspaper had promised me she would leave the funeral alone so we could mourn in private; instead, she sent someone else who posed as a mourner and got a story for more ratings and sales.

I was disgusted and shunned out the media completely after that, but the media outlets wouldn't give up. They spread unreliable facts and got everything they could to sensationalize the story more. They went on Vanessa's social media pages and assumed that her quoting a song meant she was showing signs of suicide. But where were their facts? My little girl died, and I couldn't even say goodbye and mourn her properly in peace. It all completely sucked.

There were many newspaper articles, and what should have been a human-interest story became a sensationalized story that made my family and Vanessa look like criminals. They wouldn't give up. They pulled "dirt" from my husband's and my past and shared it with the whole world, making us look like horrible human beings. They made sure the world knew we weren't the best parents. They didn't even have respect enough to give us more notice, but called the day before to warn us about the article.

My other kids were getting help and in therapy, but this wasn't fair to them. Didn't the media understand what they were doing to my family and my daughter's death? I received a call from a newspaper reporter who had some interesting news for me. I was calling around, making appointments to get mental health help for my kids, and I found out that one of the doctors I had an appointment with had called the newspaper to inform them that he was treating my kids. People are unbelievable and will do anything for their fifteen seconds of fame.

My kids were dealing with one of the most horrific tragedies that would probably happen in their lives, and here this doctor was all worried about himself and his publicity. I denied the claim that he was treating my kids and became furious. However, I do give credit to some therapists who admitted they weren't qualified to treat my kids in this situation. It gave me hope that some humanity still existed.

In the months after Vanessa's suicide, I wasn't really hit by all the pain I'd face in the next few years. In those months, it wasn't too hard for me to go to the Delaware County Suicide Prevention Walk because I wanted to do something in memory of Vanessa, and I felt like I wanted to bring awareness to suicide prevention.

My biggest fear was that people would forget her, so I remember posting her Mass cards everywhere, and each person that came to the walk had a t-shirt with my baby's beautiful face on it. People were still giving their condolences, but it was dying down more and more. It started to feel like people thought my daughter's suicide was contagious, because people were avoiding me.

I'll never forget being in a local store and overhearing a girl say to her mom, "That's the lady whose daughter jumped in front of the train."

I remember turning around and saying, "I'm still here and can hear you, and that was really rude." I was on the front page of the newspaper so much that it was easy for people to point me out as that mom whose daughter died by suicide on the train tracks. It was like I had it written all over my forehead. As time went on, things weren't getting any easier.

The blame was hitting me hard. My daughter took her life at fifteen years old, she was under my watch, and it killed me that I couldn't protect her. I started experiencing issues that were affecting every single thing in my life. I wasn't taking care of my kids to the degree they deserved, and I started putting myself in dangerous situations because all I wanted to do was die and be with my baby girl. Was that so wrong? I loved my kids that were here on earth, but I just wanted to see my Vanessa and hold her and tell her that I loved her.

Soon after, I heard from one of the passengers on the train who contacted me through social media. He said he thinks and prays for my daughter every night, but I wanted to know what it was like to be on the train. Did he feel anything? Did he know they hit someone or something?

He said it felt like they ran over sticks, and it wasn't until they stopped a mile out and he heard passengers sharing the news off their electronic devices that something went wrong on their routine train ride from Boston to Washington.

I didn't have anyone to ask if my daughter suffered, because the third girl who was with Vanessa and Gina wouldn't talk to me. I thought when people got hit my trains they bounced, but when the coroner called to ask me what shoes Vanessa was wearing, I knew my little girl was in pieces so bad that they couldn't even embalm her. No person or parent should ever have to hear that.

There was a rumor that Vanessa killed herself because she was pregnant. When the coroner called us in, I asked if she was indeed pregnant. His response was, "I'm sorry, I couldn't even begin to figure that out." I didn't know what to even think. This was complete and downright hell on earth.

I always had this stigma and misunderstanding of mental health issues. I had a friend who couldn't get out of bed due to depression, and I always told her to "get over it" and "just get up." It wasn't until I started experiencing depression and post-traumatic stress disorder (PTSD) that I could honestly feel her pain—real physical pain—so I could only apologize to her for finally understanding.

It was getting harder to get out of bed in the morning, and I was forgetting everyday, simple things. My kids would be in their rooms because I grounded them, and when they asked if they could come out, I would say, "Yeah, what are you doing in there anyway?"

Showering became a burden, and brushing my teeth was out of the question. My kids would literally tell me to get up and shower or they would hose me down. It was normal for two weeks to go by without my being able to get up and do the day-to-day activities that people take for granted.

I made the decision to have my kids stay at their dad's because I couldn't take care of myself or them, and it seemed every day they were taking more and more care of me. After I put myself into high-risk situations for too long, I was placed in a hospital in January 2012 for mental health issues. I didn't want to be labeled any more than I already was; now, being in a mental hospital, what would people think? However, my life was a mess. I was literally sleeping my days away with the help of sleeping pills. I just needed to escape the pain and this was the only way I could. But deep down, I knew it was time to face everything and get help for my kids who were still here.

I was in the hospital during the second anniversary of my Vanessa's death, my birthday, and then hers. It was probably for the best, but I feared my other kids—especially my oldest, Francine—hated me. When I got a call from her on my birthday, saying, "Mommy, I love you, happy birthday," it was the little reassurance I needed to go on.

The hospital staff and doctors let me talk about Vanessa every day until I was out of breath. It was what I needed because I hadn't done this over the years. The months after her passing, I was in shock so things didn't hit me, and when I took help right away, I wasn't ready. So after those two years went by, I just needed to vent about anything and everything.

The hospital was really good for me. I learned about depression and PTSD and was able to talk about everything that had to do with Vanessa until I could say her name without crying hysterically. I learned positive coping skills to get through and, although I would never be that same confident, outgoing person, I could learn to live as this person in my new normal.

There were only two things that comforted me through everything. A priest at the church where we held Vanessa's service said the first. At this point, I was cursing God and couldn't imagine how a merciful God would do this to anyone.

People were saying, "God doesn't give you more than you can handle." Well, I couldn't handle this, so what does that even mean?

I asked the priest why Vanessa wasn't coming to me in my dreams, and he kept saying, "Because you won't let her go."

How could I let my child go? I couldn't even protect her when she needed me most.

"God was holding Vanessa, your daughter, in his arms when she passed," he said.

I always felt like she was alone and wanted to know what she was thinking right before the train hit. Was she scared or crying? Did she suffer? What did she say as her last words? When the priest said that, I held on to it and just wouldn't let it go.

My daughter Paige, who was only ten when everything happened, said the other. "Hey Mom, do you know what I'm thinking?"

I just said, "No, what are you thinking?"

She responded with the words I'll never forget: "Well, you didn't know what Vanessa was thinking either, so stop blaming yourself."

I had never told her I blamed myself. Maybe my kids could see it on my face and in my whole demeanor. Regardless, those two sets of words gave me some comfort and sense of faith through my living hell.

Before going in the hospital, I always felt like there was a brick on my chest. Eating anything felt like I was consuming rocks piece by piece. I couldn't let my little girl go, and my life didn't matter at that point.

My husband ended up taking my kids to a psychic to connect with Vanessa. She had always called her little brother "Aiden buddy," and nobody knew that. The psychic wasn't my thing, but when she told my youngest son Aiden that Vanessa said, "Tell my little buddy I love him," and for me to "let her go and forgive myself," I was in complete disbelief.

25

Over time it was like the weight lifted, and I knew I had to let her go. She would never be forgotten, but I couldn't blame anyone or myself anymore, because it wasn't helping the situation for anyone.

Letting her go wasn't easy, but sure enough, I started having dreams about her. I could see her, hear her, smell her, but right when I woke up, expecting things to be as in my dreams, I'd realize the horrible reality that she was really dead. My dreams made me forget, but there were times I woke up in the middle of the night screaming, fighting, and crying. I was literally still in my living hell, and it sucked.

My living hell had a new date system too. Instead of referring to the year or date, it was just like the BC and AD in religion. My new calendar was Before Vanessa Died and After Vanessa Died. Literally, every day I lived with the death of my daughter, and although time was passing, the reality of losing my little girl would never be easier, just different.

I looked up all the laws and bills about suicide prevention and learned that there is funding available for all states, but Pennsylvania didn't take it like New Jersey did. When I am well enough, I want to work to get a bill passed that it's mandatory to talk about suicide and mental illness and offer support for both issues in schools.

Years ago, we couldn't talk about drugs and alcohol, and now there are programs everywhere. If suicide is the third leading cause of death among young adults, why aren't there mandatory programs in schools?

I want to make this a federal change because I don't want any other parent or child to go through what my family faced. I also want to go into schools across the country and share my daughter's and family's story. I need to let kids know suicide isn't the answer, because my baby will not have a future or experience more things in life because of her decision. Her sixteenth birthday was just six days after she died. She was going to Florida and getting a car. Everything was taken away in a split second. That decision lasts forever, and kids need to know that there is a better way.

Vanessa's death rocked me to my core. I never thought it would happen to me; until that day it was easy for me to take daily things for granted. I talked to Vanessa at 11 p.m. the night before, and those were the last words I'd have with her forever.

This is the first time I'm sharing this story. I trust Melissa and want to try to stop anyone else from experiencing what I experienced. I thought I did everything right when I saw my daughter acting different. I called the counselor at school, thinking they would call me back. I did the right thing, and it felt like after it happened, I got a slap in the face. Why didn't that counselor call me back right away or talk to her?

The day after Vanessa died, the counselor and principal both called to apologize and give their condolences, but I wasn't having it. This is one of the reasons there needs to be training and programs about suicide prevention and mental health issues in school. My daughter could be alive today, but people flirt with the idea of talking about suicide and think if we keep it a secret it will go away. The sad reality is, it won't, so we have to do something.

I need each of you to know that I am not ashamed of my daughter dying by suicide. I will talk about her with my head held high because she was an amazing person. I don't know why my child did what she did, but if she needed attention or wanted to end her life, regardless, give your child those fifteen minutes of attention they need. If they just want to talk or go scream as loud as they can and shout off a rooftop in front of people, let them.

I can't help but think, "Maybe if Vanessa had those fifteen minutes, that could have changed her life."

Today, I'm okay with her death. I know she is gone and walks with God. I still have dreams about her. When I was suicidal I had a dream that I ended my life and was in heaven and saw Vanessa. She was dressed like usual, with her hoop earrings and hair and make-up done. I begged her not to leave my side. She promised not to, but I remember asking her, "How will I know you won't?"

She came back and said, "Mom, I'm an angel, not God." That was my Vanessa, funny and cute. When I woke up, I still felt her hug from my dream.

There are some things I want the world to take from Vanessa and my family's story. To all reporters, you shouldn't exploit people's losses and tragedies for your own agenda. My family and I were going through hell, and you robbed us of a proper mourning just for sales and ratings. You made my husband and me feel like bad parents and bad people in that horror we were facing, and we didn't need you to add on to our already existing guilt and pain.

This was a human-interest story and a chance to help many facing suicide issues and to offer hope and resources for suicide prevention, yet you sensationalized it. You made it look like Vanessa received her fifteen minutes of fame, teaching other young adults that this was the way to do it and get attention. Well guess what: Vanessa will never experience the fame and attention she received because she is gone from the decision that was made on that cold February day in 2010, and she never has the chance to take it back.

Through my personal experiences from this tragedy, I had a huge realization that depression is real, and it is physical as well as mental. My mind was spinning in circles; at times it was like someone was hitting me with a bat over and over again. It's not just the "winter blues," so you shouldn't judge someone for having it and expect them to snap out of it without getting any help. There is no shame in battling depression or any other tragedy in life, and if you did lose a child to suicide, do not be ashamed of him or her or the situation.

We need to talk about these things. I'll never forget what the grade school principal, the whole school, and the community did for my kids. Besides encouraging teachers to bring us food, the principal pulled the school together and explained what happened to Vanessa. He told them it was okay to talk about it to staff and teachers, and he also guided the students in ways to talk to my other children when they returned to school. He had it right—we must talk about these things because they are real and do happen. In order to prevent more of these tragedies, we have to address the problem with no fear or stigma and be proactive.

I learned never to take anything for granted. I lived like life was promised the next day, but it never is; we never know what can happen. One moment changed my life forever, and part of me died. However, now I am more than just a mother to my kids—I am a friend and a confidant. I am much more understanding about things and realize it's not all about the big ABCs, because there are small letters in between the bigger picture. It's really important to see that.

I remember being somewhere recently and seeing people walking around without a care in the world. There I was with the weight of the world on my shoulders, and I was asking, "When is it my time to be like that, to be normal?"

Now I know, I have no idea what any of their stories were, and there is no real normal. We all have our own, and mine may be a living hell at the moment, but I refuse to let Vanessa's suicide be for nothing. It will be for something.

Kim's final words, "It won't be for nothing, it will be for something" have stuck with me since that day I learned the full story in her home just a few years back. While listening to her talk about Vanessa, I was so moved by her courage and dedication to want to help other families dealing with similar situations and ultimately stop these things from happening. When I heard certain parts of her story, I couldn't help but be filled with sorrow and anger. However, as she continued to talk about her want to help so many people through Vanessa's story, I knew I met her for a reason and had to keep going in my own quest to help others.

Chapter Four

Then and Now

What do you want to be when you grow up? That question always confused me because I literally dreamed of being a police officer on Monday, a doctor on Tuesday, and an actress on Wednesday. I couldn't understand why adults had to pick one thing and then be miserable about their choice a lot of the time.

After years of hearing this question, I realized our society, at times, defined people by their jobs, cars, clothes, houses, and how much money they had or did not have. Was that what defined a whole person?

I knew from a very young age that I was much different from most of my peers. We would always pretend to be doctors, lawyers, singers, etc., and dream about our futures, which was completely normal. However, I always wondered why we couldn't ask the questions, "How are you and who are you now?" instead of, "What do you want to be?" It was like we were trained at a very young age to go through the motions and work toward being somebody in the future—but what about who we were as children? And what about who we were in that very moment?

Alexandra Scott of Alex's Lemonade Stand is the perfect example that even youth can make an impact on our society and inspire and move people of all ages. Alex was dealt what most people would call a bad hand—an incurable cancer—but as a child, she may have offered the world more than most adults in their whole lifetime. So why do we continuously ask, "What do you want to be when you grow up or do in ten years?" or, "Where do you see yourself in the future?"

I get that these are normal questions to ask, and it's healthy to dream, work, and plan for a great future. But I can't help but wonder, isn't asking that question literally dismissing everything that person is, no matter what age they are, in that very moment? That's a lesson I learned from Ross Szabo, one of the greatest speaking coaches I would ever have. He taught me one of the greatest lessons in life: if I had a passion for something and belief in myself, I could make a difference right at that very moment.

∽

Meet speaker, author and advocate; Ross Szabo

During my senior year of high school, I went into a very deep depressive episode. I thought about death and suicide every day. I constantly cried myself to sleep, lost interest in all of the things I loved, and had no energy to get out of bed. Everything I did hurt. I spent most of my time thinking about how to end the pain. I didn't want to die, but I couldn't go on living in the depths of depression. After months of the excruciating mood, I attempted to take my own life.

Going to the psychiatric ward was a difficult experience. It was even harder to go back to my high school. I lost a lot of friends. There were terrible rumors about me. Most people just didn't know what to do. A teacher thought it would be a good idea to have a psychologist come to my classroom and talk about people with mental illnesses. As he talked about extreme examples, all of the students started laughing. I felt like they were laughing at me. I took my teacher into the hallway and told him I was upset. He asked me what I wanted to do, and I told him to let me speak.

Two weeks later, I stood up in that same classroom and spoke for the very first time. It was never my goal to be one of the only people advocating for mental health awareness. I wanted to help others find their voices. I had the opportunity to speak to over half a million people in four years. The entire time I was trying to figure out what worked, what didn't work, and what could be a replicable presentation style that could bring others into advocacy in a safe and empowering manner.

In 2006, I worked with other advocates to create a speaker training. We did a large-scale speaker search and narrowed over three hundred applications down to ten. We trained the speakers during a very intensive, week-long process. At the end, we had a whole new group of advocates. Since that time, the training I worked to develop has trained over twenty-five speakers.

I am extremely proud to have had the opportunity to create the first-ever youth mental health speakers' bureau in the country. I think one of the most important things any strong advocate can do is find a way to replicate all of the knowledge one has and bring others into the movement. Each speaker I have worked with has his or her own story, perspective, voice, and insight. The diversity of all of those attributes makes mental health advocacy stronger and reaches a wider population of people.

The goal of mental health advocacy is to create a cultural change in the ways people understand and express emotion. We live in a world where a lot of people seem to be having a competition to see who can be more stressed out, who can sleep less, take more medications, drink more alcohol, and handle more stress. To combat that mentality, we need to continue to train advocates who want to normalize mental health and not isolate mental illness.

The positive examples that speakers offer to audiences nationwide show that mental illnesses are treatable. Most importantly, these speakers embody the evidence that if you seek help and work on your own individual path, you can make a change in your life. Sustaining cultural change is not easy. It needs to begin somewhere. All of the advocates I have had the amazing honor to work with give everyone hope that one day things can be better. With passion, belief, and hope, we can start today.

Ross taught me a lot, especially when it came to my feeling different and so powerless at such a young age, but I wish I had met him many years before. Growing up, I always felt like I didn't belong. I still had this desire to help others, but I was scared to never know exactly who I was.

There were times it seemed like I was living two lives. I was an "ordinary" kid who played with friends, had innocent fights with my little brother Kenny and sister Amanda, and spent a lot time with my family. I had this awesome hot pink, battery-powered convertible car that my friends and I would race against cars that drove down the street while I rocked my cool pink shades. I honestly thought that car, my friends, and I were the coolest thing since Pop-Tarts, but I never really ventured past the end of my block. It's amazing what you learn and see when you step outside of your own world, which I learned more quickly over the years. In this interesting world outside of my own, kids had the same cool shades in different colors, and they actually had another, bigger version of my battery-powered car, which I didn't even know existed. Even today, I'm still finding surprises along the way.

I really can't complain too much about my childhood. I had a bunch of neighborhood friends, and I loved playing games, house, and especially Barbies. I do have a confession about the Barbie thing. I had a slight crush on G.I. Joe, so I would steal my little brother's G.I. Joe doll every time I played with Barbies. Ken was cool, but G.I. Joe had it all going on. Ken could be Barbie's hip brother, but G.I. Joe had to be her love interest. I mean, come on—no matter how old you are, you know G.I. Joe was tougher, had better abs, and could handle anything that came his way. At least, that's what I always thought.

As a child, I had a lot of sympathy for others, but of course I didn't have a clear understanding of the world. Don't get me wrong—I knew a bit of what was going on (even when the adults tried to hide things), but I never really understood it to the point where it made complete sense. I figured things happened and I could try to control them and make them better, but I didn't realize the way I felt and thought was actually different from most kids my age.

There was another side to me that I did my best to hide from the outside world. As a kid it's normal to have imaginary friends and play pretend, so when I started having to do these weird things—like touch the corners of tables, turn light switches on and off, walk in and out of doorways, and do things in even numbers while fighting a horrible stomach ache—I thought that was a normal part of being five years old. However, when I witnessed my mom reenacting these behaviors for my grandmother and aunt, followed by the word "weird," I knew right then that this wasn't a normal part of growing up at all.

Having control of situations was a need for me. Anytime things didn't happen my way or in a certain order, I would get terrible stomach pain, and no amount of ginger ale or tea would make it go away. The pain would get worse until I did the odd behaviors, like do things in even numbers or touch the corners of tables. It was getting harder for me to have the freedom to do them, because I felt like people were watching and scolding me more and more.

I always worried more than I thought other kids did. I was terrified of thunderstorms, driving through bad neighborhoods, plugging things into outlets, and using the vacuum. I also squeezed my ears hard when I heard any piece of bad news, as if that would make it untrue. There were things that had nothing to do with me that made me anxious, and the pain would grow a bit stronger each time. I would act out, panic, cry, fight with my parents and family, and complete these rituals until the pain would subside and I felt in control and was sure nothing bad would happen.

I knew it wasn't normal, but it was a strong part of my internal life, and I didn't know how to live without it. I wondered if any of my childhood friends had these worries too or at least experienced some struggle at one time or another. I was sick of feeling so alone and different, while pretending everything was perfectly fine in front of others.

~

Meet my childhood friend; Jessica

Growing up with Missy, as we called her, was fun. It was comforting for me to have a close friend right next door because it allowed both of us to be so available for one another. We used to play Barbies in Missy's room above her garage. That room was so cool because it had us feeling so grown up in our own space. It was almost like we had our own little house, and we were able to have time to play and be creative in there. I was so jealous of that room because I wished I had one above my garage that I could turn into my own private bedroom.

We always rode our bikes around the corner to visit her grandparents and would even put on shows for our parents, showing off our dance moves to "Wiggle It" and Marky Mark's music. I don't remember any specific fights that Missy and I had, except over Missy needing control in most things we did. She always wanted to do things her way, and after arguing for too long, I finally just gave in, because I felt it was something she couldn't help and needed.

We had many comical and hilarious memories. I remember once we were trying to fill up a blue outdoor Barbie pool in Missy's kitchen by ourselves, and we were so proud of ourselves because we did it with no adult supervision. We may have even slapped hands and danced with excitement a little. When we tried to pick it up to bring it downstairs, we realized how flimsy it was. In the blink of an eye, there was water spilling all over Missy's kitchen, and we couldn't help but laugh. However, we knew we would get in trouble. We tried to clean up the water with paper towels and the kitchen sink rag, but Missy's mom walked in, and I got sent home, but having the memory made it worth it.

There was another time when Missy's dad's weights were blocking our play area. Missy liked being in control and didn't want any adult help, so somehow she talked me into moving a fifty-pound weight with her. It didn't look heavy, but we were holding our breath and trying to pick this thing up. We couldn't even push it against the rug. I remember Missy getting frustrated, and I started to as well. Finally, we just gave it all our might and lifted the weight. We planned to drop it on three, but it started slipping, and on two, it landed directly on the top of my foot, instantly shattering my bones. I remember laughing, but then the pain sank in, and we didn't know what to do. Missy went and got my dad, and I was off to the hospital. I think we both learned our lesson that sometimes it is okay to ask for help.

Because I was the oldest, I know Missy and the younger girls on Beach Avenue looked up to me and thought I was cool, but it wasn't exactly like that when you went past the end of our block. Beach Ave. was easy because it was a comfortable world outside of school, and there were really no rules about what to wear, how to talk, or who you could or could not hang out with.

When I was in third grade, I was taken out of public school, which I had been integrated into since preschool, and put into Catholic school. The beginning of fourth grade was very difficult for me; I didn't know anyone and felt very out of place because everyone else had been together since a young age. I had a lot of anxiety, and I was resistant to even being there in the beginning. I would scream and cry, pretending to be sick just to avoid attending. When I had to go, I would get the nurse to believe I was sick so my mother would have to come and get me.

I made a few friends in the beginning, which was enough for me to feel safe. I would say in middle school I wasn't popular, but I had close friends. I had to get glasses and was different in my style and approach. This created some incidents where I was made fun of or picked on at times, but I didn't think it was anything out of the usual.

By eighth grade, when girls were beginning to get recognized, I did my best to blend in—wear the right clothes or attempt to do my hair and makeup to feel pretty. I had my first boyfriend, who was also sort of an outcast and made fun of a lot. It was interesting because he was so desperate to feel accepted that he would turn against me and make fun of me for a moment of being funny or liked.

At one point, I remember my best friend calling me, while she had all the popular people at her home, and they were making noises into the phone and saying hurtful things and hanging up. I remember being upset and feeling like people would do anything to be a part of the group, but because I related I didn't really get mad—just more hurt. As long as I had close friends to depend on who accepted me for me, I didn't really care too much. I learned over the years that I would rather have two real friends then fifty fake ones any day.

By high school, I began to come into my own and felt a little more secure, depending on who I was around, but makeup and new interests helped. High school was an all-girls Catholic affair, and this was nice because it didn't seem to be a popularity contest. It's funny when you take boys out of the equation because things change. There were your usual cliques and pretty girls, but it didn't matter because we were all able to blend together in class and at the lunch table, for the most part.

I fell into my main clique in high school and felt loved and accepted by them. They are the ones I stayed the closest to throughout my high school years. This is also when I met my high school sweetheart, who later became my husband. Meeting him and feeling desired for the first time was a new experience for me. The relationship made me more self-confident and secure within myself. I was able to become a little more open to who I was becoming and not care so much about what other people thought (I was in love of course), so nothing else mattered.

In my experience throughout school, I did pick up early on that being popular seemed to be the most important thing to a lot of people, including me. But once you realize (as I did) that you just aren't fitting into that mold, you adapt and try to find where you can at least be happy and loved for who you are, not what you have to offer or what you look like. I had big, ugly bangs, Coke-bottle glasses, unusual style in clothes, freckles and pale white skin, and not much of a body; it was inevitable that I would run into a few incidents of feelings rejected. It is difficult to experience this through such crucial years of development, but I think it made it easier for me to appreciate people who did love me later in life.

High school was hard at times, with some betrayal, back stabbing, fighting, and girl gossip, but it was also super fun to just be among people who thought we were all the fun we needed. It didn't matter at this point if we were popular or not, because in our minds we were— maybe not to others, because they defined themselves as popular, but it wasn't so much of a contest among cliques anymore.

I think that school to some degree will always be a popularity contest. On the surface, it appears superficial and important, when underneath I think it is because you have a lot of kids who don't have a clue who they are or who they want to be, with major insecurity and fear of being rejected. We are all born with the need to belong and feel accepted, and sometimes people are so afraid of being lost in the crowd that they become mean or aggressive as a defense mechanism to cover up or mask their own fears.

Being a therapist now, I've learned through watching others that the cockiest person in the room can be the most insecure within him or herself and is just trying to survive like everyone else (this of course doesn't excuse the behavior at all). Underneath it all, we all have similar fears, pains, shames, anxieties, and desires to be accepted. It's just that some approach it in a hurtful and demeaning way. When you're in school, being liked seems to be the most important thing in the whole world, when in reality, as you grow up, it's not important who you impress or who decides whether or not you're cool enough to sit at the lunch table. Don't waste time being who others expect you to be and lose the opportunity to build real friendships that will later have meaning and purpose beyond any superficial encounter.

If you are experiencing bullying, being left out, or being hurt in some way, please don't see it as the end, because no one gets to decide that you are loveable besides you. You are special and unique in your own ways, and this doesn't mean you are any less important. Don't let anyone knock you down and take power from who you are.

Kids today take bullying to a new level and don't realize the internal pain people are walking away with, or the end consequences: suicide or drug and alcohol abuse. Instead of judging someone because of what they look like or who they sit with, try getting to know them, because you could be surprised to find out you are going through the same issues.

We are all beautiful and loveable and should be accepted for who we are, no matter what. The most important thing about feeling accepted is to work on acceptance of self. Love from others is more welcomed when we love ourselves. If you have this, no one and nothing can ever get to you. Help and resources are available to guide you through, so don't shut down or isolate from the world—speak up and be proud of yourself!

Melissa Ann Hopely

I could have never imagined that Jessica, one of the first friends that I looked up to felt different at times just like me. I was reassured that I wasn't completely alone with some things, but it didn't make me feel completely relieved. I just couldn't understand how people could treat others so wrong at times to the point where people actually changed themselves to try to fit in. I knew I was starting to do this because I was so afraid of what others would think of my behaviors and issues. What scared me most was that I wasn't only hiding and trying to act differently towards my friends and peers, but to my family as well.

Chapter Five

Is this the real me?

There were many times I was in certain moments that I didn't feel like the real me. From a young age, we experience many things and form memories that tend to pop up when we are reminded by taste, smell, or sight. I always wondered if I was literally taking in everything at every possible moment while being my real self. It's scary to think that we are in these moments and we can't feel everything and be everything we want to be.

Through all the happy and horrible things that happened, was I really fully experiencing them or thinking of other things and trying to be someone or somewhere else? Every part of my past is a part of me, but it doesn't necessarily define me as a whole person, does it? There are so many internal and external factors that help shape our paths in life and who we are at this moment. I wondered what my hidden issues and distractions were causing me to miss. I wanted to believe that every experience—whether triumphs, tragedies, or obstacles—was paving my path for the future and made up every part of me. But with the constant battle to be myself, I wondered if really experiencing things in that given moment was even possible.

Sports seemed to be my escape from everything in life. I was very talented starting at a young age. My grandfathers still tell me to this day, how I would steal the basketball off my own teammates in games because I wanted to score. I got that all the kids had different skill levels, and some of them were forced to play sports by their parents, but I just wanted to score and win and have control on the court, because sometimes that was the only time I felt like I had any control.

Whenever I was on a sports field or court, I felt like somebody, and like nothing could bother me. Somehow, I had control of all my emotions and behaviors during the games. Right when the buzzer sounded, though—that's where it got complicated, and those weird

39

feelings and behaviors would come back.

Sometimes I would think to myself, "So am I supposed to be this normal kid who plays sports and has friends, or this weirdo who feels these urges to do odd things, gets overly nervous, and sometimes acts out annoyingly in front of people?" I thought I knew who I was *supposed* to be or wanted to be, but there was something in my mind and body telling me I had to be that weirdo too. I didn't know what to do, and I didn't understand why I couldn't be like everyone else all the time.

I've seen the Loony Tunes cartoons with characters depicting Jekyll and Hyde; this guy would be totally normal and then, in a split second, he'd turn green and be really mean to Bugs Bunny. I sometimes wondered if that's how the rest of my life was going to be, because at times it seemed like I was this normal kid, and in a split second I became that weirdo again.

It didn't help that people were now noticing. My aunts started becoming very vocal about my issues, and instead of feeling like they wanted to help, it seemed like they were just out to embarrass me, because they knew nothing about my issues. I wished they'd just continued focusing on their own perfect little lives, because obviously they had no issues of their own.

Meet my; Aunt Judy

For most of Missy's childhood, I knew there was something wrong and she needed help. I admit to calling her crazy and still say "cuckoo" in a loving way. I knew her behaviors and acting out were not just for attention, and I told my sister (her mom) repeatedly to get her help and to tell Missy's teachers, but she didn't want to tell anyone due to fear and embarrassment.

I always mentioned to Missy that she needed to go to a special kind of doctor, and it put fear in her mind. One particular night stands out: when I took Missy to a play in Philadelphia, and we got stuck outside of a parking garage after the show ended. She suddenly grew uncomfortable as we waited in line and I couldn't believe the amount of anxiety this little girl had. I didn't know what to do with her.

As the minutes passed, Missy started pacing and yelling, "We are going to get killed, oh my gosh; we are going to die."

With everyone looking over at us, I turned to Missy and asked her to come stand on the corner with me, but she wouldn't budge. She kept yelling about us getting shot and killed.

My response was, "We are around people and safe, and it's our home city, Philadelphia."

Missy frantically cried, "But New York City is safer—I went there, I know."

I kept trying to reassure Missy that we were on a corner with a lot of people, but she was fixated on the fact that we might get shot and die.

We didn't move for half an hour; she drove me nuts and gave me so much anxiety that I wonder what the people around us were thinking.

I felt bad for her, but even with her issues, she was still a normal kid who played with friends and went through the normal childhood issues, but I sensed my sister was embarrassed about her daughter's issues and probably didn't want to go through a repeat of what my brother had put our family through. My oldest brother, Ken, faced addiction, substance abuse issues, and mental illness at a young age that affected our whole family. I was only in grade school when my brother went to rehab for the first time. There were six kids in the family, and we had to go to family therapy because of all the issues my brother was causing. We initially thought it was mostly alcohol abuse, but I remember sitting in family therapy and learning that my brother was addicted to cocaine. It killed me because I looked up to him. He was my hero, my mentor, and I always loved being around him.

My mom and dad did everything they could to be there for my brother and try to help all the other siblings cope. I found my parents to be amazing. They raised six kids of their own and had foster babies living with us too. They tried everything to help my brother, sometimes enabling him too much, but they loved him and wanted to help their son and still raise a loving family.

Over the years, things got tough. I was a young mother struggling to raise a family and having issues with my ex-husband. Having my first baby at nineteen was really hard. All of my friends were going to college and partying, and I was changing diapers. I had the amazing support of my family, and even though my parents were dealing with my brother, they were always there for me. However, it was hard trying to live my own life when I still felt somewhat responsible to help and support my brother and family. There were calls in the middle of the night, suicide threats with the gun he shouldn't have had, frequent police visits to his house, and a family trying to hold it together, pray, and hope that their brother and son would get better.

I can't complain because I was blessed with many things growing up, but I can recall many times when my brother ruined events and holidays for us. One year he chased us around drunk, and we were scared to death. Another year the Christmas tree was knocked down and ruined. There were plenty of times when we thought he was dead. I know my parents got many calls in the middle of the night from him or someone demanding money or their son would die. I don't know how they held it together and remained so strong and hopeful, but it inspired us all.

I went to the counselor a lot at school. Part of it was to get out of class, but it also allowed me to vent about my family stuff. I learned my parents finally were kicking my brother out of the house. We were all scared, but I knew my parents were doing the right thing and trying to let him fall down so he could pick himself back up. We were all there to support and love him, but we couldn't enable him anymore.

Being able to talk to friends really helped me stay strong through it all. I learned that my brother had a disease—an addiction—and it wasn't his fault. However, he did have all the tools, love, and support to stay in recovery, but it was his choice not to take that road.

I have nothing to be embarrassed about, and neither do my parents. I know one talk show host recently said, "My kids have never been arrested, in jail, or addicted to anything, so I must be doing something right as a parent." I honestly think that was one of the stupidest things any person could say. There is so much research and talk about addiction and mental illness and the brain and it's not something someone gets specifically due to bad parenting. My parents provided an amazing life for my siblings and me, and I wouldn't change anything for the world. Yes, it was hard at times, and I wondered what would happen next, but everything we went through taught us lessons. I know what I experienced with my brother helped me realize that, as a little girl, Missy needed help, and there was nothing to be embarrassed about.

I had no idea my aunt had a story of her own or how much she did want to help me. I just felt people were so embarrassed by me that I had to hide from everyone and stay in this bubble, convincing myself that I had the perfect life and that these odd behaviors would go away, just like the common cold.

But my behaviors and bad thoughts didn't go away; they just became stronger, more forceful, and more habitual over time. I started wondering what my future would look like and if I could even survive. Every day I struggled to feel in control and make the bad thoughts go away, but they always made me obsess about bad things and kept coming back more often and when the physical pain came, the only thing I knew to do were the odd behaviors. It happened over and over again, sometimes over one hundred times a day, but as long as nobody saw and it wasn't affecting anyone else, I ultimately didn't care; it's how I survived. Unfortunately, over time, people started noticing, and I actually started affecting others' lives as well, more than I wanted to believe. I started wondering if this part of me that I tried to hide so often was actually the real me.

Chapter Six

You're never too young

At times certain people in my life have said things like, "It's all about you isn't it?" For me, that is one of the lowest blows I could face. I won't lie: part of my work and dreams are for my family and me, yes, and whose aren't? But honestly, I wouldn't be doing the work I'm doing if my genuine hope wasn't to help and inspire others. We all at some point face judgment, embarrassment, and even being called out. It's not a fun thing and not something anyone looks forward to.

I've faced a lot of judgment in my life from some of my aunts and uncles and from my peers, and even today I get comments such as, "When are you going to get a real job?" or "Wait, getting back to Missy." It's funny on the surface, and it has become an ongoing joke, but sometimes it eats away at my heart and mind. I am so focused on pleasing everyone and making sure I'm not being judged, yet here I am trying to inspire people to be themselves and not worry what others think of them.

Worrying about what others think is a normal part of being human, but don't you think we waste too much time doing this and trying to please everyone around us? I'm not saying to go out there and refuse to listen to anyone's opinions, or if someone makes a comment about you, hit them harder than they hit you. I am merely saying that those internal thoughts we experience about what people think about us are taking up time and little bits of the energy we could be using to do something helpful or enjoyable for another person or for ourselves. Sometimes it's hard to do things for yourself and make it "all about you" because you face criticism from others. But that constant battle to please others, fit in, and try to be yourself at the same time, can have you missing out on things right in front of you, and have you experiencing a lot of unhappy moments.

Grade school was the first time I experienced cliques and the constant battle of trying to fit in. Living on Beach Ave. was easy because everyone fit in and, aside for a few innocent fights; everyone accepted each other for who they were. But now that I was in grade school in a whole other town, I found myself acting out for any kind of attention and trying to be like the popular kids so I could feel a sense of worth from others and hide my issues.

The stress of fitting in added to my urges to stop bad things from happening. I no longer had to touch the corners of tables, but I continued with turning light switches on and off, plugging and unplugging things from the wall, not being able to use the vacuum, obsessing over doors being locked, and worrying about whether the oven was turned off. I also started staring at different objects like pictures on the wall or cars a certain number of times and started replaying events that happened in the day over and over again perfectly before I could go to sleep at night. The events had to be remembered exactly the way they happened, or I would have to start all over. This sometimes took up to two hours. It became more difficult when some of my classmates started to notice and at times mocked me for my behaviors.

My memories of fifth and sixth grade are a bit fuzzy, with bouts of urges and obsessions and a continuous struggle to fit in. Even though my fifth grade teacher would always say, "Missy, your mother must be a saint," she was my absolute favorite. She would always give me the attention I needed and push me to make choices and figure out math problems on my own.

Some of my other teachers, however, didn't want to deal with me. Because of my anxiety, some teachers and classmates sometimes believed I was acting out just for attention; they had no idea what was going on inside my mind and body. They just didn't understand; no one did. Maybe it was because I was the only sixth grader in the world dealing with anything like this.

I do recall hearing many times, "Get over it, you're too young to have any stress in your life." So was I really just acting out for attention and all my issues just made up? I honestly didn't know what to believe and wondered if I could just get over it. But it had me wondering, was there a certain age where you started dealing with issues or were there kids just like me dealing with things too? I couldn't be the only one, could I?

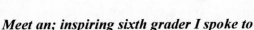

Melissa Ann Hopely

Meet an; inspiring sixth grader I spoke to

For someone my age, I don't think I've been through a lot, but others seem to think differently. Maybe they're right, but all I know is other people face horrible things, and I just want to spread some hope around to people just like Melissa does.

I did always think I was alone, but after seeing Melissa speak at my middle school I knew I wasn't, and I knew I had the power to help change the world. It's hard to do this in sixth grade, but I figured I could start one-step at a time. I guess my story is pretty interesting, but I don't want to share it for recognition, just to help people know there is hope—no matter what.

I was born in Philadelphia and lived with my mom and dad. When I was four years old, my mom took her own life. She had bi-polar disorder and depression and battled drug addiction as well. She would spend most of her time crying on the couch. Unfortunately, I was the one who found my mom when she died by suicide. My dad was a cop, and I heard a gunshot, so I went downstairs to see if his gun went off accidentally. I knew my mom was down there and thought she was doing laundry, but I remember finding her on the ground not moving and just yelled for my dad. I may have been young, but I do remember too many details of that day.

I was in therapy for my behavior, and I do recall people and even my therapist telling me my mom's death was an accident because she tripped while moving my dad's gun. Years later, I got hold of some papers, and my belief was right—my mom did take her own life.

We had some great times, but I blamed myself and thought my mom's suicide was my fault. All I wanted to do my whole life was save her, so maybe that's why I want to help people so much now. Nobody wanted to talk about what happened, so I just tried to be a normal kid and play with my friends and toys to forget what happened. My dad didn't want to stay in a house that reminded him of what happened, so two days after my mom's death, we moved to my aunt's in New Jersey.

I spent about five years in New Jersey, but we eventually moved back to a suburb outside of Philadelphia when I was in sixth grade. Moving so much was hard, and I experienced a lot of anger with it, especially because I missed my friends. It was tough to move because I

46

would get somewhat comfortable and then have to go to a new school with new people and a new atmosphere.

I tried to people please to fit in; when that didn't work, I tried to be myself, but nothing seemed to be working. It was like everyone already had their friends, and the new girl wasn't allowed to be a part. I cried a lot and lost a lot of sleep, but eventually I found some really good friends who I clicked with.

Finding friends didn't help the bullying I faced. I had trash thrown at me, got made fun of on social media and people gave me the nickname "Ms. Piggy" from the Muppets—I guess because of my nose. It was ironic because that's what they used to call me in my old school in a totally different state, and I thought I got away from that, but now I had to deal with it again.

I tried to laugh and pretend it was funny, but it hurt. There were times I would cry a lot, and sometimes I would self-harm, which didn't do any good because I was coping negatively and letting things bottle up inside. I never could make fun of others though, because I believed that if I fought fire with fire I'd just get more burned and it wouldn't help the situation at all.

I always wanted to help people, but didn't realize it could be a reality until I saw Melissa speak. I decided to reach out to her, and she responded back to me. I attended Minding Your Mind run/walk for mental health awareness (Mind Your Mind is the organization she speaks for).

It was empowering to know I did something for a cause to help people. I thought I had to wait until I was older, but I realized I could make an impact even at a young age. I'm going into seventh grade and learning that it is okay to be me. Although I still struggle with issues and bullying, I know it's okay to ask for help and talk about things. I cope by listening to music and love Demi Lovato because of her music and powerful message that you're never alone. I believe recovery is possible, and I know you have to keep going even through the tough times because life is so worth it.

I do fear that I may face things like my mom because mental health issues do run in my family, and I am currently being tested for stuff. But my family helps me, and I already know that, no matter what, I'm not alone. I refuse to be embarrassed. You can't let fear and bad things stop you from living, and you can't blame yourself for things that happened, because doing that doesn't allow you to live on. I don't blame myself for my mom's suicide anymore because I know it wasn't my fault.

These days, I'm really glad I can be myself. I still struggle with judgment and bullying at times, but I just dyed the tips of my hair pink and blue because I wanted to, and I absolutely love it. Why not do things if you like it?

The harsh reality is that facing judgment will always be a part of life, but if you're comfortable and focus on the people who care, then you're way ahead of the game. I believe in HOPE and I know that even at a young age and even with the issues I faced and will face, I have the power to make a difference and help others. That's what keeps me going: we don't know what will happen tomorrow, but today we can live and be ourselves while helping out a few others.

After hearing this young girl's story, I was moved and inspired. She was so young and had been through so much, yet she still wanted to try to help others and she had this understanding about life that most people took many years to find. When I was her age I was trying my hardest to hide my weird behaviors and only allow my struggles to stay trapped inside of me because I felt so alone. I could relate to her feelings of being picked on. It wasn't all the time for me, but the incidents happened often enough. When added on to the feelings I already had, there were times that I honestly felt like dying would make things easier for everyone.

While I was in eighth grade, I became pretty close with a group of girls. They were not the popular crowd but were cool in their own way. We usually went to the mall on the weekends and just talked at the lunch table at school. During our visits to the mall they sometimes saw my urges to walk in and out of doorways. I tried to hide my behaviors, but the anxiety I experienced had me thinking and feeling that doing these weird things would keep everyone, including myself safe from bad things. I knew it didn't make sense, but it was all I knew and understood. I remember one specific time while at the mall, my friends were all hesitant before entering a store and looking at me. It was like they were waiting for me to walk in and out again. I knew they didn't understand and meant no harm, but it killed me to know that people were seeing my behaviors and sometimes expecting them to happen.

I recall one time when one of my friends started reenacting my behavior. She was walking in and out, like, "Hey, look I'm Missy! In then out! In then out!" All I could do was laugh, but deep down I just wanted to die and end all this awkwardness and anguish.

During the middle of eighth grade, I found myself crushing on this boy. He was a blonde cutie who was one of the smartest people in the class. I told one of the popular girls I liked him to try to fit in. It actually was going pretty great. He called me on the phone and asked me out. For a couple of days we talked and smiled when we saw each other in school. I remember setting up a date with him. We were going to meet at the shopping center and hopefully have our first kiss. His best friend was going to set everything up.

The day arrived, and I was super excited. I bathed myself in fruity body spray and loaded my lips with cherry flavored Lip Smacker. I arranged a ride to the shopping center and waited and waited for him to show up. "Maybe he is stuck in traffic, or maybe his mom made him clean his room," I kept telling myself.

I went shopping for a bit to pass the time, praying I would see him smiling outside and waiting for me. But he didn't show; in fact, he didn't call after that and didn't even acknowledge my existence. I cried and screamed that night because I was so nervous to go back to school and face everyone.

Inevitably the next school day arrived, and I felt like I was about to walk into a circus. Whispers filled the room as I walked to my desk with my head down—after stepping in and out of the doorway of course. I couldn't look up and face the smirks and the laughter that filled the room. I was dreading recess because I knew I had to face this terrible situation.

One of my classmates slipped me a letter that said something like, "Missy, he has a girlfriend and this has been a joke the whole time. Actually, it was a group thing. I guess they just wanted to have something to laugh about."

I didn't know what to think. At this moment, I felt like the whole world was against me. The issue was that I was friends with some of the people who knew it was a big joke and they didn't tell me. At that point, I felt more alone than I ever had before.

My mind was racing; all I could think about was what these people were saying about me and how they were judging me. I just wanted to make it all go away and do anything I could to please the popular crowd and not make it all about me.

That's when I really started making fun of some of my not-so-cool classmates. There was a particular student who was really smart but in the eyes of others, an "outcast". People made fun of her looks, her weight, and especially her high-top, bright-colored sneakers. I would try to make jokes about her at times, figuring it would take away from my being the brunt of it, but I always felt uncomfortable and sick afterward. I knew it was wrong; however, I was so determined to get out of the negative spotlight and get the popular crowd to like me all the time that I didn't care about how she felt—until I realized I was doing the same exact things that some others were doing to me and it wasn't helping my situation, just making me a hypocrite and helping no one.

Meet my; grade school classmate

In grade school, I was very much living inside my own head and not particularly engaging with the social climate around me. I never cared about popularity and found the very concept to be bizarre and unnaturally constructed. At times, this felt like a lonely existence, but for the most part I was content and focused heavily on my studies. I did not particularly care what anyone else thought of me; the opinions of others were not relevant to my sense of self-worth. I did get made fun of a lot and was judged and picked on for being different and a loner. I remember Missy being on the fringes of the popular crowd. I suspected that perhaps she had compromised herself for the sake of popularity, but I did not judge her for it then, and I certainly hold no grudges now.

If anyone did say something cruel, I sometimes reacted, but deep down I more often than not assumed that it was just their way of dealing with social pressures. While I could certainly be furious about their lack of consideration, I was never one to hold a grudge. I did not think it had anything to do with jealousy, but that was mostly because I did not really understand jealousy or what it was to feel that. While pettiness and jealousy are certainly possible explanations for what they did to me, I think that at the heart of it, it comes down to a lack of considering the circumstances and feelings of others. That is not to say they cannot later realize this and feel regret for past actions, like Missy did.

I would say that in elementary school, being gay never really crossed my mind in any significant way; it wasn't important at the time, and so it never factored in to how I felt at an arm's length with the majority of my peers. It was in my freshman year of high school that I felt the first stirrings of a crush on a female classmate, and it was as though something clicked into place in my head. "Oh. That's what this is. This makes sense now."

And even while that sudden feeling granted me some sense of ease, it came at a difficult time. Yes, I had friends then who I was very close to, who I trusted and who I knew felt different in the same way that I did. The fact still remained that identifying as anything other than heterosexual was not exactly convenient when attending a Catholic institute. Personally, I had already been feeling distanced from Catholicism since long before high school, but I had not truly had to face the thoughts between the routine behaviors expected of me.

So while embracing my identity as queer was not in and of itself difficult, acknowledging how it affected my questioning of what little faith I had was a far greater challenge— one that I did not think I could confide in my friends.

Gradually, it became evident that some of my teachers knew, or at least suspected, that I was gay, but no one would say anything directly. That would require acknowledging something they would rather not question, but rather avoid and pretend was not a concern. At one point, I tried to tell my father, but he blew me off, saying it was a phase and that I would grow out of it. I'm certain, ten years later, that he does not even remember that conversation.

I couldn't talk to my friends, my teachers, or my family. Even with those I wanted to talk to about it, it was as though there was a table laid before me where I could set my troubles, if I so chose, but could not trust that the legs would not buckle and fail to support me. In sophomore year, I contemplated suicide, but fortunately I was too deeply ingrained in my consuming depression to act successfully on those thoughts. If I'd had any sense that I actually could trust those around me with my most vulnerable aspects, then perhaps I would not have fallen so far.

Eventually, I did reach out to some of my friends. I even told my mother and later my brother. It turned out that there really were people in my life that I could talk to, although at that moment of uncertainty before telling them, I wondered if speaking was the right thing to do. But ultimately, I would say yes, and not only was it right, it was necessary—

for my sake and for the sake of the relationships. I see that now when, years later, I can observe how very distant I have grown from my father in our differences and how much healthier my relationship is with my mother, who knows me and loves me with eyes open. I would not be half as strong within myself if it were not for her tireless support.

We all need to find someone we can rely on. Even if it's terrifying, even if it seems impossible, we need to know that at least one person is on our side, so that we can take that external strength and let it strengthen us from within ourselves as well. There is no need to be embarrassed about your sexuality; if people judge you for it or anything else, then that is because of their own personal struggle with their own personal beliefs. Through my struggles, I have gained strength and now try to empower others in the LGBTQ area with the knowledge that there is hope and support out there and that it is more than okay to be yourself.

It's amazing how we don't realize the impact we can have on others and what exactly our peers are going through. I never knew my classmate experienced any internal pain and felt like she had to keep secrets from her peers just as I did. Now with knowing her story, I feel bad she didn't really have anyone to talk to. Sometimes it's too easy for us to say negative things to each other in person or through social media. I don't think people really stop and think of how their negative actions can affect others because deep down we can never fully know what our peers experience. Whether we honestly don't like someone, we are trying to fit in or make ourselves feel better from our own troubles; there is still no excuse for disrespecting others. It isn't right and it's time we make a change for the better together. Also, no matter what age, if you are facing something it counts and no one should ever tell you that you are too young to be dealing with such things. We all deal with various things at different points in our lives. It's all part of our journeys.

Chapter Seven

Will anybody ever understand?

It's almost impossible not to feel that our struggles define us at times, especially after being diagnosed with or doing something that the outside world can't understand. I heard years ago that cancer, or "the C word," wasn't talked about because there was a stigma or negative attitude surrounding it. It was like those diagnosed with cancer were lepers and completely contagious.

With many physical issues or illnesses, people can clearly see or easily hear about the scars or casts of others. However, with mental illness there isn't always physical evidence that people can see or hear or frankly even want to think about. There are many arguments about the brain being an organ of the body; even though we can't see what it produces or does at times, that doesn't mean certain things aren't serious or real. Today, those with mental illness face a lot of stigma—people think these issues are easy to get over. But literally, everyone has mental health, and our mental well-being is affected by many internal and external factors that we can't always control.

When I found out I had been living with a mental illness since the age of five, I felt empty, completely alone. I knew if anyone found out, I'd be judged and totally alienated.

My behaviors at home were getting worse, and I could tell my whole family was getting fed up. Most of the time my family and friends thought I just wanted attention and all the behaviors were just an act. I was called psychotic, crazy, a drama queen, or annoying. At times, I was mocked for my behaviors and told, "It's always all about you, isn't it?"

I can't lie, I had a great life, parents and a family who cared for me and everything I needed, but sometimes I felt so alienated because of my issues. At times I was hit and pushed, one time my hair was pulled, and there were a few times I remember being ignored so I would stop doing things an even number of times because apparently I was an embarrassment. As I left for school one morning, my mom said she was taking me to the doctor. I remember this weird shooting pain that ran through my head down to my stomach and to my feet. I knew this wasn't the "regular" doctor. I had this scared sense that the government was going to watch me through a two-sided mirror and find out everything I had been trying to hide.

That whole day I couldn't focus on school, but only on how my whole life was about to change for the worse. I just wanted to run away. I had tried that at times, but usually only made it a few blocks from my house. I often wondered if it would be easier if I ran away so my parents wouldn't have to deal with me. I even wondered if they would actually miss me if I were gone.

The 3:00 p.m. bell rang, and it was time to head to the doctor. I had this terrible, embarrassing feeling, and I couldn't even look at my mom. It was like I was this living diary and everyone was about to find out my deepest and darkest secrets that could ruin my life even more. We arrived at a psychology clinic in Newtown Square, Pa. I dragged myself to the front door, did my ritual of stepping in and out, and plopped down on a waiting room seat. It felt like an eternity sitting there, staring at the walls and taking in the horrible, dentist office smell that filled the air.

A woman appeared at the end of the long hallway and said, "Melissa Hopely and her guardian, please come with me." I didn't know if this was it—the moment my whole world would change forever. Regardless, I wasn't ready.

As the woman pulled my mom and me into a room, she started throwing all these questions at both of us. I kept quiet and let my mom do all the talking because every time I tried to even open my mouth, I thought I was going to puke up everything. This was all so uncomfortable for me. I had never really spoken to my mom about any of my odd behaviors because I would always get faces or harsh remarks when I did them in front of her. Sometimes I was even punished because she thought I was just being defiant.

I tried to daydream during the questioning intake process, but I couldn't because I was astounded and scared at all my mom knew—the touching corners of tables, the light switches, the counting things an even number of times, the punches to my head, the moments I would squeeze my head to try and change the present, the times I would jump up and down, the things I had to tell people things twice or even four times, the moments I would make my sister and brother do things an even number of times for me, the hours I spent in my room touching things, staring at specific objects making sure nothing bad would happen, my excessive worry and obsessions about the most random things. I wondered how the heck she knew all of this. Maybe my reality TV show was already in progress. Maybe this was all an act, and I was this terrible science experiment the government was conducting on odd behavior. I was overly paranoid, but not stupid of course. I knew something odd was going on with my life, I just did not know there was a name for it and that it was actually somewhat common.

After the interview was finished, the woman left the room, conversed with a psychiatrist, and then came back to inform my mom and me that I had an anxiety disorder called obsessive-compulsive disorder (OCD). I had mixed emotions at this point. I saw the fear and embarrassment in my mom's eyes, and this made me feel ashamed, but I also had a sense of relief because I finally knew I wasn't an alien. I was just a human struggling with a chemical imbalance in my brain that had a real name.

I was partnered with a female social worker. We will refer to her as Joy. I still get chills when I think about the time I had to spend in her office. Yes, I have respect for her as a human being, but even today my OCD cannot handle hearing or seeing her name or even picturing her face in my mind. Back when I was thirteen, we were not what you'd call a good match. First, I could not stand when she would say the word "ritual." I can handle it today, but back in eighth grade my OCD hated that word. Every time I would hear it, I would have to do compulsions and behaviors to stop my obsessions and bad thoughts from overpowering my mind.

For example, my OCD would have me obsessing with, "Missy, you just heard the word ritual; now you better go touch that door knob an even number of times or someone you love will die." I would actually get in arguments with my OCD, trying to say "NO" to it. But I never won that battle and if I didn't touch the doorknob in two sets of some huge, even number, I would get even more bad thoughts, the physical pain would come back worse and I would have to continue carrying out the odd behavior until my OCD was pleased or risk the bad thing happening.

Unfortunately, there were more reasons why I disliked my social worker. Sometimes she would make comments like, "I had OCD when I was younger, and I got over it."

On the outside I was asking her, "Okay, how long did that take?" But inside my mind, I was screaming, "First, at thirteen years old I don't really care about your childhood, and second, how the hell is that going to help me right now?"

Soon the actual therapy office became a threat for my OCD. When my mom drove me, I would sprint ahead of her so I could walk all the way in the office and all the way out before she could even get to the door. Usually when she saw me doing my behaviors and compulsions, I would get "that look" that every son or daughter knows, like you just shot someone and buried him or her alive. I hated that look and also hated getting pushed into doors and getting grounded for apparently disobeying my mom when I thought I was just protecting her and the ones around me.

I really hated that place, my issues, and the fact that some stranger thought they knew what was best for me. At that time I couldn't see how much my struggles were affecting my life and those around me and how this struggle was actually going to be an asset to my overall purpose throughout my life, but how could you see that when you felt so alone, misunderstood and different than everyone around you?

～

Meet my mom; Diann

My Missy was a bundle of joy and one of the best things that happened in my life. She was such a blessing, and I knew she was different in many ways. I'll never forget when I dropped her off to the bus in first grade. She was the youngest there, and I was sitting in the car waiting for the bus to arrive. I was just watching her as she started approaching the big kids and initiating conversations with them with the utmost confidence.

I could have never done that, and all I kept thinking was, "There is my little girl just chatting away with strangers." I always admired that about her. She could talk to anyone and was so caring and outgoing. It was one of the best things about her. I knew she was special and it would pay off and be a benefit to her at some point.

It was a shock finding out I was pregnant as a junior in college at only twenty years old. Ken, Missy's dad, was only twenty-one and we both had our whole lives ahead of us. What was supposed to be the time all about us, became the time all about our baby girl. Three months after I found out I was pregnant, Ken and I were married, and we lived in a small apartment in East Lansdowne. I continued college, pursuing nursing while working as a nurse's aid, but Ken dropped out of college to work three jobs to support his newly formed family. He worked full-time at Smith and Klein in their mailroom, part-time for his uncle and part-time at a supermarket. This one decision we made changed both our lives forever.

Our parents were both disappointed and a bit angry, but when Missy arrived everyone fell in love and knew she was a blessing. Getting used to changing diapers instead of going out all the time was hard for both of us, but we knew we had a responsibility and not once did we ever think about putting Missy up for adoption or not having her at all. Ken eventually went back to night school to get his degree at St. Joseph's University after I finished at West Chester University. We were a beautiful family, and I would say what we did wasn't easy, but possible.

As a little girl, Missy had terrible strep throat with a rash all over her body. Today they are relating strep throat to PANDAS (Pediatric Autoimmune Neuropsychiatric Disorders Associated with Streptococcal Infections) and OCD, and it makes me wonder about how it relates to Missy's struggles. However, even before her strep, Missy showed signs of something unusual because she would have to complete these odd behaviors that drove me nuts!

Starting at the age of five, she was always too anxious about things she shouldn't have even been aware of. Whether it was thunderstorms, driving in bad neighborhoods, or seeing strangers in certain situations, Missy seemed to be overly concerned. I would see her touching the corners of tables and turning light switches on and off, and she wouldn't plug things in or use the vacuum. We would always fight over these things, because I thought she was being defiant when she wouldn't stop after I repeatedly told her to. I was honestly embarrassed about the way she acted and some of the things she said and did. Even through my anger, deep down I knew there was something more going on with my little girl, but I wasn't ready to admit it. I guess I felt guilty and as a parent I wanted to do everything I could to make my daughter's life the best it could be.

Missy's odd behaviors and overly anxious ways had been present since her younger years, but I always thought it would just go away. My family members kept telling my to take her to the doctor; even as a nurse, I just couldn't find the strength to. I couldn't face the fact that my beautiful little girl was struggling.

In October 2000, during the fall of Missy's eighth grade year, I took her to a local psychiatric center to get evaluated. I was not confident in this practice, especially because it was a random place out of the short list my insurance offered. I remember answering questions during Missy's evaluation and feeling the discomfort and horrible aura that filled the room.

After being diagnosed with OCD and evaluated, Missy was teamed up with a social worker who had no professional training with treating OCD, but I just wanted a quick fix for my daughter. As a nurse and mother, it almost felt like malpractice having someone with no expertise with OCD treating someone with the mental illness, especially a child. To me, it's just not right because they are not trained to deal with this issue and could potentially make it worse, which did happen to Missy's OCD over time.

Every appointment was useless and a permanent dead end, so I was feeling hopeless, but I would never give up on my daughter, no matter how hard it would be. She would get the help she deserved and get her life back, no matter what I had to do to make that happen. I am proud to be her mother and in this fight for her and others, and I know there is no need to be embarrassed if your child battles a mental illness— or anything for that matter. They just need love, support, and the knowledge that you as a parent or guardian will never give up on them or the fight.

Seeing the frustration of my parents killed me. I was too young to be taken seriously, but old enough to know something wasn't right and that I was different from those around me. I admit to not taking therapy seriously and not taking my antidepressants everyday like I should have. I also admit to flushing my medicine down the toilet at times because I didn't want to admit what was happening, but I later learned that those actions weren't helping anyone. It was obvious things weren't working with this therapist, and I just wanted to run away from anything that had to do with realizing I had OCD, but my mom would not let me give up.

I absolutely hated going to any form of therapy until I was matched up with a therapist named Addie, who was young, pretty, and really cool. I was always anxious hours before my appointment because it was the only place I felt safe and comfortable with myself besides on the sports field. I could talk to Addie about anything and knew that unless I threatened to hurt myself or someone else, she could not disclose any of my secrets. It was like having the perfect best friend and mentor who could pass on some much-needed advice about life, but you knew wouldn't judge you.

But over time there was a huge issue: I wasn't focusing on therapy for my OCD at all. I was just using it as an escape from my life. It was becoming more of a venting and hanging out session and getting Addie to notice me—not just as her patient but as a little sister as well, and I didn't know how much harm I was doing to myself.

After many sessions with my Addie, I started getting comments from family members about my relationship with my therapist. Every time someone made a negative comment, I would get brutal, shooting pains in my stomach; it felt like my intestines were in complete knots. It was like they were trying to ruin my relationship with her. I didn't know how to respond, because deep down I knew my family members were right. I was becoming obsessed with going to see my therapist and could not even imagine not having her to talk to.

I was still in eighth grade and playing on four softball teams, two soccer teams, and one basketball team because sports were my only escape. I started experiencing these strange shooting pains in both of my feet. I figured it could have been my OCD, so I decided to ignore it. As I continued to play on my softball teams, I tried my best to push through the pain, but as I booked it to first base in my varsity eighth grade softball game, I stumbled over the bag, looked at the first base coach, and knew that was the end of my eighth grade softball career.

It was a tough time in my life because sports were honestly the only thing that gave me some sense of worth and relief from my OCD. It was like my home away from home, but somehow safer; I felt so alive and unbreakable. Now, instead of putting on my cleats, I was getting two hard casts put on my feet for at least six weeks, and I'd be rolling around in a wheelchair. It's funny; I was actually excited about the attention I would get from being in the wheelchair, especially because I wasn't getting any sympathy or understanding for my OCD. Was that so wrong? Plus at least it was two casts; an even number so my OCD would be pleased.

I honestly didn't think it was wrong of me to want sympathy from others, because people couldn't see that I had obsessions about bad things happening and got unbearable physical pains. They didn't know that the only way to take those obsessions and pains away was to do these odd behaviors, like turning light switches on and off and doing things in even numbers. At least now, they would see evidence that I was facing an issue. I had the two hard casts and a wheelchair, and I knew somehow I would get some kind of compassion and understanding.

Chapter Eight

Supposed to be the best years of your life

I was recently at sitting at a coffee shop with my headphones on and completely focused on my computer screen. I heard some background noise, but I didn't pay it too much mind because when writing outside in a busy town like West Chester, Pa., that's normal. After only a few seconds I saw a shadow over my keyboard and looked up to see a young man trying to spark a conversation with me. He asked if he could sit with me at the table. I surveyed the area and saw two other tables open, so I was confused as to why he wanted to sit with someone who was paying no attention to any of her surroundings.

I also wondered how he had enough confidence to ask a complete stranger to keep him company. I was a bit creeped out and somewhat hesitant. He did seem like he had a disability, but who was I to judge? So I couldn't say no to the innocent look on his face.

I remembered hearing about the European culture and how it was completely normal to sit and converse with strangers. I had often wondered why it was so hard for Americans to do this. In the past, I had been afraid to sit by myself, but over time I realized I was confident enough to do this. I wasn't self-assured enough to ask to sit with a stranger—I talked to strangers all the time, but to literally walk up to someone obviously busy to just say hello and spread some love was way out of my comfort zone.

That shadow over my keyboard turned out to be a guy named Ryan who was a resident of West Chester. I explained that I loved conversing with people but had to get my work done. There were moments he interrupted me to tell me how gorgeous the day was and thank me for letting him sit there. I tried to focus on my work, but every two minutes or so, passersby were coming up to my table, greeting Ryan, conversing with him, and sharing moments that had me smiling and thinking a lot.

What was Ryan's story? Why were people so attracted to him? How was it so easy for him to talk to strangers? I was impressed and inspired by this guy and kicked myself for being so hesitant in my first few words with him. I saw the joy he easily brought into others' lives, but was it like this all the time? I was too busy to ask, but I wondered what his high school experience was like. Did he ever face any judgment or criticism for the way he was? Did he try to fit in and please everyone around him just as I had years before?

These thoughts left me reliving my high school days, which some say are supposed to be the best times of your life.

I was always focused on trying to fit in, please others, and come off as normal and cool to my peers. Grades were not my biggest worry. My first two weeks of school consisted of getting used to my teachers and finding my place with my peers. It was immediately known who the cool kids were, and I knew I wasn't close to fitting in with them, but that wouldn't stop me from my people-pleasing and attention-seeking behaviors.

After being diagnosed with OCD, I knew I had to try to distract people from seeing or noticing my behaviors and anxiety. I did everything I could to hide behind this external life that looked fairly normal. I was involved in almost every activity at school, was one of the best softball players in my grade, and also flaunted this smile that made it seem like nothing could ever bother me. I talked to anyone and everyone, even those who weren't always nice to me.

Sadly my internal life was completely opposite from what people saw. In my own reality, I hated the person I was, coped negatively by hurting myself physically to ease my anxiety, and always talked down to myself while comparing myself to others.

Just two weeks into my freshman year of high school, the tragedy of 9/11 occurred. It threw me for a loop; everything I thought I knew about my OCD seemed to be a complete lie. I always had to do things in even numbers to prevent any bad thing from happening. On this particular day, I thought I did everything right—all the important things in even numbers—but after my principle announced the tragedy over the loudspeaker, I second-guessed everything I had done that morning and the night before. It was literally like I was trying to find a way to blame myself for this tragedy. I needed to feel safe, but at that moment, I was losing all sense of control, and my peers were noticing.

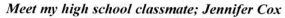

Meet my high school classmate; Jennifer Cox

September 2001 was one of the most influential months of my life. Not only was I a freshman in high school entering a whole new chapter of my life, but I would also learn of the most tragic attack on American soil in a classroom essentially full of unfamiliar faces.

At the time the first tower was struck, I really didn't understand what was happening; I simply thought it was an accident. I had no reason to assume otherwise. This changed very quickly as the teachers and other students began to talk about the possibility of a terrorist attack. For me reality really sank in when I got to my sixth-period science class. As soon as we entered the classroom I could tell things were far from okay.

Everyone's eyes were glued to the TV screen, which was full of horrible images of the burning and then crumbling towers. I hadn't been in my seat for more than a minute when I looked to my left and noticed my classmate with her head down and hands over her head. This classmate was Melissa "Missy" Hopely. Missy was one of the first new friends I had made since coming to high school. I couldn't help but notice how physically uncomfortable she appeared to be, and very quickly it began to make me uncomfortable as well. I remember asking Missy if she was okay, and she tried to reassure me that she was, but it was very apparent that something was seriously wrong.

As time passed, Missy became more and more upset. Initially I thought Missy was overreacting, but her demeanor only seemed to get worse. Missy repeatedly asked our teacher to turn off the TV. Within a matter of fifteen minutes, Missy could not even sit still in her seat. She was visibly becoming more upset, and I would even describe her as frantic. Our teacher tried to reassure Missy that everyone was okay, and he took her out into the hall to try and calm her down. Nothing seemed to be working, however, and eventually he had another student escort Missy to the counseling center.

It's no surprise, considering the events of the day, that almost everyone was upset and concerned; however, I will never forget the look on Missy's face. As I left sixth period that day I could not stop thinking about why Missy appeared to be so scared. None of the other students seemed to be as upset, so I knew something was different for her.

I remember there was a parent-teacher conference the following week, and when my mom came home, she specifically asked about what had happened in my science class on 9/11. She told me that a mom in the classroom had made a statement about her child panicking in front of the other students and that she was sorry. I knew exactly whose mom had spoken up that night, and it worried me even more. I now knew that the fear and panic I saw in Missy that day had followed her home as well.

Throughout the next four years, Missy and I had several more classes together and remained friends. We did not hang out outside of school because our friends were in different groups. I remember Missy confiding in me about a boy that she was interested in who happened to be someone in my group of friends. I encouraged her to let him know, but she almost laughed at the idea and told me she knew she had no shot.

I know that Missy never let this boy know, and I also know her crush came and went just as it does for many young girls. What concerned me was how Missy couldn't even consider that there was a potential for something to happen. Missy was always a fun and exciting person, at least from my perspective, but from the various conversations we had over the years and from different situations I saw her in, I knew deep down Missy was struggling to be her true self out of fear of what others might think.

I have always attended what I considered large schools. As a result, I have interacted with people of all different ages, races, genders, and religions. One thing my experiences have taught me is that you can *never* judge a book by its cover. It's so easy to see someone and make a judgment about how you think their life may be. It's also impossible to come to any kind of conclusion based solely on appearance. I would bet that many people would be surprised to learn some things about me.

High school is a tough time in a young adult's life, and it's a time when people can be cruel. For some of us, these were the best four years of our lives; for others, they can be the most damaging and sad years a person may ever experience. Throughout high school and college, I was actively involved in all types of activities such as cheerleading, swimming, softball, and student council. I had friends from all different groups; however, I had a very close group of friends for the majority of that time. I felt comfortable with this group of friends and therefore kept them close.

Fortunately, I do not recall being teased or bullied to the point where I was physically upset or uncomfortable. Unfortunately, I witnessed this occurring all around me and *that* made me upset and extremely uncomfortable. Seeing this brought me back to a dark personal experience of my own—one that may potentially have been forgotten by everyone except me.

My personal experience with bullying goes back to my fifth through eighth grade years at St. Joseph's School. As dramatic as it sounds, I can honestly say that fifth grade was the worst year of my life. I was constantly made fun of by a group of girls and boys in my grade. I had no idea how, in what felt like overnight, I had lost all of my friends.

I felt absolutely awful about myself. I was told I was ugly and that a classroom pet died "because it saw my face." I was told that I could not walk home a certain way from school each day, which resulted in my walking alone a much longer way along a cemetery. I can even recall a time when one of the girls sang a nursery rhyme in front of everyone at recess and changed the words to "Go away Jenn."

In addition, I was the target of a sexual joke that resulted in a formal meeting, led by the school's principal, with the entire grade. On top of my being embarrassed about a sexual joke at the age of eleven, the principal ended the meeting by calling me out into the hallway to discuss the matter further. I felt completely singled out, ashamed, and embarrassed.

Each of the situations I described above felt as though they were completely out of my control. I had no idea what I had done to warrant such treatment. I began to think, "Maybe I really am ugly," and, "Maybe there is something wrong with me." I could not figure out why it felt like no one wanted to be my friend.

Finally the bullying in fifth grade stopped. It was as if everything went back to normal overnight, and I had all of my friends back. I remember a time when one of the ring leaders started to pick on another girl. I stood up for this girl and was told to "stop being the peacemaker." Peacemaker seemed to be such an odd choice of words to me, as I was unaware of what this girl had done to disturb the peace.

My most vivid memory of outright bullying occurred in seventh grade. It was the cool thing to do to share a notebook with a friend. We would write notes back and forth and pass the entire book. We thought it was more discreet than actually passing a note during class. I had a few books with different friends. To be honest I really enjoyed this activity. It was almost like a journal that I could share with other people—a way to put what I wanted to say into writing.

Halfway through the school year, I found myself at the home of one of the other girls in my grade. I noticed that one of her notebooks seemed to look a little different from the ones I had seen before. I asked her about it, and she became uncomfortable for a split second but then eagerly began to reach for the book. It was almost as if she was proud to share.

What I saw in that book can almost bring me to tears as I write this. For anyone who has seen the movie *Mean Girls,* you are well aware of what the "burn book" was. This notebook I paged through was exactly that (mind you this was four years before the movie even came out). Each page was dedicated to a certain girl in the grade. The pages contained negative comments and listed each girl's flaws and imperfections. Nearly every girl was given an awful nickname. I was horrified but tried to conceal my feelings.

I got to my page and my heart sank. The girl told me that my page was going to be taken out since "they didn't have a problem with me anymore." My page contained a picture along with comments that I was fat and ugly and had a double chin. (At this time I was thirteen years old and probably weighed ninety pounds.) I fought back tears and pretended it didn't bother me at all, since of course my page would be taken out.

I remember leaving her house that day and walking home. I don't think I was half a block away before the tears started pouring down my face. I got home and told my mom that night that I was interested in switching schools for my eighth grade year.

She was very taken aback. It was a big change at such an important year. She told me we could discuss it later, but that talk never occurred. Things got better at school, and I realized that maybe I could deal with it.

Our eighth grade year started, and it was time for high school visitation day. I made the decision to visit Cardinal O'Hara rather than the other local high school. There were five of us who went to O'Hara that day (five out of seventy). I knew instantly that O'Hara was where I needed to go. I needed a fresh start and to separate myself from the group of girls I had attended grade school with. I think this was one of the most important decisions I have made to date. My life was changed, and I am forever grateful for it.

I have come to realize that high school was just a small part of my life. While very influential, it certainly has not defined me. Although I may have been considered a part of the popular crowd, as soon as I walked out the doors in June of 2005 that label vanished, and it was time to start fresh.

I found that same thing to be true for Missy as well. After high school, we were not in contact for years. I remember when I first started seeing posts from Missy on her social media pages about all the new things she was involved in, I couldn't believe how far she had come. I specifically remember watching a video she had created; it literally brought me to tears. It was a true reminder that anyone can overcome obstacles. Missy has proven to be an inspiration to many, and she certainly has inspired me.

Looking back it is hard to think about that time of my life because it's very upsetting. I feel sorry for that young girl, and I feel angry that anyone has to go through that. I know now that no matter how it may appear, everyone has a story. This was mine.

I couldn't believe that Jenn ever experienced bullying. To me she was one of the nicest and prettiest girls I knew. It really is unbelievable to think that things like the "burn book" really do exist and that people think it is okay to be so mean to others. For Jenn this happened many years ago, but sadly bullying is still a reality and what Jenn said is right, "You can never judge a book by its cover." But in our sad reality, people are still so mean to others and really don't think about the negative effect their actions can have.

During my sophomore year, I was diagnosed with depression, which made things even harder and it was just one more thing I had to hide from the outside world. Now I felt even more embarrassed. I was living with not one but two mental illnesses, dealing with people making fun of me, making fun of others to fit in at times, growing angry towards others for no reason but trying to hide behind a smile and athletic abilities, forcing myself to get out of bed and go to school (or were my parents doing that?), ignoring the fact that I was losing interest in the things I once loved like playing sports and hanging with friends and pushing aside the realization that I truly needed much more help than I was getting.

My internal and external lives got a lot more confusing after that diagnosis because, as each second passed, I was losing sight of who I was. People kept telling me to "get over" things, but telling someone to get over their depression is like telling a person with blindness to just look harder.

I started losing friends more and more, and I was sick of all the cliques in my school. It wasn't exactly like TV portrays, but close enough. There was the popular crowd, which consisted of the cheerleaders and football players, the "ghetto" group, the stage crew group, the theater geeks, the outcasts, the brainiacs, the nerds, and the students involved in literally every activity at school. I never felt like I fit into to any group exactly—not even the outcasts—but I hate even using these labels. Each person in each group was a unique individual but sometimes got too caught up in their own group dynamic.

There were times I felt like I was living a lie because most parents and outsiders thought I had a perfect little life. However, I knew my overly anxious ways and desire for attention came off to my peers as more annoying than anything. I always wondered why I couldn't be normal and fit in anywhere. It seemed everyone around me had a place on the high school scale, and I was continuously ringing the wrong doorbells and missing invitations. The popular crowd seemed to have it all figured out. Mostly everyone liked them and wanted to be exactly like them. I'm not saying it was easy for everyone in the popular group all the time, but seriously—what did they have to worry about?

It wasn't until I really talked to one of the most popular girls in my high school outside of school that I realized even the popular crowd had insecurities and issues. Ironically enough, I would later learn valuable lessons from some of those people, even the ones who put me through some of the toughest muddy waters of my life. But thinking about it, back in high school how could I have seen that I could learn anything valuable from any of those popular people?

In reality, most of them were very good at putting up a front and never letting anyone on the outside in. How could anyone else ever realize that they too sometimes needed saving and support?

～

Meet; one of my high school's most popular girls

I truthfully have no idea how I became popular. I think it carried over from grade school into high school. It all stemmed from the people I hung out with in grade school. When you knew a lot of people from different schools that all happened to be in the popular group and you started high school with all of these kids, the group became bigger: suddenly there was one big popular group.

It was like a force, because there were now so many groups of friends all in one circle, all under one roof. I don't exactly know how I initially became cool in grade school. Again, it had a lot to do with the group I hung out with, and who the guys wanted to get with, and what you did on the weekends and with whom. All of these things carried over into my high school career.

I had a lot of friends in high school, and I guess I became well known. Anyone in my crowd could pick on our less popular peers because they were easy targets and they didn't, in our eyes, have a bond with their friends the way we did, so we thought it was okay, funny, and cool to talk down to them. They were different than we were.

When someone said something inappropriate to someone in the less popular group, the popular group laughed, which made us feel a sense of belonging, and that our group would stick by our sides through whatever. They would always stick up for us, even when we were wrong. I wasn't afraid to say hurtful things to people because of this. Someone would always laugh and have my back, even if we didn't agree with it. That's what friends do. They'll stick by you even when they know you're wrong, and that's exactly how it went.

No one stood up to anyone in my group and told them to chill out or ease up; the person getting bullied sure as hell didn't stand up for himself or herself, and this, again, made them an easy target. It was like we could say whatever we wanted, and the fact that they said nothing in return made them seem weak. I've said this over and over, but it was easy.

I can remember Missy from sports in grade school. I think she stood out the most because of her red hair and great athletic abilities. I didn't know her to be annoying, because I didn't know anything about her besides her hair color and how she hit the softball. I did know other girls on the team though, from dances, mutual friends, or through the guys.

When we entered high school, I really can't recall if Missy stood out to me right away or if, again, I just knew her as the girl on the St. Pius X grade school softball team. I do recall one day in class when

Missy would not stop talking to the teacher and asking question after question and debating everything. A classmate of mine who happened to be one of my best friends told Missy to "just shut up already!" I guess I agreed with her but didn't have the courage to say anything to Missy myself. When my friend said this, though, it was funny to me. Funny because that's exactly what I was thinking, and I'm sure other people were too. It's just that this particular classmate actually said it. We saw it as annoying that Missy wouldn't stop talking and kept persistently asking questions. We just didn't get it and wanted her to shut up, to put nicely.

I remember Missy constantly going to the counselor—like every single day during this one particular class. People said things like, "There she goes again," because we didn't get why she got to leave every class and not have to make up her work or do anything. We didn't know where she was going. We didn't know why she had the privilege of leaving class, but we all had to sit there and endure X amount of minutes with this god-awful professor who talked about his freaking tree house and Beowulf mask. It was beyond annoying and it made Missy stick out. Where was she going? Why didn't we get to go? Who decided that she got to get out of this class every single day? Was she doing something fun, and if so, how do we get out of class to do something fun?

I don't remember Missy touching doors or flipping light switches. And if I did ever notice this, it didn't stick out enough for me to remember now.

I vaguely remember chatter of Missy being in the psychiatric hospital. I remember people being in shock, and at that moment I am certain that people thought about their actions in the past.

I have no idea why I started being nice to Missy during Kairos, our senior class retreat. I can assure you, though, that twenty-five percent of it was because I was supposed to and because that's what Kairos was all about. Kairos was, hands down, a great experience, and I don't regret going—I cherish what I got out of it. I gained friendships that I thought I never would, even with people in my own in-crowd that I didn't get along with.

I wasn't brainwashed when I got out of it, like people said I would be. I even got made fun of by girls in my group that didn't go. I talked about it and was proud of my experience there. During Kairos I may have had the chance to talk to Missy, and feeling obligated to get along with everyone, I gave her a shot. If I remember correctly, she wasn't so bad.

Being in the popular group wasn't as easy as it looked, however. There was pressure to look good, date guys, get with guys, throw parties, and get drunk. You had pressure to wear cute clothes and do your hair and, of course, your makeup every weekend when you went out, no matter where you went. You still got made fun of.

I got made fun of in high school too. Sometimes it was because of my weight, how I dressed, or some things I did. That's right: a popular girl got made fun of and even called fat. We all got made fun of, some more than others. If you didn't look perfect, you were picked on for something. In everyone's eyes, though, we could take it; we had thick skin, and it just rolled off our shoulders. For most of us, however, this wasn't true. We all had our own things and issues going on, and I guess being the popular ones and hiding behind our reputations helped us keep these things from our peers, but it didn't make things easier.

After leaving high school, I learned it's important to stand up for yourself and ultimately be you. Don't be afraid to talk to the pretty girl sitting in front of you just because she's in the popular group. And girls, don't be afraid to date the "nerdy" guy just because he's a nerd. Tell your friends to back off when they make fun of people. At the end of the day, it doesn't make you cool—and deep down you know it's not right.

If you're bullied, I disagree with walking away, to be honest. That's the cliché way to do it, but really, what does that do? It makes you look weak, and you continue to be an easy target. By standing up for yourself, you will show the bullies they're no better than you. If it gets bad enough, don't be afraid to talk to someone about it, or address the person about it. People dig that.

Above all, please yourself before pleasing others, and don't be afraid to stand up for others. I admit I made mistakes and am sorry for hurting anyone I did, but remember—sometimes the ones dishing it out are hurting as well. I'm not saying that makes any of it right, but the trick is realizing you're not alone, which is hard to do at times. There is always someone who cares about you. It only takes that one person to stand up for people to see they aren't alone. You aren't and never will be.

∼

I know now that the high school years are not the "best years of your life" for everyone. But before I started speaking, I was honestly shocked to hear that some of the popular crowd struggled at times as well. However, I think what surprised me most was years after high school, when I started speaking, the popular girl that just shared her story actually sent me a Facebook email and apologized for what happened in high school. She also offered her help if I could ever use it with my work. I give her so much credit for sharing her story because this gives another important point of view of high school popularity and bullying. I also give her so much credit for admitting that things like this do happen and hopefully someone reading this will stop bullying others and maybe even step up to his or her own friends if they are bullying someone else. Because believe it or not, whether you are in grade school, high school or even older, but still stuck in your "high school ways," you have to realize the high school years aren't the most important years of your life. Yes, they are important and can be great, but think of it this way, when you look into a straw your eyesight is restricted and you can only see a tiny bit of your surroundings. But when you put the straw down and look around you see so much more. To me that's what high school was like. It felt like I could only be focused on what was happening in front of me because of all the pressures I was facing from others and even myself. It was hard to see that there were better things ahead of me, but I had to keep that little bit of hope I had alive.

Chapter Nine

Hitting rock bottom is really just landing on solid ground

There are many things in life worth forgetting, things that leave us asking, "Why did I do that, what the heck was I thinking, and why me?" We want to make it go away. We're embarrassed and want to just pretend it didn't happen. We fail to realize that the thing that happened, although it shouldn't define us, is a part of us, and sometimes it's the reason we are in this very place at this very moment—whether good or bad.

Sometimes we lose the energy to move forward and remain stuck, or we become reckless and cope negatively, thinking it will push away the bad. The truth is, until we actually deal with things, they will always be there. We don't want bad things to define us and yes, at times they make life a lot harder, especially with the fear of embarrassment, but what happened to the resiliency every human being holds?

The cards we are dealt can have the power to change our lives forever. However, everything we experience and go through—whether hitting rock bottom or even being lucky enough to win the lottery—is a part of us, but a part that doesn't define us as a whole.

I always told myself I never wanted to be defined by my mental health issues and the fact that I actually thought ending my life would make things easier for everyone. Growing up, I just wanted to be seen as an amazing athlete with a great smile and, one day, become completely defined by my career. However, each day as I meet new people and experience new things, I realize that I don't even want to be defined by the one big thing I do in my lifetime. There is so much more to a person than just a diagnosis, an outstanding performance, good grades, making a diving catch to save the game, or earning a million dollars. I refuse to be defined by one thing, but also become stuck in the mindset that my rock bottom didn't happen because of my fear of people judging me for it.

After thinking a lot, I realized I wouldn't be in this moment today—speaking, singing, and writing this book—if certain things in my life hadn't happened. The beauty of my rock bottom was that I actually hit solid ground, and there was a hand helping me to my feet.

During my sophomore year, I met my bully. This guy was a year older than me and, with every chance he got, he called me out. He called me horrible names, hit my books on the floor, and always had me feeling completely naked and exposed. My response was to laugh and slap his hand because I was trying to protect myself from letting anyone know it bothered me. I also wanted to look somewhat cool.

With every encounter, I had tears, and my internal scars kept getting deeper. I would ask God, "Why is this happening to me and why doesn't anyone like me?" I knew there were some people who cared, but overall I felt out of place and started losing the will to even want to live.

One day I had to get a ride home from my bully's best friend, Mary Beth, who was also my neighborhood friend. We would play sports at the park and sometimes have sleepovers and hang out. I looked up to her because she was a year older and, to me, a perfect person—caring, loving, smart, athletic, and pretty both inside and out. She represented everything I tried to be in my external life. We had a little sister–big sister relationship that I cherished every day. She was always there to stand up for me even when her friend, my bully, tried to put me down.

After the bell rang and I packed up my schoolbag with homework and books, I walked to Mary Beth's car in the back parking lot. I knew my bully was getting a ride home as well, so I tried not to make eye contact with him. When Mary Beth was around, she was my crutch: she was always there to stick up for me, or anyone for that matter. But at this moment, she was too far away. As I looked up, I saw my bully staring and smirking at me. There were about six people surrounding him, chatting about anything and everything.

Right in mid-conversation he looked at me and said, "Hey faggot, go away," and waved a middle finger right in my face.

I was used to laughing and trying to put on a smile, but everything that was going on—my battle with OCD and depression, the bullying, my constant struggle to fit in and please others, not being the daughter my parents had hoped for—started replaying in my mind. With each second that passed, I started losing control and the will to stay strong. Tears filled my eyes; a fire sparked throughout my body, like someone lit a match to gasoline. I felt like I wanted to punch this kid.

I started screaming, "Why do you have to do this to me? You're an asshole and I hate you."

He just laughed and, as we got in the car to drive home, the situation grew even worse. He wouldn't stop tormenting me. With every emotional punch he threw, the pain grew worse.

They say, "Sticks and stones may break my bones, but words will never hurt." I think that is a load of crap because words can hurt badly, sometimes way more than the physical blow. One minute I was looking out the window with tears rolling down my cheeks, trying to ignore him; the next minute I was kicking the car door and screaming, "Is this what you want? Do you want me to die, to kill myself? What do you want from me?" With every emotional punch he threw, I found myself getting closer and closer to an uncontrollable emotional state.

Everyone was dropped off before me because Mary Beth and I lived three doors down from each other. I couldn't even look at her the whole way home, only stare out the window trying to fight off my thoughts. When we pulled up to my house, I left all my bags in the car and sprinted right up to my bedroom. I felt a tremendous amount of fear and embarrassment. My body was trembling while my mind was going crazy. When things got this bad, I usually hurt myself physically— punching a wall, pulling hard on my hair, or hitting something over my head just to ease my anxiety and feelings of discomfort. That pain seemed better than the emotional pain for me, but I knew it didn't help the situation at all.

As I turned my head, I saw my bedroom window was open a crack, and I had an urge to walk over to it. More tears filled my eyes, and I started having eerie thoughts about how easy it would be to just kill myself. I couldn't believe how much of an embarrassment I was to my family and such a burden and annoyance for so many people. I just wanted to be me and love myself, but living with OCD, depression, and the fear of being myself were taking over my life. It wasn't helping that other people added to my own self-hate.

As I opened my window, and then the screen, I became numb. I wiped my tears away and took a look down at my deck. I thought, "It's only two stories, but if I got lucky I could end it all in an instant."

More thoughts filled my mind: "Do you really want to die? What about your family and sports? You still do have a good life even with all your issues." However, the earlier event and the constant struggle to be myself and fit in overtook any thoughts of wanting to live. Minutes passed; I was contemplating suicide—or was it merely hurting myself badly enough to get attention? I honestly didn't know which one was better, but I remember saying, "Maybe if I break both of my legs again or break my back and have to stay in the hospital, people will feel bad for me, and my name will be announced over the loudspeaker at school. Everyone could think it was an accident, but for once I'll get sympathy and some sense of care from my peers."

The tears started again. I grew more fearful because there were parts of my life I loved, but even more that I hated. I knew this would be my rock bottom; I felt like there was no getting back up.

What felt like hours but was really only seconds later, I heard the front door open and someone running up the stairs. Usually I would scramble to look like nothing was wrong—wiping my tears and smiling—but I just didn't have the strength. I started crying again, and when I saw Mary Beth's face, I fell to the ground whimpering uncontrollably.

She stood in the doorway, scared but concerned. The first thing out of her mouth was, "Are you okay?"

I was shocked because I was used to people calling me crazy or a drama queen or telling me I just wanted attention and to "get over it." This was honestly the first time I felt like a peer genuinely cared and wasn't going to judge me for my issues. Mary Beth sat with me for over an hour as we both cried, and she reassured me that she wouldn't think of me differently and that she loved and cared for me. She also reminded me that I had a lot to live for and that things could be okay one day soon.

At that moment, I knew Mary Beth helped save my life. Although my return from rock bottom wouldn't be easy and quick, knowing someone cared for me was all I needed. I realized that hope existed even in my darkest hours.

Realizing you've hit rock bottom can be hard to grasp. I've always heard that term, but when you are literally in the moment of hitting it, you try not to believe it is actually happening—or you don't realize it until way after. I could sense this was my rock bottom during my incident in high school, but sometimes you do everything you can to ignore the truth, which can unfortunately lead to getting trapped in a vicious cycle that keeps getting longer, faster, and more complicated because you stay in the mindset of denial.

I found that there is no real easy or right way to come back from rock bottom, but having someone by your side can make a difference; that's why it's so important for people to genuinely respect others. We never know what that one smile or second of care can do. Moreover, when you find some sense of strength within yourself, you realize you have the power to get back on your way—no matter how you do it or what path you choose to take.

I learned this from a man name Lafayette, who was dealt a hand at birth that no one should have to deal with.

~

Meet Lafayette Kanard; a HIV awareness advocate

I'm twenty-five years of wisdom and have been living with HIV my entire journey of life. I contracted HIV at birth from my mother. She contracted it from my father, who was using drugs at the time without knowing he was HIV positive. My father has been in and out of prison ever since I could remember, even around the time of my birth.

My mother, grandmother, and doctors didn't find out my mother and I were HIV positive until after she gave birth to me. Doctors said I wouldn't make it past a year old. God and my grandmother's prayers thought differently. During my early childhood days, I remember spending most of my Christmases hospitalized. I didn't think much of it at the time because I enjoyed meeting other sick kids and making new friends. It helped me feel like I wasn't alone.

I began to have fewer visits to the hospital around the age of eight or nine. Then, when my teenage years began, my mother got really sick; I had no idea why. She passed away on September 3, 1999. A month later, I found out she passed away from kidney failure, which is a complication of HIV, and that she and I were HIV positive—what a rough time, right?

My doctor prescribed a cycle of pills for me to take, so I did. To deal with all the hurt, pain, and confusion of my life at that time, I began having sex. Using sex as an outlet made me feel loved. I started hearing more about HIV, knowing I had it but not knowing exactly what it was. So I just kept it to myself; I didn't tell anyone. It was a depressing, angry, lonely, and scary time of my life. I felt as though I couldn't be myself. I had to get counseling, I hated taking my medications, and I was angry with God, my mom, my dad, and even myself. I felt like I didn't deserve to have to deal with this burden.

Being the ladies' man I was, I had many relations and relationships with girls. I loved having sex and I loved women, so it worked. I then got bored and wanted to have more of a connection with a girl as I got older.

My first real relationship helped me to grow. The girl was amazing and very compassionate. At this time, I still had anger, and she kept asking why I was angry all the time. I got up enough courage to disclose my status to her. I thought she would treat me differently, but she didn't. Until it came down to having sex, we never did. Times came up where it almost happened, but it just didn't. We were together for a year and a half, and then mutually decided to part ways.

The second girl understood, as well; I disclosed my HIV status to her too. She treated me no differently and didn't mind having sex. I was very much in love with this girl—so much that we were having unprotected sex. We both knew better than to do what we were doing because it was reckless. She got pregnant, and had a miscarriage. Thankfully, she didn't contract HIV. We were together for almost two years.

Now on to girlfriend number three: she was amazing as well. This girl and I had protected sex first, and then I disclosed my status to her. She was shocked but still stayed with me. We fell in love with each other, and in no time I was back to being reckless again. You think I would have learned my lesson, right? Nope, she got pregnant and had an abortion. Thankfully, she didn't contract HIV either, but I broke her heart and we broke up.

I also had unprotected sex with my most recent girlfriend, who is now my ex. I got her pregnant too, and I made my second trip to the abortion clinic, which is too many in my book. It was the worst experience ever for me, and even worse for her. Again, with God watching over me and over us, she did not contract HIV. We both wanted to keep the baby but knew we weren't in a position to take care of or provide for a child, and she and I agreed to go our separate ways.

So you see I was reckless for years with these relationships, and so were the girls. Some unfortunate events occurred, but the most important thing is that none of the girls came up HIV positive. I learned my lesson and began living right and protecting myself and my partners.

I disclosed my status to the world through an article by Brooke

Minters in the *Philadelphia Inquirer* in 2011. As a result, my grandmother kicked me out of her house. She felt as though it wasn't my right to tell my story about being positive and that it wasn't right for me to tell my mother's business. I thought differently because it was my business now. I had the right.

I had nowhere to go and no one to call. I worked with a Philly-based brand called Commonwealth Proper at the time, and the only person I could think of to call was Craig Arthur Von Schroeder, the CEO. I had to disclosed my status to him and explain my situation of not having a place to live. He had a huge heart and understood, so he allowed me crash at his place for some time until I got on my feet. I'm thankful, and I love him for opening up his heart and home to me.

I worked for the brand, but I had no real income. I ate at Craig's spot sometimes, but I didn't want to be a moocher or a bum. There were times when I went days and nights without eating. I walked everywhere instead of using public transportation, and I had a bike I had borrowed from my cousin. That bike soon got stolen, and I only had my skateboard left, which didn't help when it rained.

I remember sleeping in Craig's car one night because I had no key to his place and got locked out. I also slept in the park some nights. Technically I was homeless, and I kept losing more of the little bit of hope I had left. It was a rough time; I felt like giving up. I also stopped taking my medications.

A lot of doubt crowded my mind while I was down and out. It was the lowest time of my life—I'd hit rock bottom. I kept believing, praying, and reading the Bible. Even though I didn't have a lot of food, clothing, or transportation, I still had faith. I was still alive and well, and I was making it through what I called hell.

Things began to get better, days began to get sunnier, and I reconciled with my grandmother. I moved back in with her, and right after this, I found a job and started my life over.

Somehow, I overcame adversity, even when things got super tough. Having gone through so much in my life, I decided to give back to the youth by sharing my story as a source of information, inspiration, and hope. I travel around the world to motivate and speak to teens and young adults about HIV, life choices, and how to keep faith when life gets hard.

I spoke at my old high school in Philly, Benjamin Franklin High, on WAD12 (World AIDS Day 2012) about my life with HIV. I talked to the students about how they can take my experiences and learn from them by using protection, and that the best way to not contract the disease is: no sex! I had a feature and got the cover of the 2011 September Issue of *POZ Magazine*. I will continue to share my story to everyone.

To anyone struggling with HIV—or anything for that matter—remember that you're not the only one dealing with it. You don't have to deal with it alone, and I want you to know that you are not alone. Keeping faith, praying, and believing are important; but know that things, you, and life will only get better if you want them to. You have the resources and people around you to help you become a stronger, happier, better person.

If you find it hard to keep faith, just look at me and my story. If you have HIV, you don't have to die from it; you can live a long, happy, productive life because God said you could. My rock bottom gave me strength, because even when I was down, I was never alone. I had a friend; I had faith; I had strength.

I was honored to work with Lafeyette on iChoose2live and Take Control Philly's Department of Health's youth documentary film where we first met. Lafeyette opened up right away about his story and I knew he wanted to help as many youth as possible. I was so impressed with his confidence and his will to live and succeed even though he was dealing with what most of us would see as a death sentence. People, especially young adults can learn a lot from Lafeyette and I am proud to be able to share his story. When you hear from others about how they overcame adversity and their rock bottom, it just gives you that little bit of extra hope to know you can get through things as well. I know hearing his story made me take another look at my life and realize that my rock bottom didn't make me a weak person; it just made me stronger.

Chapter Ten

You're not alone

I've found over the years that being alone doesn't necessarily mean the same thing as experiencing loneliness. You see, I was surrounded by people all the time and, from an outside standpoint, it looked like loneliness wasn't even in my vocabulary. But no matter how many people surrounded me, I felt lonely more times than I wanted to count. I knew it mostly had to do with my mental health issues because it wasn't something other people talked about. I've realized that some people are afraid of what they don't understand, so at times they tend to hide, ignore, or run from those things.

Living with two hidden mental illnesses wasn't easy. Although sports, friends, and high school kept me busy with activities, laughs, and things to do, I couldn't escape feeling like I was the only one living with issues and completely alone. I wondered if there were people around me struggling with the same issues, but who lived in fear just as I did.

Today I hear from a lot of kids who say, after they hear me speak, how comforting it is to have someone around their age come in and talk about real-life struggles. They realize they aren't alone. Even before speaking, I knew there were others struggling with things, especially when I sat on a panel with many brave peers in college who shared their very different, empowering stories. Yet for all kids and young teens, I wished there was something like this in grade school and high school. I knew a lot of our youth felt very alone at times, even the popular ones and as a society we weren't getting it through to them that they weren't alone and that asking for help didn't make them weak.

Meet my friend, public speaker and advocate; Jordan Burnham

I suffer from depression and bi-polar disorder. I was diagnosed with depression at the age of sixteen when I was just a sophomore in

Melissa Ann Hopely

high school. I wasn't educated on what mental health really is, and I certainly didn't understand how to cope with my mental disorder in a healthy way. I decided to hide my secret of having depression from all of my friends because I didn't want to be judged in a negative way. I figured people would look at me as just trying to seek attention. I smiled, laughed, told jokes, and looked happy, but no one knew what was going on inside me, so I tricked myself into believing that I could keep that façade.

Things just got worse when I wasn't taking my therapy sessions seriously, wasn't taking my anti-depressant on a consistent basis, and started using alcohol to cope with my dark times. By the time I reached my senior year in 2007, I was constantly having suicidal thoughts. I didn't necessarily want to die; I wanted the part of me that was suffering to die and go away.

That year, in September 2007, I attempted to take my own life by going out of my ninth-story bedroom window. When I hit the ground I broke my left tibia, left fibula, pelvis, jaw, and left wrist. I was bleeding from my brain and organs and was in a comma for five days. The injuries were devastating and led to a grueling mental and physical five-month recovery.

During this five-month span, I was interviewed by Mike Vitez, a reporter for the *Philadelphia Inquirer*. The story ended up being on the front page and was the main article. I got a lot of feedback from people across the country, but I also got a phone call from the executive director of the mental health foundation Minding Your Mind. The founders were a married couple, Amy and Steve Erlbaum. They wanted to start an organization that educated young adults in middle and high schools around the Philadelphia area. They were hosting a forum in May 2008 that featured four speakers; two of them really sparked my interest.

The first was speaker and author Ross Szabo. I had read his book *Behind Happy Faces,* and I was excited to know I could finally meet and talk with him. The other speaker I was excited for was the *Sopranos* actor Joey "Pants" Pantoliano, who was there to discuss his struggles with depression and trying to find happiness in the midst of his success with his acting and films. Joey felt it was important to tell his story and to let people know that depression and other mental disorders have no bias toward certain people; anyone can struggle with them. That's what prompted him to name his organization "No Kidding? Me Too!"

82

During his speech, Joey mentioned how he was speaking to Congress that month about why they should help fund resources that would enable people to seek help or treatment. The entire program was very moving, and I was more than happy that I got the chance to come and hear such moving stories involving the same subject that I felt I was so alone with in high school. I thought I was the only one struggling with understanding and coping with my mental disorder, so to hear others talk about theirs was truly touching.

At this point I was still weak, around one hundred twenty pounds, and dependant on a wheelchair. I was planning on leaving early because I couldn't stay up late due to my energy level, but I stayed and wanted to ask a question. I wheeled up to the microphone, introduced myself, gave a one-minute snippet of my story, and asked how we could help young adults talk more about suicide prevention and depression.

After hearing Ross's answer, Joey asked me how I was doing. I said I was doing better, but every day was still a struggle. When I wheeled away, there were people who shook my hand, people who said they had read the story, and people who said "God bless you and your family." It was a great ending to a great night. Joey actually invited me to come speak to Congress with him that month, and Ross read about it in the newspaper and offered me the option of speaking for the National Mental Health Awareness Campaign and Minding Your Mind. It's amazing what one question can do.

After my parents and I officially became a part of Minding Your Mind, we were invited to a photo shoot to put pictures up for their website. Once we got to the studio, the executive director was there to greet us and let us know how the photo shoot would go. She said that I would have some photos taken by myself in a couple of different shirts, as well as with my parents and with two young ladies named Kristen East and Melissa "Missy" Hopely. Both were a part of Minding Your Mind as well and shared their own stories. Other than that, I didn't know anything about them, but I was looking forward to meeting young adults who had the same mission as I did.

We actually met while we were having our pictures taken. Looking back, meeting someone while they're inches away from your face and smiling for the camera isn't the most ideal way to strike up a conversation for the first time. Nonetheless, we met and they both seemed really nice.

I found out that they were students at Immaculata University, which was only twenty minutes away from me, so I knew it was possible I'd be able to see them and become friends. We exchanged numbers and names for our social media pages so that we could keep in touch.

It was very refreshing when I first got to spend time with Kristen and Missy. I had talked to people who worked in the advocacy of mental health but rarely got the opportunity to speak to people in my own age group. I also got to learn about them and why they decided to get involved.

Missy talked about how she battled obsessive compulsive disorder and depression and how difficult it was for her having to go through high school, dealing with being made fun of at times while hiding behind her smile just because others couldn't understand or accept her. I was inspired and touched that she had the willingness and strength to speak out after dealing with her negative experiences.

Kristen was diagnosed with generalized anxiety disorder; she explained how much of a struggle it was to find the right medicine and the right therapist. I knew from that moment that we had created a friendship not only on a work level but on a personal level as well. I'm very grateful that our paths crossed at the time they did.

There were certain events that I wanted Melissa to be at, not only as a friend but also as a fellow advocate of mental health. It was important to me for us to go to events like these together, because support is often the biggest fuel for determination of a mission or goal.

It was also nice to know that you weren't alone in the fight. After feeling like I was the only one struggling in high school, it was comforting knowing I had a fellow speaker, advocate, and friend there to support me. That's what our youth needs today, so I'm honored I get to share my story and try to offer them some hope and understanding, so people know they are not alone and that it's okay to talk about these things.

After meeting Jordan for the first time, it didn't click that this was the kid whose story made the front cover of the *Philadelphia Inquirer*. It wasn't until on the way home that I realized what just happened. We meet people everyday and hear so many stories, but sometimes we don't even think twice about them. As it started to hit me, I couldn't believe how inspired I felt, but also how clear something became. I wasn't alone in the fight to decrease the stigma of mental health issues. It was so nice to know there were others my age that wanted to share their stories to help others and it was all so important because too many young adults felt so lonely far too often and somehow we needed to change that.

For me, loneliness didn't start disappearing until I made my way to the adolescent unit at a psychiatric hospital. It sounds ironic, but this was going to be the first time I would meet young adults who weren't afraid to talk about their issues in fear of being judged and where I would find that being myself was actually more than okay. Just hours before, I was sitting in the corner of my room surrounded by family members who were saying things like, "This is so sad, I feel so bad for her." Surprisingly I felt more alone at that moment than I ever had. After being evaluated at a crisis center because of my suicidal threat, I was taken in an ambulance to a psychiatric hospital. These would be some of the most challenging but rewarding days of my life.

I woke up groggy in an empty, dull room, realizing I was only fifteen and alone in a mental hospital. The walls were off-white and dirty; I had only a nightstand, a bed, and the clothes on my back. I felt lonely and scared. The nurse let me sleep in because I hadn't gone to bed until after 2 or 3 a.m.

When I woke up, I wasn't sure if I should stay in bed all day or get up. After I heard laughter and people's voices, my curiosity got the best of me. I walked into a room filled with teenagers, all different in race, gender, age, and persona. I was scared, so I sat quietly on the couch. Some of the patients started to circle around me continuously, like they were playing a game.

One girl said, "Yo girl, what's your name?"

I responded, "Hi, I'm Missy and just got in last night."

"Oh, cool—this is my third time here," another girl said, laughing. Her laugh made me a bit more comfortable, and before I could say anything else, we were led into group therapy.

I was still wearing the same clothes as the night before and was growing increasingly uncomfortable. In group therapy, we had to say our names and one thing we liked to do. Some of the teens talked about liking music, sports, hanging with friends, video games, and going to the mall. I was shocked to hear their responses. These teens were in a psychiatric hospital, but not one of them was wearing a straitjacket, conversing with themselves, or locked in a room with padded walls.

I remembered seeing many TV shows and movies depicting psychiatric hospitals; I couldn't believe how inaccurate they were. I know for emergencies and special cases they have those things, but it was honestly very nice to be around other teens who were experiencing similar issues in life and not judging me for mine.

I'm not comfortable mentioning some of the things that happened in that hospital, and there are some things I'll never forget. Overall, knowing there were other teens struggling was really comforting. I had always felt very lonely and thought everyone around me had the perfect life; during my stay I found proof that maybe someone I knew was feeling the same way I did—or very similar.

Many of the other patients had been judged, seen as outcasts, alienated, beat up, kicked out, or stigmatized due to their mental health and personal issues. Here they were, pouring their hearts out for a better life and a chance at normalcy. Even though we all didn't share the same issues, we all shared one thing: the fear of feeling alone in the outside world and being judged and defined by our struggles and prior choices. For the first time, I felt like the real me and felt less worry and stress than I had in years.

I think my parents were pretty surprised at how happy I seemed when they visited me. It wasn't an overall welcoming environment or a place where you would want to see your daughter, so my smiles brought much discomfort to them. My dad didn't like to talk about my struggles. We had a great relationship through sports, so that left my mom with the role of pursuing help and trying to find good treatment for me.

One day the doctor switched my medication, and I ended up sleeping for twenty-three hours; my mom wasn't happy about that. She also wasn't happy that I was on the adolescent floor, because the kids on my unit were a lot more mature and had been exposed to things I was sheltered from.

I actually signed out of the hospital against medical advice (AMA) because my parents didn't think I belonged there. I was so mentally drained at that point that I couldn't argue with them. I honestly don't think my parents ever knew that this experience, although frightening and so new to me, actually helped me more than anyone could ever understand. I finally understood that I wasn't alone in my issues, and that fact would never leave my mind through the years to come.

Chapter Eleven

Does this now define me?

When something tragic or unexpected happens, there are times you can feel total discomfort and out of place with those around you. It's like everyone is looking at you, and the more you try to blend in, the more exposed you feel. Usually people are good at sensing others' emotions because professionals say that ninety-three percent of communication cues are nonverbal, but sometimes people try to hide behind a front, pretending everything is okay and totally normal.

When I left the hospital and transitioned back into school, I felt completely exposed and uncomfortable. I had always been the annoying, outgoing student; now I was quiet and disconnected, so people could sense something had happened. Having to see Mary Beth for the first time was awkward, too.

After taking almost a week off, I went right into taking midterm exams and trying to get mentally prepared for softball season, which was just a few weeks away. Walking the halls was the worst. I felt the unwanted presence of loneliness again, especially knowing rumors were spreading quickly about my absence. There was talk that I had been in a psych ward, which left me wanting to disappear again for good.

A few teachers and counselors at school made everything a bit easier. I was close to some of my teachers and enjoyed their attention, so I didn't hesitate to tell them what happened. However, after realizing I had told my teachers about my issues, I started feeling more and more naked and alone with each day that passed. I tried to stay involved in school and didn't like going home, because I felt even more awkward and exposed there. Sometimes it felt like a no-win situation; I started losing friends more and more, and I was so sick of all the talk in school.

While in the hospital I wrote my three closest friends that I've had since early grade school, trying to explain what had happened and that I would be okay. When I saw them for the first time, it was awkward and painful for both sides. I knew there was a stigma surrounding me and my issues; trying to transition away from that stigma seemed almost impossible. My friends now would see me as their friend who thought she had it so bad that she had wanted to take her own life. Once again, I had drawn unwanted attention to myself like I had done many times before.

As the weeks passed, I was hearing from my friends less and less. I found out that my three friends took a trip to Florida without even telling me. I was completely torn up and angry, so I called one of the girls at home on her house phone. After I'd argued with her for a while, her mom got on the phone and didn't hesitate to tell me I was crazy and couldn't be friends with her daughter anymore. It was ironic because this same mom had called my mom to offer help and support while I was in the hospital. Apparently, after my discharge I should have been cured and completely "normal" again.

At that point, all I wanted to do was disappear back to the hospital and be among people that didn't judge me for the struggles I faced. I hated how this one situation apparently changed the way everyone looked at me. Did this one event now define everything I was and did? Did people forget that I was an excellent athlete and mostly happy-go-lucky teen who was just trying to find her place in this world?

It killed me to think that I was now looked at differently. All I could do was totally engross myself in sports and school activities and put on the act of being that overly outgoing, fully energized teen, because at least people would be talking about me for other reasons. Again, I started to wonder if anyone else could relate. Maybe someone else out there was trying not to feel defined for the rest of their lives by something that had happened to them.

~

Meet my close college friend; who lost her younger brother to drug violence

During the summer before my junior year of college, I lost my little brother, who was only eleven months younger than me. He was still a baby, only eighteen years old. I don't know why he died, but I do know it was a senseless act of violence. That was the hardest thing I have ever had to deal with.

Many people knew about the tragedy, and I hated the attention I was getting from it. I didn't know how to live day to day after that, because this was something that was affecting me with each minute that passed. I didn't want to be defined by it for the rest of my life.

You honestly never get over something like losing your brother—especially when he's shot and killed over a misunderstanding for a drug like weed—but somehow you try to keep living. I honestly don't know how I survived it.

I quit my job for the summer and locked myself in the house. It kind of felt like I was living in a dream, just floating through life and remaining stuck in the loss of my brother. I remember my friends trying to be there for me, but I completely blocked them out for fear of being judged and having to relive the situation over and over again.

Once school started back up, I kept myself incredibly busy with school, work, and lots of parties. I didn't want to be the girl whose brother was murdered; I just wanted to be the fun, outgoing party girl. At one point, I realized I was drinking two bottles of wine and half a bottle of vodka on a normal night. I guess it was my way of coping, whether right or wrong. I seemed like a great person on the outside, but I was a mess on the inside, and at times, I still am.

There is no one way or right way to deal with a death of a family member, let alone a younger sibling. Somehow you have to keep pushing forward even through the pain. There are nights when I still wake up crying because I miss my brother and I don't have the luxury of hugging him. Not one day goes by where I don't think of him, even though it's been over six years since his passing. The pain doesn't lessen; you just learn to live with it while trying to live your life and not being defined by that one event.

I have not moved on, but I have learned to live with it.

I got pregnant while I was in graduate school. It was a hard time, knowing I was going to be a single parent, but I also knew I would have help and support from friends and family. I did have to deal with my parents, more specifically my dad, who was so angry about my pregnancy that he didn't talk to me for months. I also had to deal with having a poor relationship with my daughter's father and the fact that my child would never meet my brother. On top of that, I had to work full time and finish graduate school to provide for myself as well as another life.

Melissa Ann Hopely

My daughter, who is the most amazing child I have ever known—yes, I'm biased—is now two years old. She gives me a reason to keep moving forward; without her, I sometimes feel like I would have no other reason to be here. Because of her, I have finished graduate school with a master's in education. I found a job with an amazing charter school, and I am working on owning my own home and finally being on my own.

I have to remember that life is not guaranteed—only death is. I know I will never be able to hug my brother again. As time passes, though, I am proud to be seen as much more than the girl whose brother was murdered. I am a graduate school graduate, a teacher, and a mother. I am making it a point to keep living every day as if tomorrow doesn't exist.

In the same breath, however, I won't be careless to the point that today could be my last, because I know how much pain and struggle an unexpected death can bring.

When I first met this college friend, I had no idea she had lost her brother. She literally was the outgoing, cool girl and I felt as if I wanted to be more like her because it seemed she was always the happiest, most confident person I hung around. It wasn't until one of our mutual friends told me about her brother that I started realizing that my friend was seriously hurting, but wasn't ready to talk about it. I didn't realize that she was coping negatively and feeling so defined by this tragedy at times. She and I have become closer over the years. When her brother died, I only knew her through my other friends and felt I was in no place to say anything to her. However, I wish I would have. I wish I would have let her know I was here and that there were people that cared about her. I knew she knew it deep down, but my hope was she realized that she would never just be seen as the girl whose brother was murdered. She would be seen as a great mother, sister, daughter, teacher and friend.

Chapter Twelve

What would you do?

I never want to be that person caught on a hidden camera who doesn't do anything when something happens. The bystander effect occurs more than we even want to realize—actually, way too often. Situations happen around us where we don't do anything to stand up or step in.

Maybe we fear being judged by others or becoming an instant target, or maybe we feel like someone else will do something so we won't have to. Deep down, I always wanted to be that person who stood up for others and myself, but my fear of criticism and judgment usually kept me in the background. Mary Beth, the girl who helped me at my rock bottom, was always so confident in doing this. She would stand up for anyone at any moment. I wondered how she did it so easily without the fear of being called out too.

There were times when the popular crowd in my high school pushed their peers to their limits. I always wanted to stand up to them, but I was put down so many times that I didn't have the energy or self-confidence.

I saw my classmate Chuck get picked on often. He was in my senior Spanish class and sat right behind me. He was a kind redhead who was considered a nerd by some. He took the brunt of most of the bullying by the popular kids throughout high school. He seemed to be a loner, and at times I could tell the bullying bothered him, but I figured he was used to it.

I witnessed one particular day, however, that pushed him to the edge. It made me wonder, "Did the bullying affect him even outside of school?" The fear of being judged and made fun of too almost stopped me from saying something—until this particular day. It would be the first time I stood up, stepped in, and did what I should have done many times before.

Meet my high school classmate Chuck; a bullying victim

I'd always heard people talk about Missy when I was at Cardinal O'Hara High School. Her name seemed to come up a lot. She sounded like one of those people who was involved in every possible school activity, from sports to the yearbook. Up until senior year, I couldn't have picked her out of a lineup.

Back then I really didn't go out of my way to get to know people's names unless I had class with them; if I didn't see you there, you were just another nameless face in the crowd to me. So when I actually officially met her in our senior Spanish class, I kind of went "Oh, her!" because she happened to be one of the few faces in the crowd that I actually did recognize.

I can't exactly say Missy and I were friends, because I didn't really go out of my way to make a lot of friends with the people in my classes, although there were some exceptions. Had I bothered to try, I would have made an extra effort to get to know her. She seemed pretty cool—a little perky at times, but that's not a bad thing at all. Most of the time she had a smile on her face, or something that resembled one anyway.

To me, Missy seemed like one of those people who had it all figured out: she was involved in everything, people talked about her all the time, and she wasn't going to let anyone or anything hold her down. Above all, she was just nice—so nice that I never understood why some people made fun of her.

My lunch table loved to make horrible jokes about her that always made me feel uncomfortable. But they weren't the only ones who made comments about her. I remember, when the yearbook was published, all people seemed to do was rant about how she and her co-editor put too many pictures of themselves in it. It all just seemed so petty.

Bottom line, if you had told me that Missy had issues back then, I would have looked at you like you were, well, you know…Now, if you said that I had issues, I would have said you were flat-out wrong. I didn't have issues: I had subscriptions.

School was always tough for me. And when I say school, I mean K through 12, not just high school. I wasn't like a lot of the other kids.

First and foremost, I was a complete and utter dork. I wasn't into sports of any kind; I liked things that nobody else was really into.

To make matters worse, I was the fat kid, and being dorky *and* fat essentially puts a huge bull's-eye on your forehead. Every day of grade school was hell for me. To make matters worse, when I tried to talk to my teachers about the bullying, they told me to stop being a tattletale. Nothing was ever done about the problem. In fact, things would usually get worse. My fourth grade teacher even bullied me for no apparent reason, a fact that the school agreed with and still did nothing about.

By the time I got to high school, I'd already been put through the ringer. As a result, I just kind of shut myself off from the world when I wasn't in school. While everyone else was going out, having fun, making new friends, and dating, I just stayed home. I'd go to school, get on the bus, go straight home, and just disappear into my own little world—mostly movies. As a result, I could pretty much quote by heart any movie I had ever watched, but I had extremely poor social skills, and my self-esteem and self-confidence were non-existent.

My parents tried to get me to go out and have fun and join stuff, but I didn't want to hear any of it. I was so beat down that I just didn't want to be around people at all. Eventually, after a little prodding from a guy named Dave, I did finally get involved in the theater program, acting as part of the stage crew and then becoming a performer in the shows. While my shell started to crack by senior year, one thing hadn't let up: the bullying.

People were a lot nicer to me in high school, so it was only a few people who were bullying me, but the attacks grew more intense and more mean-spirited. Eventually, the abuse started following me home, as a couple of the kids who were bullying me also lived on my street. I'd get harassing phone calls, and occasionally they'd barge into my house when no one else was around. They'd take embarrassing pictures of me and pass them around at school. They even filmed some of what they did.

I couldn't even get peace at home. It was so bad that at one point, I briefly considered just ending it all. Thankfully, I didn't, but I didn't say anything to anyone about any of it. In my mind, telling my family or any school officials would do nothing except make the problem worse, just like it had in grade school. I was doing my best to hold it together, stay strong, and not let it all get to me.

One day at lunch, things got so bad that I couldn't handle it anymore. Two of the guys at my table just wouldn't let up. One of them was a friend who would be nice to me in private, but then turn into a total monster in school just to fit in. The rest of the guys at the table tried to get them to stop, but nothing would dissuade them from tormenting me. I did my best to not let on that it was bothering me.

When the bell rang, I left the cafeteria and made my way to my senior Spanish class. I sat down and got ready for a quiz, just wanting to put it all behind me. As I tried to answer all of the questions, I saw Missy talking to the teacher. She'd been watching what happened at lunch and had decided to tell him about it.

A few seconds later, the teacher walked over to me and took my paper away. Tears began to stream down my face and I started to protest, telling him I needed to finish the quiz.

He said, "I'm not going to let what's going on right now affect your grades." He had Missy escort me down to the counseling office and stay with me while I talked to a counselor. They brought in one of the lunch moderators and, from that day on, while the bullying didn't necessarily stop, things were a lot better.

One night about four years later, I was on the Internet. Missy and I were social media friends, but again, I didn't talk to her much. I'd seen her posting links to a mental health organization called Minding Your Mind that she was a part of, but I'd never really thought to check it out. That night I decided to click on one of the links she posted. When I did, I discovered something that shocked me: Missy had OCD and depression and had been struggling with it throughout high school.

I was thrown for a major loop. Whenever I was around Missy, she seemed so normal, strong, and sure of herself. I never would have guessed that she was struggling with any mental health issues at all. The fact that she was now using her struggles to help educate others was absolutely amazing to me.

It was at that moment that I thought about how, in the midst of her own personal struggles, Missy had bothered to take the time to help me with mine. Here was someone who didn't have to do anything but decided to help—because it was the right thing to do.

I realized I had never thanked her for doing that, so I wrote to her. I told her how I never knew that she had struggled with OCD, suicide ideation, and depression. I thought it was amazing that she was using her own experiences to help erase some of the negative stigmas that surround mental health disorders. I told her to keep up the good work. Apparently, my e-mail was well-timed, as it helped her out with something she was working on.

Missy and I have been in touch ever since, and she's been a bigger help to me than she knows. For years, I'd been struggling with issues of my own, but I didn't want to talk about or acknowledge them because I was afraid that people would think I was crazy. I finally reached a breaking point last year after a particularly painful personal experience. I started acting out and alienating people around me. I even sat up at night wishing I would just die already.

When I finally realized that I needed to do something about it, Missy was one of the first people I turned to; I knew she would be able to help dispel some of the stigmas I had about seeking help. She told me she'd write back to me, but I didn't hear back from her until about two months later.

In those two months between messages, I started seeing a therapist. I'd learned a lot and was eager to share it with her. It turned out that the years of bullying had affected me in ways I didn't even realize: the doctor told me that I not only had low self-esteem and self-worth, but I also had post-traumatic stress disorder (PTSD). Ignoring the problem— just trying to forget it and move on—was only making things worse for me. By not dealing with it, I allowed it to build up, and it started to create problems for me in other areas of my life.

Six months later, things are a lot different. I feel like a whole new person, and for the first time in forever, my outlook on life and the way I view people in general have changed. I decided to share my story for two reasons: first and foremost, because Missy asked me to. Second, I did it because my story shows the effect that bullying can have on a person's state of mind.

The years of constant harassment caused me to hide from the rest of the world in a sense. Not dealing with it or talking about it actually made things worse. Had I not reached out and started to deal with my problems, things could have gotten much worse than they already were.

The first thing I would tell anyone who is having issues with bullying or even just mental health issues in general is this: don't be afraid to reach out and ask for help. I know that's a tough thing to do. People were telling me to talk to someone for a long time. I'd entertain the thought briefly before deciding I didn't need to talk to anyone and that only people who were crazy sought help. I had that mindset for seven years before doing anything about it.

The prospect of getting help is a little scary at first, but in the long run, it will be a great help to you. Don't be afraid to talk to someone, be it a therapist or a school counselor.

Another thing I would like to make clear is that even though it feels like you're the only the person in the world who is experiencing these issues, you're not alone. Everybody has something they're dealing with personally; some people are just really good at hiding those issues from the rest of the world. That person you know from class who's always joking, smiling, and having a good time could be masking a lot of pain inside. You never know what other people are going through in their personal lives.

Finally, if you see someone who you think may be in need of help, reach out to them—talk to them. I'm not saying try to diagnose their problems and tell them that they need serious help; just ask if they're okay and let them know you're willing to listen if they want to talk. Sometimes, something as simple as that can change someone else's life for the better and maybe even help save them.

Several years after Chuck and I graduated high school, I received a message from him. He wanted to thank me for the work I was doing with anti-bullying, mental health, and suicide prevention, but also thank me for what I did for him in high school. I immediately got choked up because as time passed I had forgotten that event even happened.

It was right then that I realized how important it was to stand up for something or someone; when you do this, that person never forgets. I knew there were other people out there standing up for things. When I came across a web page called "Stand for the Silent," I couldn't help but be moved and inspired by a father's fight to stand for all those who were bullied, including some who were driven to suicide—just like his son Ty. I knew I had to reach out to him; I felt an overwhelming need to join him in this fight so I too could keep standing for the silent.

Meet Kirk Smalley; an anti-bullying advocate and founder of Stand for the Silent

The boy's name was Ty Smalley, from Perkins, Oklahoma. He was eleven years old. On May 13, 2010, after two years of being bullied at school, he took his own life.

This boy was my son, whom I loved and would do anything to protect. On the day of his death, Ty was suspended from school for three days after he retaliated against a bully who had picked on him for two years. His mother, Laura, worked at the school he went to. She picked him up and took him home and had to return to work, as they were shorthanded that day. She told Ty to do his homework and chores and that they would talk about it when she got home.

When Laura got home that afternoon, she found that Ty had taken his own life. Instantly my family's world came crashing down.

I wanted to sink into isolation in my overwhelming grief, but I knew my wife and I couldn't do that. Somehow, over time we rose up and said, *"Enough!"* And in response to this unimaginable tragedy, "Stand for the Silent" (SFTS) began.

I didn't know where to start or even how to use the Internet, but I knew it was a quick way to reach masses of people. I dove in and learned the social media ways as fast as I could. I just knew we had to do something.

As my wife, Ty's mother, said, "We are doing this because we don't ever want another child to feel that hopeless, and we don't ever want another parent to lose their child to bullying."

On July 1, 2010, the OSU-OKC Upward Bound students decided to take a stand against bullying. Inspired by Ty's story, they wanted to make a difference and do something for all those out there facing bullying. I went to speak to the students about Ty, and that was the beginning of this huge movement.

On July 11, 2010, the Stand for the Silent (SFTS) social media page was launched. As of today, there are over 100,000 members. On August 1, 2010, SFTS held a rally at Western Heights High School. Then on August 24, 2010, SFTS held a vigil at the Oklahoma State Capital and around the world. There were at least nineteen vigils in the U.S., one in Ireland, one in Spain, one in Africa, and two in Australia.

We went global with our message.

Purely by word of mouth, SFTS Inc., a nonprofit organization, has seen unbelievable growth and support. The message is one of unity. The SFTS program addresses the issue of school bullying with an engaging, factual, and emotional methodology. I show students firsthand the life-and-death consequences of bullying.

With the help of Upward Bound participants, students are presented with testimonials, videos, and role-play activities. With this unique approach, minds are being opened, hearts are being touched, and lives are being saved. Students—some for the first time—develop an empathetic awareness through education and understanding.

The goal of the program is to start an SFTS chapter at each participating school. Each chapter consists of a group of students committed to change. These students will no longer stand for one in four of their peers having to suffer at the hands of a bully. At the end of each event, pledge cards are given to those who agree to Stand for the Silent. The pledge speaks of respect and love, hope and aspiration. Above all, it illustrates the main lesson taught through the SFTS program: "I AM SOMEBODY!"

In the last year alone, we have presented the SFTS program at over 650 schools, touching the hearts of more than 650,000 students and educators. We have established 365 chapters of SFTS in over twenty states, as well as several chapters in six countries. More school programs are scheduled in California, Alabama, Texas, Louisiana, Delaware, and Oklahoma in the coming months, and many more program requests are coming in daily.

The Stand for the Silent program is offered to schools and organizations free of charge. My family and I have funded the endeavor up to this point, with a few small private donations and sales of "I AM SOMEBODY" wristbands and T-shirts offered on the SFTS website, www.standforthesilent.org.

SFTS is about students teaching students not to bully. It takes all of us to teach students that bullying hurts and changes lives forever. Sixty-eight Upward Bound students and a handful of adults decided to make a difference, to make a change, and to be part of the solution.

My wife and I have met many amazing people through this journey and gained so much support from people like President and First Lady Obama, Lady Gaga, Oprah, Shawn Crahan (the drummer from the band Slip Knot), actress Ksenia Solo (who is now a board member), actor Tiny Lister, and Peter Yarrow from Peter Paul and Mary Singer. Our story was also told in the movie *Bully* and we have recently become an alliance member for the *Be a Star* program sponsored by the WWE and The Creative Coalition.

We are very grateful for all of this, but to me, the most important people to focus on are the more than 780,000 kids we've spoken to and whose hearts we've touched—kids who have decided to change this world. Every single one of them is the greatest!

Never forget to tell yourself, "I AM SOMEBODY," every single moment of every single day. You are so important in this world and can be that person who will make a difference in someone else's life. You have the power, and you have our support.

How could I not be inspired to keep standing up and stepping in after hearing Ty's story? It pains me to know that this little boy took his life because of bullying, but I couldn't help but be inspired by the tireless efforts of his parents. When I emailed Kirk, I was nervous about getting a response because I know he receives thousands of messages everyday, but it just shows there are many caring and dedicated people in this world wanting to unite with you to make the world a better place. I haven't met Kirk and his wife in person yet, but I believe one day our paths will cross in this fight to end bullying. Until that time, we will continue to work for the same mission and support those around us letting every one know they have the power to do something because they are and always will be an important somebody.

Chapter Thirteen

Recovery and accepting help —
"I could use somebody…kind of…maybe"

Asking for or accepting help isn't always the easiest thing to do. For some people, it's easier to stay in their own vicious cycles and relive the same path and outcome over and over again. There are those who think crying makes us weak and getting help takes away from our overall strength and independence. I used to think this way, and I did everything I could to push away and deny any help my mom got me, such as medications and therapists. After hitting rock bottom, I knew that it wasn't rock bottom that made me weak, but the fact that I was too stubborn and scared to accept help.

During my junior year, I was leaving school numerous times a week to participate in an OCD study at the Center for Treatment and Study of Anxiety at the University of Pennsylvania. My mom had tried countless times before to get me help; she and my grandparents had paid hundreds of dollars so I could see one of Philadelphia's leading OCD child psychologists. Honestly, the psychologist was great, but I wasn't ready to accept help and with each pill I flushed down the toilet and each therapy session where I acted out, stayed quiet or just didn't listen, I knew I was being selfish. But I also knew there was work to be done and effort to put in. I was already so exhausted from dealing with my OCD, depression, and the bullying on a day-to-day basis that I ultimately just didn't think I had the strength to fight.

My mom was literally running out of options and optimism, so finding a study at the Center for Treatment and Study of Anxiety was like a last hope for her daughter to have a somewhat normal life. My stomach would be killing me in the hours leading up to the study. Of course, the ride there included neighborhoods in Philadelphia so ironically every time I drove to get help, I was experiencing a significant level of anxiety just minutes before, but I guess I was used to it. My

OCD became my way of life. I let it control everything and did my best to never disobey it. There were times when people stared at me and mocked my behaviors, but it was getting so bad that I would take the embarrassment over the feeling of losing control, risking something bad happening, and having to deal with the physical pain.

I was the number one subject of the study at Penn. After the initial intake, I was told that I'd be in one of three groups. The groups differed in medication and how often the patient would receive cognitive behavioral therapy (CBT). During my many past attempts at therapy, there was only one doctor that had introduced me to CBT, but it wasn't until the study that I realized CBT might be the one thing that could ultimately save my life. After going through so many tries at therapy and medication before, I was skeptical but realized this was my best, and maybe only, chance.

I was introduced to a man named Dr. Martin Franklin. I wasn't too keen on seeing men, especially ones that were my dad's age. Why couldn't I be teamed up with a hot, young therapist for once? At least I'd actually want to go each week. Was that too much to ask? I was allowed to call Dr. Franklin "Marty," which made me feel a little more comfortable. There was only one problem my mom and I found with the study: I was put in the group with medication and very limited CBT, which meant I wouldn't be seeing a psychologist in sessions and doing much work with my OCD, which I desperately needed. Although this was the case, Marty promised that he would see me right after the study because he knew how bad my OCD was.

I really connected with Marty and trusted him. He was one of the few doctors who treated me as a person, not a patient, and who got to know me and not just my OCD and depression. We connected through softball—any chance he got, he would use softball as a part of my treatment. The talk of softball, which was my number one coping mechanism at the time, really had me wanting to see this guy every chance I got.

Besides Marty's realness, he did one other thing that most of my past psychologists didn't do: he explained OCD and depression in terms that I could understand. For so long, I had been confused about why I had to do these things and how CBT would even help anything, because not doing my behaviors and giving in always made things worse. Marty knew I was losing hope each day, and I could tell he genuinely wanted to help me.

He explained that you have to treat the OCD and depression a little differently; the key was knowing which thought went with which. It was getting easier for me to figure this out—I learned that if I had a thought from my OCD, I had to play with the thought and make it worse than it was. If I thought I would get in a car accident if I didn't do one of my behaviors in an even number, I would literally have to picture the accident and everything that led up to it and after it without doing my behaviors, so I'd realize it was an irrational thought and a false alarm, not a reality. It was very difficult and uncomfortable, but I knew it would eventually make my OCD weaker. For depression I would do the opposite and reassure myself that I was beautiful, talented, and worth it. If I thought that the world would be better off without me, I would have to think of accomplishments and positive things I did for others. It was tiring at times, and the thoughts were taking over, but I knew this was how I was going to get my life back.

I'll never forget the moment Marty told me something that changed the way I thought about my OCD forever. He said, "Missy, OCD is like a dog begging at the dinner table. Each time the dog begs and gets food, the dog becomes stronger and smarter, knowing it will get food over and over again if it keeps begging. However, if the dog was not fed from the dinner table, it would beg and annoy the owner, but eventually become weaker, bored, and go away. The dog is just like your OCD, and each time you feed your OCD, it becomes stronger. I know the physical pains are hard to handle, but they are false alarms—just like the dog's begging."

I couldn't believe it. It was literally the first time I had understood myself and realized, "My OCD and depression don't define me, they are just parts of me that I need to work on."

Accepting help was one of those things that changed my life forever. Over time, it became easier for me to fight my OCD and depression outside of therapy, and I started accepting and loving myself for everything I was. I can't say it changed everything and made things perfect, but my anxiety levels were at a lesser rate, I wasn't hiding as much behind my external life, and I gained the strength to ask for help in other situations.

I understand a lot of people don't believe in talking to anyone. Some people give up after pursuing psychological help and hitting a dead end. I always try to compare getting that kind of help to treatment for cancer and heart issues. If a doctor told you that you were going to die tomorrow, would you go get a second, third, or even fourth opinion? And if you didn't like your physical care doctor, would you seek out another one? It's funny that it's so easy for us to do this, but when it comes to our mental health, we tend to think every psychologist, psychiatrist, and therapist are the same, which I can tell you from personal experience isn't true.

I'm not saying everyone needs help or medicine; however, even those not diagnosed with mental illness pursue and accept help. Mental illness may affect one in four people, but everyone has mental health issues, and we all go through things both good and bad that affect us. There are those little things that upset us, like stubbing a toe, dropping a cell phone in a toilet, or getting in a fender bender. Then there are those more extreme things that hit us hard—like a death in the family, being diagnosed with a disease, or being in the middle of your parents' divorce. Everyone handles things differently, and everyone is affected in their own personal way. Sometimes the littler things hit people harder than others, while the bigger issues don't affect some people. There is no wrong way to feel about situations or an ultimately right way to deal with tragedies; it's just your way that you may need help with at times.

I want to commend my mom for never giving up on seeking proper treatment for me. If she had given up, or if I hadn't accepted the help, I can't confidently say I'd still be here today. However, in the beginning, even when help was available, I wasn't willing to accept it because ultimately I wasn't ready.

I don't hate myself or think it was necessarily wrong of me, because everyone is different, but I do think living in a vicious cycle and letting the same issues and feelings happen over and over again without doing something is completely unhealthy. There comes a point where we have to make a change or try something else to see a different outcome. Unfortunately, sometimes there comes a point when we have to force ourselves to ask for and accept help, and really come to terms with the fact that needing a little help doesn't make us weak. It was nice to know I wasn't alone with this.

Meet my college soccer teammate Casey Kehoe; in recovery with an eating disorder

I entered Immaculata University at the end of summer 2006. I was coming into a new environment, meeting new people, and beginning a new chapter in my life. Luckily I had something to look forward to—soccer. Yes, I was going to be on a different team than I had been in the past four years, but the familiarity of the game kept me excited and brought ease (even at a time in my life with major crossroads and underlying difficulties). This is how I came to meet Missy.

I met her during my first pre-season of college soccer and automatically loved her spunky, upbeat, and passionate attitude. Unfortunately, I saw her being criticized by other girls on the team for the same reasons I thought were her best qualities. It must have been very difficult for Missy, knowing that these other women were on her case for nothing but being the outgoing, motivated person she was. Still, she always seemed to have a smile on her face and a positive attitude. It always gave me a little hope when I saw the way she interacted with those girls and how she seemed so confident, even when others wanted to bring her down.

I even related to her in some ways, because I felt different too. At that point in my life I was struggling with a demon within myself that prevented me from accelerating not only in soccer, but also in life. I had a severe eating disorder.

My eating disorder began about a year and a half prior to entering college. At that time, I was eighteen and had learned all the things that health class and the media would have me absorb about the dangers and health risks of eating disorders. I remember beginning to exercise more than I would have in months past. After practices, I would still have to get in an extra run. Then I started to cut back on certain foods and educate myself on nutritional info—mainly calories.

I replaced lunch at school with exercise. When I did have to eat, I followed it with severe purging, either by vomiting, exercising, or laxative abuse. A few months went by this way, and I had dropped a noticeable amount of weight. Logically I knew that something was wrong, but by this point, the line between rational and irrational thinking was broken. I had gotten into a cycle of starving, exercising, food rituals, binging, purging, and then starving again.

After my parents found out, I went to the doctor for a check-up. I found out I was severely underweight and moments away from entering into a diabetic coma from dangerously low blood pressure and a heart rate of only 34 beats a minute. A week later, I was sent to the Renfrew outpatient program, where I gradually digressed from once a week to the day-treatment program, which is five days a week for eight hours. Before leaving for college, the team suggested that I take a year off and focus on treatment—getting better in an inpatient facility. I declined and chose to leave for school.

After that, I went in and out of programs, saw therapists, and even went to an inpatient facility for about two months. Not fully committed to recovery, I left the program. I had to leave school because I was not physically or mentally stable enough to be on my own. I did have times where I was better than others, but my eating disorder continued to hold a tight grip on my life—and that life even began to slip away. I didn't know who I was anymore and couldn't fall asleep at night for fear my heart would just give out and I would not wake up. It wasn't until about a year later that I decided for myself to get the help I needed.

In May 2010, I went to a residential treatment program in Lemont, Ill., called Timberline Knolls (TK). TK is a twelve-step based program that treats eating disorders, substance abuse, and mood disorders. At first, I was very reluctant to accept the help the program offered. Accepting help is more difficult than one would think. I believe it was the fear of giving up my disease and what life would be like without my eating disorder.

As crazy as that sounds, I didn't know who I was without it, because I had identified myself as someone with an eating disorder for years. But the constant support of my family, staff members, and other patients encouraged me to give recovery a fair shot—so I did. Treatment helped me learn how to cope with my symptoms and taught me how to feel again. I slowly began to learn about things I liked to do and things I liked in myself. I saw myself growing out of my disease and into a person.

Now, treatment by any means is not easy. I had to learn a whole new way of living life, leaving my eating disorder behind.

Throughout my disease and recovery, I've learned there is a large stigma associated with mental illnesses. It is no one's choice to have an eating disorder, OCD, bi-polar disorder, self-harming behaviors, or any other mental health issues, just like no one chooses to have a physical disease.

There were times when I was criticized about the way I looked or how I acted around food. I remember one time I was walking into a store when a complete stranger said, "Damn girl, eat a sandwich." It is important to become educated about these disorders and to reduce the judgment society brings on the people who suffer with them—or anything for that matter—because you just don't know.

Although it was not my choice to have an eating disorder, it was my choice to get the help I really needed. In fact, I still choose every day to live in recovery and ask for support when I am feeling triggered. Asking for support is sometimes hard, but I've come to realize that I am worth fighting for it. I have been symptom-free and stable for over two solid years. It has been a struggle, but I can finally say that I am happy and healthy—and more important, I have hope. Without hope there was no point in even trying. Having hope got me to where I am today because I had the belief that anything is possible—even recovery.

Casey was always a really cool, self-confident person. I'm glad she came into my life. Even through her struggles the way she carried herself always amazed me and she didn't know it, but she taught me so much. She wouldn't change her style or interests to fit in with anyone and she always stood her ground when it came to sticking up for others and her beliefs. When I was around her, it gave me greater hope that I too could be myself one day and not try to people please and also fall victim to my mental health issues. By this time, I was really starting to take control of my life and the ironic part about it was that I was letting go of some of the control I thought I once needed to have and actually letting people help me.

Chapter Fourteen

Be that somebody

E very person has a passion or craze for something. Some of those passions or crazes are for things that others view negatively, don't understand, or disagree with. Martin Luther King, Jr., and Harriet Tubman were frowned upon by many in the white community for their passion for the equality of African Americans. Susan B. Anthony fought for women's rights even after receiving criticism and being arrested for her beliefs. And today many are fighting for gay marriage equality rights.

Even with the inspiring stories of these amazing activists, many times people don't take a stand or fight for their beliefs due to the fear of being judged or the dangers of the unknown. Some also have issues with self-confidence and the fear that they may not have any support. They may wonder if it's worth even trying. Through much questioning and going back and forth with myself, I realized that it definitely is worth it.

For a long time I was afraid to use my voice. I kept hearing there was nothing wrong with that, but I was missing out on the important lesson that my passions and beliefs mattered in the bigger picture. I, just like everyone else, had the chance to make a difference in the world, through avenues like speaking, sports, art, music, or poetry.

For most of my life, I worked to please everyone around me and make sure I didn't say or do anything that went against what most people believed. It became a vicious cycle, in which I found myself agreeing with "cooler" people even though inwardly I completely disagreed with everything they said. I just wanted to fit in and feel somewhat accepted. When I finally decided to step out of my comfort zone and speak up about my passions and beliefs, I was scared at first, but I realized it was going to be a life-changing experience that would have me connecting with people and doing things that I could have never imagined.

In the fall of 2009, I attended Immaculata University, one of the only colleges that accepted me. My first year was almost a complete replica of my high school experience, with people pleasing, seeing where I fit in, and trying to gain people's attention in any way I could. I did experience some bullying from my peers, but overall I found some friends more easily than high school allowed.

It wasn't until sophomore year that I started growing comfortable in my own skin and realized that life wasn't always about people pleasing and blending in with the popular crowd, but sometimes it was about stepping out and standing up for yourself and your beliefs while still respecting those around you.

I found myself on a panel at school with other students I saw around campus every day. It was a small school, so there were benefits to knowing everyone, but that also led to gossip and rumors spreading easily. People thought they knew everything about everyone.

As I looked down the panel, I wondered what these students had to say, because this panel was supposed to be students with personal issues sharing their stories so administration could make the school more fitting for everyone. From the interactions I'd had with these students, I in no way would have realized some of the personal issues they faced day to day and how they sometimes had to put on a happy face for those around them. The students struggled with diseases, birth defects, accidents, mental illness, family troubles, drug and alcohol issues, and learning disabilities. I was stunned. I also had to share my story for the first time with a large group of acquaintances, but after hearing from the other students, I became more comfortable: I realized that no one was there to judge me or look at me in a different light.

After the panel discussions closed, I was approached by one of the counselors at school who mentioned Active Minds, Inc., an international mental health organization. She explained that I could share my passion for mental health and raise awareness by starting a chapter of Active Minds on campus. I was hesitant but knew the only way things would get better for anyone is if someone did something. I wondered if there was anyone else feeling trapped with his or her issues—as I did—but feeling too afraid to take a stand. At that point in my life, especially after being reassured that I wasn't alone by hearing my peers' stories, I was ready and willing to risk even my reputation to make a little bit of a difference. At the same time, I wondered if any of my fellow students would be willing to help me and do the same and that's when I met Kristen East. We didn't get along when first meeting, but after realizing we both had so much in common and a want to help others, we formed a bond that was going to help more people than we could have imagined.

Meet my college friend and mental health advocate; Kristen East

When I first entered college, I wasn't in the best place in my life. I was trying to figure out who I was and the person I wanted to be. Because of my attitude, I viewed people in a more negative light. One of those people was Missy. She stuck out like a sore thumb to me. She was loud and she was obnoxious. I can remember in math class, every Monday and Wednesday morning at 8:45 a.m., she would stroll into class with the same maroon sweatpants with the word "softball" down the left leg. Her smile was wide, but that wasn't the only thing that lit up the room. Add her braces to the mix and that was the icing on the cake for me. However, the cherry on top was at the end of the class when our professor would ask, "There's a few minutes left of class, does anyone have any questions?" Missy would almost always be the one who raised her hand.

Over the next year, I did my best to ignore her and focus on my positive college experience, but our paths continued to cross. Shortly after I changed my major to psychology, I realized that I wanted to do more than just be a therapist. After working with one of my psychology professors on extracurricular activities within the field, she set me up with a fellow psychology major who had the same idea about doing more.

When I found out that it was Missy, I was hesitant to work with the girl with the maroon sweatpants who had annoyed me every Monday and Wednesday the previous year. My opinion of the girl in the maroon sweatpants changed in a heartbeat after talking one night in a parking lot. It turned out that we were more alike than I ever could've imagined, and I had been way too quick to judge.

Ever since I was a little girl, I always felt normal. I enjoyed being with my friends, going on bike rides and vacations, and obsessing over boy bands. However, there were some bumps. I had struggled with chronic stomach pain, which kept me from being able to have sleepovers at friends' houses and even attend school at the end of the year. When I experienced the stomach pain, I felt dizzy and nauseous, and my muscles were so sore that I felt as though I had done a long workout.

I experienced this pain occasionally and I dreaded going to school every Monday. However, this all came to a head when I was a freshman in high school. I was in the emergency room almost every week for chronic stomach pain. I was unable to eat because I felt as though I was unable to swallow, which caused me to lose about twenty-five pounds.

I had been through numerous doctors, tests, and medications to find an answer to my pain. Every doctor was looking for a physical diagnosis, but they were unsuccessful.

During the summer, I was becoming my normal self again. However, I entered the following school year very differently. While doctors were focusing on my physical pain, my attitude was deteriorating. I was arguing with my mom, my grades were slipping, and I was obnoxious, loud, and manipulative. I was ditching my friends and exposing myself to the wrong crowd.

In February 2003, I attempted to end my life. I didn't tell anyone about it, and when I was unable to go to school the next day because of how sick I felt, I told my parents that it was because I had a presentation in my French class and was too nervous.

During that entire day I spent home alone, I felt physically sick from my suicide attempt. I lay in bed praying for God to take my last breath and put me out of my misery.

By the next day, I felt so guilty about what I had done that I told my basketball coach, and I was taken to the local emergency room to make sure that I was physically and emotionally okay. However, once I was released, things continued to go downhill.

My parents didn't understand what was going on with me, which caused more animosity and arguing between us. I started to miss the compliments that I'd received the year before when I lost the weight, so I purposefully started to lose weight until one day, I snapped. I came home from school to find that my mom had found the many goodbye and self-hatred letters I had hid throughout my room. When she confronted me about them, I physically attacked her, destroyed my room, and made suicidal threats. In the end, I landed myself in a psychiatric unit for a week, with a diagnosis of major depressive disorder.

My experience in the psychiatric unit wasn't the most positive because I wasn't ready to tackle my own issues, but instead focused on the issues of those around me. After spending over a week in the unit, I came out with a case manager and an in-home therapist for the summer that I didn't connect with.

I still wasn't ready to take my issues seriously and would lie to my therapist. I transitioned to meeting with a new therapist once a week. It took about eight months for me to trust my therapist and open up to her, but I never gave up. Although I didn't open up and literally didn't talk, I was forced to listen to what she was saying. Once I was ready, I began opening up to her.

Senior year went pretty smooth, as I was accepted into college, enjoyed my time with my friends, and finally graduated high school. Though college was a great experience, I still had my ups and downs. Throughout high school and the beginning of college, I had felt alone; it wasn't until I met Missy that I realized there were people my age experiencing similar issues.

When I had started working with Missy, having someone else who understood what it felt like to experience internal issues made it easier to volunteer. I realized that my story was more important than I had thought. My experiences put a positive spin on my diagnosis, and I was led to focus my career on mental health and helping people.

I recently graduated with my masters in social work from Widener University, and I'm an in-home therapist for children and adolescents. I am also beginning to speak on behalf of Minding Your Mind, the same organization Missy and our mutual friend, Jordan, speak for.

One of my first speaking engagements was at my high school; I spoke in the same health class I had sat in many years back. It was the same teacher, same seats, and same lessons. After I finished speaking, he asked if he could say a few words to the class in front of me.

He said, "I thought she was a bad kid. I had no idea the battles she was facing. It's so important not to judge before you really know the facts." It was right then that I knew I was supposed to be sharing my story.

Although I feel as if I've accomplished a lot in my life, it wasn't all glitter and unicorns. I still experience struggles, but through therapy, I have gained a self-awareness in which I am able to help myself and ask for help.

My message is that you are not alone. You may feel alone and lost, but there is at least one other person who has felt the same way. If you feel hopeless or alone, reach out to someone you trust. Reaching out and getting help can be difficult, but it's not impossible.

Advocacy was difficult at first because of how much negativity surrounded mental health. However, the support Missy and I received was overwhelming. What stuck out the most was the fact that other students shared their own stories with us, and we were all able to stand and support each other. But we knew our stories didn't define us; we continued to live our lives and build careers and independence, although with a new perspective: that we were never alone.

It is pretty remarkable how Kristen and I ended up being friends. I always looked at her so negatively and honestly thought she was miserable for no reason. I had no idea she was experiencing anything let alone mental health issues like me. I always thought about the quote, "Don't judge a book by its cover" and this proved it so I knew I was wrong for judging Kristen too quickly as well.

Right after our talk in the parking lot that night, Kristen opened my eyes to so much and not only did I feel less alone, I knew I had someone there to support me and that's when I decided I was ready to form a chapter of Active Minds on campus with her help. It was one of the best decisions I ever made. There was so much support for the group, even from people I wouldn't have expected to care or get involved.

With the growing support, I was learning that when you put effort and positive energy into something, people become attracted to it and feed off your passion. I gained a lot of confidence in that time frame, found the most supportive friends, and started feeling like I had a true purpose in life. Of course there were bumps and bruises along the way, but overall I couldn't believe how many of my peers were facing their own challenges—even the ones I least expected to have these struggles.

That got me wondering why and how someone actually started the first Active Minds chapter many years back at the University of Pennsylvania. What was her story? Did she ever feel alone as well?

Meet Alison Malmon; suicide prevention and mental health advocate and founder of Active Minds, Inc.

I started Active Minds when I was a junior at the University of

Pennsylvania, following the suicide of my older brother, Brian, one year earlier. Brian, also a college student, had been experiencing depression and psychosis for three years but had concealed his symptoms from everyone around him. In the middle of his senior year, he returned to my family's Potomac, Md., home and began receiving treatment for what was later diagnosed as schizoaffective disorder.

A year and a half later, on March 24, 2000, as I was wrapping up my freshman year at Penn, Brian ended his life. Shortly after, I knew I had to do something or no one would.

Recognizing that few Penn students were talking about mental health issues—though many were affected—I was motivated to change that culture on my campus. I wanted to combat the stigma of mental illness, encourage students who needed help to seek it early, and prevent future tragedies like the one that took Brian's life. After searching unsuccessfully for existing groups that I could simply bring to my campus, I decided to create my own model.

I was so astounded to really dive into the issues and learn that they were so real, and so prevalent, but at the same time know that they were so quiet, that "taking a stand" was the only answer in my mind. My brother deserved a more supportive and open society when he was struggling. Thousands of my peers did too. There was no question in my mind that something needed to happen and that I was fully dedicated to making it happen. I knew I had to be that someone.

After a great first year, the Penn student group gained enough support that it expanded onto other campuses. The national headquarters was established in Washington, DC, during the summer of 2003, and the organization was incorporated as a 501(c) 3 organization later that year. In just over eight years, the nonprofit organization has grown into a well-recognized entity in the field, respected as the voice of student mental health advocacy. Featured on CNN, in the *New York Times, Chronicle of Higher Education,* and the 2013 Mental Health Conference at the White House, Active Minds has become a voice of young adult mental health advocacy nationwide.

With over four hundred campus chapters, hundreds of thousands of young adults all across the country are benefiting from the Active Minds model. Active Minds has grown substantially, and quickly, because of the need: students and staff identifying the need for students to feel comfortable seeking help at any point that they are struggling, and knowing where to seek out that help.

Everyone has a story, and Active Minds provides a place for students to be able to share their stories and help change the way society thinks and talks about mental health. I'm thrilled that there's a new generation taking the reins and helping move our society toward acceptance and respect of mental health disorders. This is an ageless cause; all ages need to be involved so we can reach all ages where they are and with the language they are using.

I've always believed that what I was doing was critically important and would work; I wouldn't have started the organization if I didn't. If and how it would work is a different story. I knew it was important, and I knew I had to do it or no one would. And I had told myself that, if things didn't pan out after a couple of years, I could find a different path for myself, and that would be just fine.

Happily, that hasn't had to happen; there has been more support and growth than I could ever have imagined. Mostly, having the support of the amazing, dedicated, creative, and passionate people that surround me has helped give me the strength to keep moving forward and continue to change the conversation on mental health.

In my junior of college, I was keeping up with what Alison and her organization were doing. I felt inspired and wanted to do something big with my college chapter of Active Minds, something that people would remember. I decided to host a "Stomp Out Stigma" 5K run and walk on campus, inviting the whole community and advertising it to every local media outlet, community group, and campus group that existed.

At 7 a.m. on the day of the event, over fifty students gathered at the event registration site to volunteer for the day. I was completely overwhelmed and ecstatic that people were so open to supporting the cause—and my passion. I couldn't have asked for more. The day was gorgeous, I saw a cardinal (which was a symbol of hope for me), and, as registration started, the numbers kept growing. Then an Action News van pulled up to cover the event. My initial fear of taking a stand was disappearing as the day went on.

It was a great feeling, knowing this was my passion and all could see that, but I couldn't have done it alone. My friends, family members, peers, teachers, Immaculata staff, community leaders, and community police department were so willing to volunteer their time to spread a little hope to others. The event raised over $3,000, which was given to two mental health organizations including Active Minds, Inc.

I knew this event was going to leave a mark at my school; however, that wasn't the most significant thing to happen that day. As I looked around and took in the event, I realized something really important: each person in attendance was unique, with his or her own personality, issues, likes, wants, friends, and views, but here we all were at this event, putting our differences aside and uniting as one to fight for the hope of others. I knew this couldn't just be happening here, because there had to be more people my age, across the country, battling their own personal issues and wanting desperately to share their stories, volunteer and ultimately help others as well.

∽

Meet my LA friend Allison Bickleman; a mental health advocate

I had fallen into a major rut. I was nearly finished with my first year of graduate school; one year down and three to go on my way to becoming a doctor of psychology, but I found myself dreading the coming years instead of feeling excited about what my educational and professional future held.

Although I was completely immersed in the study of psychology, which included classes such as abnormal psychology and psychopathology, I had been completely hiding and denying my own struggles with psychological issues. I spent nearly all my waking hours at school or at home with classmates studying for school, and yet not one of these colleagues knew the truth about me. They saw me as a mature and composed individual, strong and organized, always prompt and dependable. How would they have known that I had spent eleven days in a psych ward on suicide watch? How could they have known about the medications flowing through my veins or the number of hours I had spent in therapy sessions?

On May 23, 2011, I reconnected with a good friend from my early college days in San Diego and discovered that she worked for a nonprofit organization that focused on helping young people understand the importance of erasing the stigma of mental illness. She invited me to attend an event, a youth summit, in downtown Los Angeles. I RSVP'd that I would attend, but I nearly backed out at the last minute. I was stressed with the completion of the school year and was feeling rather depressed and isolative. Still, something pushed me to go to this event, which would become the catalyst for many amazingly wonderful changes in my life.

She was wearing purple leggings, and so I just knew that we could be friends. Not only was she so boldly wearing my favorite color, but she seemed to embody everything I hoped to someday be—beautiful, confident, enchanting, and fascinating. There were just so many things to love about her—about this girl who, I quickly learned, was named Melissa Ann Hopely.

We ended up sitting next to each other for lunch at the summit, and we began to talk. I found out that she was not merely a volunteer and guest as I was, but that she was the primary public speaker for the event. She nonchalantly told me that she had OCD and depression, and that after graduating from college (with a BA in psych—just like me!) she had been trained to speak publicly about her experience with living with an anxiety disorder, as well as a multitude of other mental health topics such as bullying, suicide prevention, and self-esteem.

To say that I was in awe would be an understatement. The job and lifestyle she had just described to me sounded exactly like what I had long been searching for. I suddenly felt completely invigorated—more motivated and passionate than I had ever been before. The next day, I submitted the necessary forms to withdraw from graduate school.

Somehow, amazingly and wonderfully, Melissa and I clicked instantly and right away became very close friends. For the entire week that she was visiting LA, we were inseparable. After only knowing me for about forty-eight hours, she even spent her final days in California residing in my apartment with me. I had not had that much fun for a very long time. I had, perhaps, never laughed or smiled so much in my entire life.

The week I met Melissa is one of the best in my entire lifetime collection of memories. We stayed up late chatting about everything and anything. We ate huge bowls of Baskin-Robbins ice cream and sprinkled a whole container of rainbow jimmies on it. We went to Universal Studios city walk, hiked to the Hollywood sign (belting out Miley Cyrus' "Party in the USA!" at the top of our lungs the entire time), sang Taylor Swift karaoke in my car, and read long excerpts to each other from our respective memoirs.

Being diagnosed as an older teen, it may seem as if my childhood and adolescence were all fun and games. But rather, it was quite the contrary. I struggled to maintain my standing high upon the pedestal of elementary school grade point averages and community theater groups. Somehow, I managed to portray an outward image of perfection, but on the inside, I was falling apart.

As far back as I can remember, I have engaged in obsessional thinking and compulsive behavioral rituals. The themes rotated, based on the seasons and my interests and my age—from fires to earthquakes to death to burglars to forgetting my homework. I also remember throwing raging fits and having tremendous outbursts of emotion. I would scream, cry, and throw objects at the walls. I was purely, simply, angry.

Bullying was a word that came into my repertoire of language at a young age. I was born with nerve damage in my face and was teased about that, as well as having to be pulled from class to go to speech therapy. It was also clear to the other kids that I was the teacher's pet and a goody-goody. I spent my recess and lunch times engrossed in solitary activities, such as reading a book.

In my teen years, it was all of that, plus new and intense feelings of emptiness and sadness and dread. I even contemplated suicide at the ripe, young age of thirteen. Somehow, I managed to pull through the middle and high school years, graduating in the top eight percent of my graduating class of nine hundred students.

At age nineteen, I began attending college at UCSD, which I was very proud of because I had worked so hard on APs and the SATs throughout high school. But San Diego brought a whole new slew of challenges for me. I had dealt with many personal issues all throughout grade school, but focusing on academics and extracurricular activities had kept the monstrous demons inside of me at bay. When I found myself out of context, however—away from my hometown, family, and friends—I became lost in the dark abyss of a major depressive episode. It was then that I was finally diagnosed with major depressive disorder, obsessive-compulsive disorder (OCD), and generalized anxiety disorder.

My college years were lost to me in a whirlwind of medication consults, therapy sessions, hospital stays, and treatment centers. I eventually made the very difficult decision to leave UCSD behind and, halfway through my undergrad career, I moved back home and

117

transferred to the Cal State system. Even with all of these tremendous challenges, I managed to graduate in the typical four years with a bachelor's degree in psychology.

Life today isn't perfect; I've learned that nothing is. I have come so far, but the journey is still not over. Although my disorders are currently under control, I stay on medication and in therapy because I am well aware of the uncertainties and inconsistencies of mental illness, and of life itself.

Soon I am going back to school to obtain my masters of science in behavior analysis, as I currently work as a behavior aide for young children with autism. I find that I can relate to my young clients in a very personal and unique way: I use memories of my own past struggles to understand their own intense thoughts, behaviors, and feelings.

I'm also going to share my story at the American Foundation of Suicide Prevention's (AFSP) Out of Darkness Walk in California, which will be the first time I get to speak publicly about myself. And finally, my greatest and proudest accomplishment is working on writing and publishing a full-length memoir, with the title *Perfectly Imperfect*— because I am, and we all are, living perfectly with our own unique imperfections and have the power to make an impact in others' lives.

With each new person I was meeting, my fear of taking action was become weaker. Instead, I felt inspired to know there were others wanting to make a difference even so many miles away. I also started to realize that it was so important for people to bring their unique qualities and passions to work together and support each other in order to really make a positive impact in the world. I was beginning to see a much bigger picture and realize that I always had the power to "be that somebody," it was just hidden away for so long. Now, together with those trying to make a difference as well, instead of just being one somebody, I recognized that we could all band together in some way no matter what cause or passion we believed in and become an army of somebody's who provided hope.

Chapter Fifteen

Standing up and stepping out of your comfort zone

My friend and mentor Mariel Hemingway's wise words about trusting the magic in the unknown are ones that I'm really trying to live by. There is no way we can experience our dreams or live the life we want if we continue to stay stuck in our comfort zone and cycle of doing the same old thing.

How do we allow ourselves to experience the magic in the unknown if we live in fear and are afraid to venture out? And how do we even attempt to step out of our comfort zone if we fear the judgment of others and failure? Sometimes we gain confidence from those around us, and sometimes it comes from surprising opportunities that we can't resist. There is no right way and frankly no "easy button," but as the ancient proverb says, where there is a will, there is a way.

Deep down, I always had dreams of being on stage and in movies, as some kids do. However, I didn't exactly look or fit the part because I was a tomboy who never dressed up. Sports became my comfort zone and safe place; I always did well and received compliments from others about the way I played. When I mentioned I wanted to try acting, speaking, and singing, many people were shocked and mostly brushed the idea off. I understood why, but their reactions had me feeling incapable and left me living in my own personal comfort zone. I just wanted to step outside of the lines, dismiss my broken record, put on a new CD, and dance the way I really wanted to.

During my junior year of college, I was doing more stepping out of the box than holding back. This was the first year I hosted the "Stomp Out Stigma" Run and Walk Event, the first time I did an interview on radio, the first time I felt like an individual among my friends and peers, and the first time I would have any real acting experience. My college, Immaculata University, had a powerful women's basketball story from the 1970s that got picked up by a production company. Students at the school were allowed to be extras in the film, *The Mighty Macs,* which played in theaters across the country. I loved every second of being on set and, after a few days of filming, I wanted more.

At that point, I had more confidence than I had felt in most of my life. I felt very comfortable in my own skin, but there were still areas that I wanted to work on. I heard about another film shooting in the area called *The Happening,* which was M. Night Shyamalan's new film starring Mark Wahlberg. I sent my photo to the casting company and received a callback to go to a wardrobe fitting. I was told to bring any cute outfits I had. Part of my struggle with my comfort zone was with my wardrobe. I usually hid behind my tomboy image and sports clothes because it was easier to blend in than stand out in the physical sense. So this posed a problem, but I gathered everything I could find and brought it to the fitting.

I felt like I was on the show *What Not to Wear.* The look on the stylist's face was priceless, and I knew this was going to be more of a challenge for her than she wanted. As she sorted through my clothes, I started looking around the room, seeing all of these other young adults who were going for the same parts. My stomach started turning in knots, and all I wanted to do was run and hide. Why was I even here? This was way too far out of my comfort zone.

After getting into the outfit the stylist worked out and having my make-up and hair done, I found myself looking into a full-length mirror and not recognizing myself. I was wearing a huge smile and thinking to myself, "Dang, who is this chick and where has she been?"

I scanned the room and spotted Mark Wahlberg and M. Night Shyamalan about ten yards away from me. They were looking around, trying to see who would fit perfectly in the classroom scene. I couldn't help but notice that they glanced at me a few times; if that doesn't build your confidence, I don't know what would. I honestly felt truly beautiful on both the inside and outside for the first time, and I decided to go out on a limb and talk to both of them. It turned out that introducing myself was going to open doors to one of the coolest things I would ever experience in my life.

The next day it happened. Because I had stepped out of my comfort zone the day before for less than five minutes, I was now sitting in a desk playing Mark Walherg's science student in *The Happening.* My only job: to say a line in unison and stare at Mark Wahlberg during the two to three hours of filming. What did I have to complain about? Absolutely nothing!

At one point, however, the camera was set in my chair because they were filming another actor's lines. I was bummed because I had to take a break from staring at Mark Wahlberg, but I did have my time. As I went into the hallway with another young actor named Jeff, we both turned around and saw Mark Wahlberg following close behind. He was on break too, so things were about to get even cooler.

Mark, his assistant, Jeff and I were all just shooting the breeze. We talked about sports, life, goals, and many other random things. I was in complete awe but felt so alive in that moment, like I was living in my unknown magic. After filming ended, I wanted to shake Mark's hand and just thank him for being so awesome. When I extended my hand, he put out his arms and gave me a huge hug. Now, have you ever seen his arms and how perfect they are? Well, they feel better than they look! The hug felt like a lifetime.

That amazing, breathtaking experience—which it was and much more—would never have happened if I hadn't stepped out of my comfort zone, even before my wardrobe fitting. I'm not saying stepping out of your comfort zone will always be easy and land you in Mark Wahlberg's arms, although it would be nice. And I'd be wrong if I didn't tell you that on many other occasions when I have stepped out of mine, I've completely failed or faced embarrassment. However, from my failures, I learned lessons and from my embarrassment, I gained confidence. Living outside your comfort zone is easier said than done, but it is possible and at times worth it.

Right around the same time I met a friend named P-Track in college. I never understood why it was so hard for him to say "hello" and talk to me at times. When chatting on social media, he seemed so outgoing, but in person it was the complete opposite. After I learned he lived with Asperger's syndrome it started to make sense. With each encounter we would have, I became more and more inspired to want to keep stepping out of my own comfort zone.

Meet my college friend; P-Track who lives with Asperger's Syndrome

I was going into fifth grade when I first learned I had Asperger's syndrome. I didn't completely understand how it made me different, but I could kind of tell I wasn't getting along with too many other kids for whatever reason. I was bullied, but I don't know if it was because of Asperger's or just the usual behavior of boys ten or eleven years old. Regardless, it stunk.

People didn't really know I had the diagnosis when I was being made fun of; in reality, they probably didn't know what it even was. I could sense it was hard for me to express myself like others. It was easy to communicate online or through texts, but it was more difficult for me to connect with people in person.

I fell in love with dancing my freshman year of college and pretty much starting dancing during the summer of my orientation, because I watched a classmate have no fear or embarrassment and completely own the dance to Michael Jackson's "Thriller." It was one of the coolest things I had ever seen, and this kid didn't know anyone, yet he was dancing his life away. I was inspired, and dancing seemed really fun, so I started doing it a lot, and I seemed to make a name for myself.

My high school had been pretty small, so life seemed to be a lot easier at college, especially with meeting people who also loved to dance and express themselves. I've always known I don't have the worst case of Asperger's, but I know it has probably made me less interested in getting involved with a lot of different clubs at school. I don't regret it all that much.

I know people judged me for what I have, but I didn't ask for it, and honestly I am cool with being me, because Asperger's isn't who I am. I connect well with others through dance and found some awesome friends. I was a bit nervous to just rock out and dance like I never danced before, but it was empowering, and I loved every second of it. I encourage anyone to do what you love because it can be a great way to get to know people.

Before I loved dancing, I was really into baseball. It was just something to talk to people about. Not everyone's going to have the same social challenges as me, but it can't hurt to have specific interests in common with other people.

With dancing, though, I don't feel the need to show off when I'm out there; I just have fun. I know it can take me some time to get used to different people or warm up to somebody, but that won't stop me from meeting new people and enjoying my life. Challenges are a part of life that make us strong. I live with Asperger's, but it doesn't define me.

I honestly wouldn't change my life for anything, unless of course I got the chance to dance on national TV—now that would be something I'd totally love to do, but the song would have to be "Thriller" or at least "The Cupid Shuffle." But seriously, don't be afraid to take chances, step out of your comfort zone and try new things. You never know the cool things that can happen.

From the moment I saw P-Track dance at orientation to the moment we became friends, I knew there was something inspiring about him. He reassured me that it is more important to be myself and do the things I love than to live in the fear of being judged and the fear of the unknown. That was something I knew I had to take with me as I continued my journey of speaking and advocacy work.

Chapter Sixteen

We affect one another—so pay it forward

Sometimes we don't realize the impact we have on others, both positively and negatively, and the impact others can have on us too. It's easier to blame others than to face our own emotions and issues. Many times people aren't aware of what mean words or actions can do to someone else (or they don't care).

When my peer in high school gave me the middle finger, his action triggered something inside me. Although he didn't mean for it to have that much of an impact, his selfish act still affected my life in ways he'll never know. I understand people deal with issues and sometimes take things out on others, but no one knows exactly what someone is going through, so we can never know what our actions have the power to do. On the other hand, we have the power to make someone's world just a little bit better with actions such as holding a door for someone or offering a smile in passing. Those small acts can go a long way—even if we never know exactly how.

I once heard a story of a man who promised himself that if one person smiled at him before he reached the middle of a bridge, he wouldn't jump off to his death. He walked miles, passing hundreds of people, and not one person smiled at him. This man, who died on that day, could have been saved by one stranger's simple act—or at least he could have been reassured that he had worth and a reason to get help and live. Now, each time I pass someone, I always make it a point to do a good deed or at least smile, because I often wonder what their story is and how I can make their day or life just a little bit better.

I completely believe in the power of paying it forward and always coming off as a positive person. But what happens when you experience something that rocks your core, affects your whole character, and starts affecting others negatively? Are you supposed to pretend that everything is okay and smile all the time, or is it better to live out your emotions—

even if they affect others in a negative way?

On July 3, 2008, I learned some devastating news that would change my life. I was hanging out at my friend Tracy's when I received a phone call—the call I had been dreading for about a year. On the other end of the phone was my aunt Judy, my mom's sister, asking if I had heard from my dad. I could tell something was wrong, but she wouldn't tell me. All I could do was call my dad and confirm my suspicions.

The call was muffled, so I couldn't make out all my dad was saying, except that the marriage was over, he was on his way to New Jersey, and everything he thought he knew was a lie. I remember calling my mom, screaming because I knew that one of my biggest fears was now a reality. My parents had been having problems and, although they had been together for twenty-one mostly strong years, their bond was dead. My mom had found love with another man, and our family core was being ripped apart. We had been living a lie of being the perfect family for far too long.

We had a lot of support from both sides of the family, but I was the big sister, so instantly I became the middleman for my mom and dad and the homemade therapist for my little sister Amanda and brother Kenny. I tried to hold it together for everyone, but there were times I felt completely broken, as if there had been a death in my family. My whole sense of security completely vanished. People started treating me differently, knowing the pain my family was facing. It was awkward seeing my parents' friends and having to respond to their questions with fake answers and fake smiles.

There were times when I couldn't control my emotions; I would cry, break things, hit things, and scream. I wondered why the hell this was happening to me when I had thought the worst was behind me and my life would be a straight ride of happiness—especially after making it to the big screen in *The Happening* and hugging Mark Wahlberg. But it was clear at that moment that it didn't matter who I was or what I did; disasters and misfortunes were bound to happen.

I never wanted to bring down anyone around me, and I tried not to use my issues as an excuse, but there were times when I couldn't make social events, hang out with my friends, focus on sports, or even take exams at college. My friends, some teammates, and some professors were worried about my obvious issues. I knew I had to get help; I couldn't go on, knowing I was affecting others and taking so many steps back because of this one situation.

It was hard having to interact with the outside world when people had no idea what I was facing. I would get smiles here and there, but sometimes people were cruel and just added to my feelings of anger and sadness. I was overly sensitive to those who thoughtlessly cut me off, closed doors in my face, or flipped me off while I was driving.

If anyone on the road disrespected me, my usual response was to turn up my music to the highest volume possible and sing along loudly while smiling obnoxiously at the other driver. I figured killing people with happiness would be the best revenge; sometimes it worked because, if I added the hand motions and dance moves, people might crack a smile or even laugh. Unfortunately, after everything happened, I found myself cursing and screaming back at people. And I was disappointed with myself. As the saying goes, "Two wrongs don't make a right"—although these people had no consideration for my feelings, it bothered me to know that I could be affecting their lives negatively as well.

Most of my friends supported me during this hard time, but some made things worse. After this situation, I lost two of the best friends I had. I faced criticism from them because they thought I was too happy and outgoing at times, but ultimately I knew that was just me, so I didn't think twice about it. However, on July 4, 2008—the day after I found out about my parents—I had to cancel plans with these two friends because I couldn't face going out in public.

I told them something bad had happened and that I couldn't go, so I was going to hang out at Tracy's. Tracy and my friend Lexi were the only two people who knew what was really going on; I was literally too embarrassed and sick to tell anyone else. When the other two friends learned this, they started giving me grief. They were upset that I hadn't come to them first.

It wasn't anything personal—I was so consumed with denial and confusion that I didn't even think twice about calling them.

Frankly, I don't think we had a healthy relationship at that point, and maybe this was the straw that broke the camel's back. My parents' situation wasn't something I talked about lightly. It was like those stories you see on some talk shows. Rumors were spreading, and people were finding out what happened. I still tried to hang on to a relationship with these two girls, but it just wasn't working.

My twenty-first birthday was only two weeks after everything happened. I hadn't talked to the two girls during that time, but I heard from one of them on my birthday. A simple "Happy Birthday" would have been nice, but instead I got an earful of how ridiculous it was that I hadn't told them about the situation and how I had hurt them. Didn't she realize that my birthday was already ruined because my family was completely broken?

The situation with my parents made me want to die. Most days I couldn't breathe, I felt like red ants were crawling all over my body, and I started losing the energy to get out of bed or even eat. I couldn't believe that once again my world was falling apart. I needed the people closest to me more than ever, but it seemed like the only thing I could do was turn off my phone, force myself to go to my internship, and try to put on a happy face. I had to stop affecting and being affected by those around me.

As the years passed, things got a little easier. I even became friends again with the two girls; ultimately, we wanted the best for each other. It seemed the more time that passed, the more things filled up my time and took away from the constant reminders and emotions that had come with my parents' horrible divorce.

Eventually my mom and dad both found significant others, and I gained two new families. One day I visited my old neighborhood, reminiscing about the old times; it's amazing how many emotions crossed my mind. It seemed ironic that my visit happened on July 3, 2012, exactly four years after I found out about my parents' separation. That whole day I'd been feeling bitter, anxious, and angry, even though I had no reason to be. When my sister and I got into a fight over absolutely nothing, we looked at each other and realized that both of us had subconsciously known this was the day that had changed our lives.

That day I was made aware that my moods were affecting those around us. My usual happy smile was nonexistent, replaced by a constant aggravated state and forced grin. I can't say things didn't work out great with my family over those four years, but I guess I missed my old life and was pissed that I couldn't have it back. I know it wasn't right, and I did my best to show respect to others, but I couldn't get out of my bad mood. Part of me wondered if I somehow ruined someone else's day because of my own personal issues. I prayed that wasn't the case and, as my bad mood improved over time, I tried to pay it forward and smile again.

Those efforts didn't take away from my actions toward others before my mood changed. I hoped those I affected could sense I was having a bad day and didn't take it personally. At one time or another we all deal with something that affects our whole being. In times of distress or aggravation it's hard to force a smile, but the best part about a smile is that it's the same in every language and completely contagious.

On the other hand, taking your "something" out on others can do much more harm for both parties than you may ever realize. Your actions toward others can last a lot longer than you think and have a negative impact on someone's life. You may live in regret and feel sorry for yourself.

I'm not saying it's easy to cope positively and not take some things out on others, but just think—your smile or good deed can impact someone and inspire them enough to pay it forward. Then another person pays it forward, causing a domino effect of positive actions. That's exactly what I learned when a local, talented artist named Jamall Anthony promised to help me with my music, even though he was working through and dealing with issues in his own life.

∿

Meet local musician; Jamall Anthony

I grew up in a poor part of Coatesville, Pa., in a big family: three sisters, a little brother, and a bunch of half sisters and brothers. It was hard, and money was always tight.

I had this dream as a kid of being a wrestler; I never thought I'd be a singer. I was pretty sheltered growing up—not so much bullied but definitely picked on at the beginning stages of school, so I learned to keep to myself at a young age. Sadly, kids can be cruel, not knowing what people are going through, but I always kept a golden heart, not giving it back to them.

I got into music at the age of eleven when my uncle Walt began teaching me piano. I became a member of my church's worship team, and my passion grew from there. My first performance was in middle school, but my first real performance was in high school. I got a solo for a school concert, singing "Seasons of Love" from *Rent*. I was nervous because all eyes were on me, but it was the moment I learned what I wanted to do with my life.

I've always felt like the underdog in life, so I had to be my own biggest supporter and make believers out of nonbelievers. I got confidence in myself to never give up. I saw my parents struggle and do their best to push through; that taught me many lessons about working hard. To me, failure is not an option. Music is what I love to do, so every day I strive to get better and be a better person, especially paying the gifts I was given forward to others. Hard work has gotten me into the situation I am in right now.

Recently I did a cover of the song "I Can't Wait." The band, Runner Runner of Capital Records, actually listened to it and said it was the best cover they'd ever heard. Believe it or not we started working together, and I have learned so much. Guitarist Nick Bailey and singer Ryan Ogren of the band have become like big brothers to me. They actually flew me out to Hollywood to record some songs to pitch to the record label.

As I was looking around and staring at the Hollywood sign, I couldn't believe it—this nobody kid from nowhere was about to record music with a famous band. I know my dreams were always a long shot, but I always knew in my heart I'd get out of Coatesville. I'm even performing live with them at their concert this year, which I could have never imagined.

I'm proud of where I came from, but most people get stuck there. I wanted to inspire these people to know they have a bigger purpose in life than the cards they were dealt. I just started volunteering with my hometown community council to get youth more involved and turn the town around. I want to inspire the kids and I want do it by letting them know you don't have to put yourself in a box. If you have a dream, protect it and don't ever let anyone tell you that you can't be whatever you want to be. There's nothing cooler in the world than being yourself, so be you, work hard and follow your dreams.

I hope to let people know they should always stay true to themselves. When it comes to life, don't just live loud—live louder! Yes, you're going to fall; I did many times and still do. It's not about how many times you fall; it's about how many times you get back up.

I've fallen a lot but I never stay down—I just keep coming back better than before, working to inspire others through my music, give back to the world and pay it forward. There is a much bigger picture than we can see, and if we give back the gifts we were given, we'll never know how many people we can truly help and inspire.

      I never really knew Jamall's full story until we talked one day after doing a volunteer musical performance at a youth event. I honestly thought he was a talented musician, but never really gave two thoughts about what his story could be. What fascinated me the most was with every performance he did in the community, he did for free, using his own gas, unloading his own equipment and continuously doing it without complaints. I knew he ultimately wanted his dreams to come true of become a well-known musician, but in his heart, he was always willing to pay it forward and help the youth in any way he could and that inspired me.

Chapter Seventeen

New normal

Transitioning to a new normal is never easy. There's hesitation, fear, moments of missing what was, and a level of discomfort when everything you once knew is now different or distanced. We get caught wishing things were different and sometimes saying, "Coulda, shoulda, woulda," which tends to get us nowhere.

It's completely normal to have those feelings and to remember the past. It makes you look at situations and people in a new way, giving you the ability to learn, grow, and also appreciate what was. However, asking those questions all the time and remaining fixated on what you can't change can make your head spin at times, and make it even harder to transition to your new normal. I'm not talking about completely skipping the stages of grief, but about moving on after you've gone through those stages. Living in the past, even though it's comforting at times, means staying stuck—which can never make for a better future or give you the chance to really be alive and in the moment.

I had a hard time transitioning to my new normal after my parents' separation. I was used to going to my house on Crescent Hill Drive and seeing my mom, dad, brother, and sister, and walking by the hallway pictures of our family at sporting events and family functions. Now this was no more. My dad took down most of the family pictures because the constant reminder of our broken family was too much for anyone to handle.

Each of us experienced the stages of grief in our own way. I was lucky enough to be in my senior year of college just a month after everything happened. It was a nice distraction and escape, but I wasn't fooling anyone, because I wasn't dealing with my emotions properly. I would have random freak-outs and panic attacks at school and have to call my grandmom and best friend Lexi to come rescue me almost every time, before I ended up punching another hole in the wall or breaking something. It seemed I was going back to my high school ways, but that was the only way I knew how to deal with this sucky new normal.

I tried to run away from everything while at school. I thought pretending it didn't happen at times would make all the pain go away, but it didn't. Deep down, I was pissed off, wondering what more could happen and if this unwanted change in my life would cause any more discomfort. I also wondered what I could have done to stop any of this from happening. Maybe I was blaming myself for what I put my parents through in the years before. Regardless, I could tell that I was going back to my old ways with OCD and depression.

Going into my senior year of college, I knew things were going to be hard, but I didn't realize how many new, unwanted things would become part of my normal that year. There were three distinct moments I recall that my parents' separation affected and essentially ruined— moments that were supposed to be huge milestones in my life. This was supposed to be the biggest year of my entire athletic career. I was going to be in my fourth year of playing two NCAA Division III sports: soccer and softball. That's how my normal was during the three previous years, so I figured it would remain the same, with the exception of a few minor issues.

Even during my junior year of college, I knew my parents weren't doing well, and that distraction started interfering with my abilities and concentration when I was playing softball. I started making rookie mistakes and, after previously being one of the best players on the team, I became a distraction and burden to my team. Some of my teammates already had issues with my personality and disliked me immensely, so there were comments thrown around as well as some looks, and I started feeling more and more uncomfortable being around my own team.

Things started to go haywire at home that year. Although I was at school, subconsciously it was affecting me. I kept it quiet, not wanting to use it as an excuse for playing so badly. The things I ignored actually seemed to affect me more, causing my OCD and depression to spike up and allowing them to impact my daily life again. I knew going into my fourth year of college that I would have to make some unwanted changes; not playing softball, the sport that had made me feel alive and at home my whole life, would be one of those changes.

I decided to stick out my fourth year of soccer. I was the only senior and I wasn't starting, but that was okay. It was our first winning season, and we actually made the playoffs for the first time in the history of the school's sport. My coach, Fran Tacconelli, cared about us both on and off the field, and when I would break down and confide in him, he always reassured me that what happened off the field wouldn't take away from the good player I was on the field. It was refreshing to know I wasn't being defined for my struggles, like I had felt at times before.

Of course, all good things can't last. After I had built a trust with him for four years, Coach Fran's cancer returned, and I was left with the assistant coach, who didn't have the same understanding of my game as Fran. Soccer became more of a burden than an outlet, unfortunately, that wasn't even the worst part. My parents didn't want to be in the same vicinity as each other, which posed a huge problem because my senior game was approaching, and it was something I had looked forward to for four years.

I had a back injury midway through the soccer season, but the trainer did everything he could to let me play at least five minutes of my senior game. I was so excited and, being the only senior, I knew all eyes were on me—at least for the beginning of the game. There was only one big issue: the game was only a few months after my parents' big blow-up. It was the last time they ever spoke to or saw each other, so knowing that they would be in the same vicinity brought concern, fear, and nervousness to my mind and body.

During the opening ceremony, I spotted my mom and dad on opposite sides of the field. It didn't help that both sets of grandparents were there, and my brother and sister had to go back and forth between my mom and dad. I can't even recall if we won the game, but what was supposed to be an awesome milestone in my college career sucked, because one of my parents got so overwhelmed that they left the game early. I don't blame either one of my parents, but I remember sitting on the bench in embarrassment and heartbreak. I was tearing up, and the only one I knew to turn to, Coach Fran, couldn't even be there because he was in the hospital fighting his battle with cancer.

As my final college days came to a close, my Baccalaureate Mass and graduation ceremony were approaching. I had mixed feelings: being excited to graduate and join the outside world, but also losing that sense of comfort I had felt for those four years. I knew things were going to change and that I'd be experiencing a new normal, but I didn't know it would be even harder with my parents' issues.

I found myself panicking at my Baccalaureate Mass. I entered the church thinking I would be sitting with classmates and not having to make one of the hardest decisions of my life—which parent to sit with? I was aggravated that the school would allow this; they should have known that not all families were together. I was crying in front of all of my college classmates, their families, and the college community while running out the back door of the church. I saw so many happy families, and I couldn't bear to pick between my mom and dad's families. I ended up sitting by myself in a seat basically in the middle.

With each new song, I tried to hold back my tears, but it was very difficult. My best friend Lexi, who had been with me through everything, saw what was happening and grabbed my hand while we walked to communion. She knew this was hard for me, but it was then that I realized that, although my family was "broken apart" they were all there to support me. That should have been my focus.

As I returned to my seat, I took a deep breath, looked around, and wondered if anyone else in my college had to deal with such an abrupt, unwelcome new normal.

~

Meet my college classmate Ryan Carson; an amputee survivor

On May 5, 2012, my life changed forever. Some people would think it should have been for the worst, but I can't help but see that my "new normal" became the best thing that could have ever happened to me.

I boxed for eleven years of my life—as a professional boxer for some of it. I got to travel, got to meet people, and was known for what I did. I was strong mentally from all my training, in amazing shape, and at times cocky. I thought I was one of the toughest guys in the physical sense.

I stopped boxing to focus on school. Immediately my grades went up, and I made the dean's list. I was about to graduate with a physical therapy degree because I wanted to help people and their injuries, instead of being a boxer who sometimes caused injuries. After I had my accident, my personality changed in terms of looking at life differently, but I knew the core Ryan—outgoing, happy, and determined—was still there.

It was Cinco De Mayo 2012, and my roommates and I had a party at my townhome. We started drinking early; I don't know how intoxicated I was, but I don't remember anything before my accident happened. I didn't black out—I never let myself get that intoxicated—but everything is still very hard to recall. Maybe it was the trauma.

The pool had opened the week before, and my roommates had been talking about swimming all week. If we were quiet enough, we could jump the fence at night and take a dip in the water. When we jumped in, the water was freezing, so my buddy and I looked at each other and rushed out to get in the house.

As I went to jump the fence, I slipped, and the fence post got embedded in the back of my knee. I immediately pulled my leg off the fence. It was like someone turned on a faucet; there was blood everywhere.

My friend saw everything happen. We both looked at each other and had that "oh crap" moment. Then he ran to call 911. I have no idea how I walked to my patio, but I got there and lay down while putting my leg in the air. I had learned what to do in extreme situations from my PT training, and I did everything by the book: applied pressure and told my friend John to put a tourniquet on my leg.

John took the shirt off his back and did it. It worked pretty well; the bleeding slowed down a bit. Looking around, I swear I was the calmest—most people were freaking out. There were about twenty people at the party, and they all were now out back, squeezed onto my patio to see what was going on.

People kept saying, "You're going to be okay."

I just laughed and said, "I know, dude."

I knew the cops and ambulance would be there any second. I could see there was bright red blood everywhere, so I knew it was arterial bleeding; I must have severed an artery in my knee.

When the ambulance arrived, I was focused on staying calm. I wanted to keep control of the bleeding since I was losing so much blood. The EMTs rushed me to Paoli Hospital in less than ten minutes, and the whole time I was joking with them. Even when I got to the OR I was just joking around, trying to stay calm. I don't now how I did it.

The hospital staff started asking me all these questions: who to call, if I had a living will, and whether they could amputate my leg. It was too much in such a short time, and I was in the state of mind that everything was going to be fine, so I was just laughing and saying, "No way."

I didn't want to call my dad and worry him because it was 2 a.m., and he was a single dad who would have to hear that his son might die. I was his only kid; I couldn't do that to him. I wanted to wait until the next day to call, because I was confident I wouldn't die. My friend called my stepbrother, so eventually my dad was called and showed up.

In reply to the nurses who were asking about a living will and amputating my leg, I told them to let me wake up the next day with two legs. I don't think I would have been emotionally okay if everything had happened that first night. I needed to wake up with my leg the next morning.

I was in surgery for nine hours so the doctors could put a bypass in my leg. I had lost a lot of circulation and blood to the lower part, but they were trying to save it at my request. At first the doctors said I'd just lose half of my foot, and I was okay with that. I eventually woke up with a fasciotomy on my leg, but *with a leg,* so I was mentally strong. I think if I had awakened without a leg, it would have been more traumatic.

I was heavily medicated; I remember feelings but not specific events. I was happy but in a lot of pain. Although it was the most painful thing I had ever experienced, I maintained hope because I knew in some way everything would be okay.

After the third day in the hospital, I was confident I would keep my leg. Each day the nurses would come in and check it for feeling. They would start at my toes over my foot to my ankle over my calf and eventually to my knee. I never regained feeling from the middle of my calf to my foot. My leg was numb, but it still hurt. It was the weirdest sensation.

After the fourth or fifth day, I realized from everything I learned from school that I wasn't keeping my leg. I mentally prepared myself days before the doctors told me. In my mind, it sucked, but I still had to be strong and happy overall that I was alive.

By the eighth day, I had lost ten pounds, and things weren't looking great. The doctor came in and asked where my parents were. I was just hanging out and eating when the doctor said, "There is no easy way to put this: we have to amputate your leg."

I didn't get upset, cry, or even get angry; I just sat there for ten or fifteen seconds. My mom and dad were upset. I remember my dad asking if the doctor could take his leg off and give it to me.

After that, I just needed time for myself, so I kicked everyone out and just sat there. I don't know what emotions I was feeling. I was numb and simply shut my brain off for about two hours. Because I had prepared myself for this moment, I never really went into a deep depression or came close to losing my mind. Boxing had helped me to be mentally strong.

The nurses and doctors were shocked by how positive I was throughout the whole thing. All of my friends kept saying, "If anyone can get through this, it's you." That was great to hear, but honestly, I didn't want to be that guy; I just wanted everything to be okay. I didn't want to admit it to myself, but I believed this had happened for a reason. I knew it would be a new normal, but I'd still have the same friends, we'd go out and have a good time, and one day I'd walk, run, and play sports again. I kept reassuring myself of this.

Two days later, my leg was gone. It was like a death in my family. I was still joking, relaxing, and trying to get the nurses to let me wear street clothes because I hated the hospital gown. I don't remember the day I lost my leg because I was on so many medications and sleeping a lot, but the next day I let certain people visit.

I did need a day to accept the fact that I had no leg, and I wanted people there who would be strong for me and not make me upset. I couldn't handle people freaking out; I needed people to talk to me like a normal person. It was a rough day, the worst I had ever had, but I was still in good spirits even with this huge change—my new normal.

I ended up at Bryn Mawr Rehab Hospital and started slowly getting better and much stronger. The first day I could only stand for thirty seconds because there was so much swelling, but the second day I stood for two minutes and the third day, six minutes. I was progressing, and so happy to be in a rehab center because this was what I wanted to do for a career. I finally got to take a shower for the first time in a month, and I could also crutch around. My new normal was getting easier to handle.

On about the fifth or sixth day of rehab, I was progressing rapidly. Since I'd had a puncture wound, I had to wrap it with cloth and stick it in the wound. I was going through my normal day and eating breakfast when I felt something squishy around my knee. I just kept eating while thinking, "What the heck is that?"

I started patting it with my hand; it felt like there was something in the bandage. I peeled a quarter of the bandage off, and blood starting pouring out everywhere. I sat there for a second thinking, "There is no way this is happening; I'm totally dreaming."

I didn't even ring the call bell—I just started screaming at the top of my lungs for help. The nurse ran in and screamed even louder for help. There I was lying in bed with my leg in the air, just as I'd been on that day I got stuck on the fence. Could this really be happening again?

The nurse put a tourniquet on my leg, and I applied pressure. As I looked around in that moment, there was a janitor cleaning up all the blood, four nurses and two doctors all working on my leg, and me, lying there wondering what the heck was happening.

Another ambulance was called, and once again, I was rushed to the hospital. By the time I got there, the bleeding had stopped, but I was living a harsh reality that I might lose more of my leg. And, for the first time during this experience, I thought I was going to die. I have never felt anything like that day. It was a near-death experience, more extreme than my first, and I never want to feel that again. When I was bleeding out, I was telling the nurses to tell my dad I loved him, tell my family I cared, and my friends too.

I ended up in surgery again. It went well, but my mind was completely drained. I was in a horrible and extreme state of mental distress for two to three days. I lost a lot of my positive attitude and kept wondering what else was going to happen. I thought with every little muscle twitch that something was wrong. I was living in fear, and my new normal wasn't going so well.

I was still grieving the loss of my leg but had been doing well until this shook me. I was extremely scared. I would wake up thinking everything was supposed to be okay, but now I didn't know who to believe, and I struggled to keep myself calm. It was a cluster of a lot of crap in a small period of time. My anxiety started going through the roof, and I started asking people if they thought I was going to die.

It took me four days to get my positive attitude back, because I knew I had to be optimistic. Without hope and belief, you can't do much, so I knew a positive mental attitude would help push me through. I didn't have control of what would happen in the coming days, weeks, and even months, but I would have to keep moving and maintain my hope.

It took a week to get mentally strong again. When stuff like that happened, there was no turning back.

The grieving process really started when I was sent home. In the first week, I cried more than I ever had before. I'm not sure if it was because I was really upset, but it felt like the right thing to do. I had been strong most of the time, but until then I'd never given myself a chance to release all the emotions I had built up. It was funny because I'm a man and still pretty strong, but there I was crying at any commercial, movie, or song that triggered any sort of emotion. Getting everything out really helped.

After the first week home, I felt a lot better. I was on fewer medications, in my own comfortable bed, and not getting woken up twelve times a night by nurses. I started focusing on how I could get better, both physically and mentally. I came up with things I wanted to improve in my life: I wanted to be a nicer person, appreciate things more, and be happier.

It's funny how something so horrible can make you appreciate the things and people around you. Now I'll admit, even as a guy, the little things make me smile—like the first time I stood up in the shower, I couldn't help myself. I smiled for days. It's the stuff you take for granted—you don't realize until you've lost something, or something in your life changes drastically, how nice it actually was.

My main focus today is being able to rationally think about how everything will work for me. I won't lie; at times, I think, "This sucks." Getting upset won't change what happened and make my leg grow back, so I have to go on.

I contacted CHOP and Paoli Hospital because I wanted to volunteer and speak to amputee patients. Someone came to speak to me after my leg was amputated, but I wish someone had come to me before the surgery to say, "I made it through this, and so can you."

I recently got to talk to a young kid who was going to have the same amputation as I had. I told him to keep pushing through, and I let him know that he was strong and would make it through everything. It was a cool experience. I want to help people in any way I can, and I figure when I'm walking again, I'll be able to do it a lot more.

I don't think I was ever angry that it happened, but I was angry at *how* it happened. It's like a "cool story bro" kind of thing. After I tell people how it happened, I always wonder if a shark bite story would have been cooler to tell. Regardless of how it happened, I know somehow it happened for a reason because, where the fence punctured my knee, it was just too much of a perfect position; just a centimeter over more, and I would still have my leg.

I'm still the same guy, although in my new normal. I still go to the gym, I play certain sports, and I just started boxing training again. I'll still talk to anyone and have many things I want to do. I will rock climb, sky dive, and travel very soon. I'm coping with everything by positive self-talk, meditation, and making goals for myself.

I thought I had so much time to do everything, but that cliché that "life is too short" hit me right in the face just months ago. People say it, but they don't comprehend it. I guess when you have a near-death experience or two, your eyes open wide. I came to feel that I'd rather be rock climbing or skydiving and die than live in fear and not experience anything.

I almost died because I jumped over a fence. If I had died that way, I would have been so mad. It was a totally innocent act gone completely wrong, but it's true that anything can happen. I had a friend who died in a car accident at seventeen years old. He had his whole life ahead of him. You just don't know. Worrying is an option, but I don't want to let worrying consume me; I want to really live.

Overall, having a positive attitude has kept me going. I'm not saying it didn't suck and that I didn't get depressed, but I took the cards I was dealt and am using them the best I can. I still plan to be a physical therapist and help people push through their injuries, both physically and mentally. I hope my story can encourage them to never give up.

I honestly realized that with anything in life, it's important to never lose hope. Losing hope means losing a lot. I can't go back or control anything that will happen, but I do have the power to keep my hope and never give up. My new normal hit me when I least expected it, but I know it was for the best because I've never felt more alive in my life than I do now.

∼

New normals are inevitable in life because things can constantly change. The hardest change comes when we least expect and are forced to live out a new normal we were never prepared for. After I learned Ryan's story I could only feel less angry and more appreciation for the strength and resiliency that others can have when faced with certain hardships and change. It helped me realize that just because I had something so unexpected and negative happen, that didn't mean my life would be completely worse, just different. And now after being inspired by Ryan's story, even though it was completely different than mine, I knew I could make my new normal work and really start living in the moment again instead of focusing on how things could have or should have been.

Chapter Eighteen

There is no place like home...

The Wizard of Oz's catchphrase, "There's no place like home," has become a cherished quote passed down for many years. It brings a feeling of comfort to your mind and body, giving you a sense of safety and security. "Home is where the heart is" is another quote that can produce the same emotions and safety net, except that it also illustrates that it's not about one particular home base; your "feeling at home" can be anywhere or with anyone toward whom you feel love.

Both quotes are heartening, but what happens when the home you knew is completely broken—or you come to realize it never fully existed the way you always thought?

Growing up I believed that every family had the fairytale-behind-the-four-walls type of story. Most of my parents' friends had beautiful homes that gave you the sense that things were perfect, and there was never any trouble in paradise. As I started growing up and understanding more, I realized that behind every family, every person, and every door was something that affected people or caused a family-bond to be weak, distanced, or even completely invisible. I also realized that there were some people in this world who picked up and left their secure homes to find new ones—sometimes involuntarily—and there were others who never had a real home at all.

After my parents' separation, my dad did his best to keep the four-bedroom house where my siblings and I had lived for most of our lives. It was filled with memories that we couldn't even try to replicate. Between the mini-hockey games, quick family dinners of fish sticks before sports, huge back yard with the trampoline, and scuffs on the walls from our careless play, it was my perfect home most of the time. Of course, there were moments when I hated it and wanted to run away, but it was usually my safe place. I couldn't imagine not having a place to call home.

That had me wondering about all the people out there who never had the chance to experience that constant feeling of security and contentment in their own home. I couldn't help but feel some sense of empathy towards them.

~

Meet Steve O'Neill; my brother's friend, an advocate against domestic abuse

As a little kid, I didn't know my biological dad because he was in and out of jail. My mom looked for love and support from other men, and it seemed like I was constantly meeting potential stepdad after stepdad. My mom just wanted to be loved, and she deserved it.

We seemed to move from town to town and from house to house; I never felt like I had a proper place to call home. My mom's relationships didn't stick too long, and with my biological dad still in jail, she decided to try finding a place in Havertown, Pa. I was in fourth grade when we moved there.

My mom fell in love with a man who had two kids of his own, and I felt left out at times. I actually threatened suicide at times and locked the doors so no one could get in. I wasn't ready to open my home to other people. I just wanted it to be my mom, my other brothers and sisters, and me.

With my suicide threats and even attempts and moments of acting out, I was 302'd (involuntarily committed to receiving a psychiatric evaluation). The doctors felt the best way to help me was for me to stay in Haverford School District, because they thought it could help me. Things were rocky in my house: we had good times, but blood and tears were shed, my stepfather was drinking and using drugs, and I never knew what mood he'd be in, so I tended to stay away.

Because of so many domestic abuse fights, both my mom and stepdad were arrested. Eventually they split up. My mom ended up keeping his kids and taking care of them, but I knew that this was his way back in. Over time, the two got back together, but there was a lot of fighting. They would take it out on all the kids, including me, by grounding us and making us do chores.

I got sick of the atmosphere in my house because it never felt like

143

a home to me. I decided to run away to Cape May and stay with my aunt. My mom knew this was probably better for me, so she allowed me to stay.

On July 4, 2005, my mom and stepdad had a huge fight. He beat her, and she was rushed by ambulance to the hospital with the fear she'd also had a stroke. When I saw her, I pulled him out of the room and told him he'd pay if he ever touched her again. He was always manipulative, but he promised, so I let it go for that moment.

I told my mom I wasn't coming back home unless she kicked him out. Basically it was him or me. On August 16, 2005, we kicked him out, and I was finally going to be home with my mom.

Unfortunately, my stepdad drove her to work the next day. He dropped her off, went home, grabbed a knife, and went back to my mom's work, where he stabbed her to death. He had the intention of killing himself to be in a happier place with her. He was under the influence of drugs, and I heard he lay down next to her for hours, smoking cigarettes, while my mom lay dead on the ground. No kid should ever have to know that kind of information especially about his or her own mother.

I was in New Jersey when I saw the breaking news out of Havertown, Pa. I saw the store's logo show up on the screen and knew right away that my biggest fear was now a reality. I didn't want to believe it, but I called my brother, who knew too. I drove right to the police station (about two hours away) and confirmed the picture of my stepdad. The next day the police found him in Philadelphia seeking drugs. I couldn't believe it.

The trial was exhausting and difficult. Ironically, it started on August 6, 2006, which comes out to be triple sixes, which is known to most as the Devil's number. It was eerie to experience, but having to be a witness and testify against my stepdad was even worse. I had to relive the moments when he beat my mom and me, all the moments I was scared for my family members' lives, and all the horrible times back in my unstable home.

The trial lasted three days; the verdict was reached in just one and a half hours. After he was found guilty, I came to terms with the fact that my mom was really gone, and I was never going to have the home I had dreamed of as a little kid.

This tragedy changed everything in my life. I was once this kid who minded his own business, just trying to get by, but now my face was plastered all over the front page of the newspaper. I was in an unwanted limelight, completely embarrassed, and I kept seeing the eerie headlines like, "I think I killed Lori." This rocked me to the core. Now everyone knew my business, my life, my struggles, and the fact that I had a broken home. People looked at me differently. The reporters were everywhere, trying to get any bit of information from me. My neighbors were doing interviews, people were spreading rumors, and I felt exposed. I had just lost my home, my family, and my mom, and now nothing seemed to matter.

I had a lot of support, which got me through, but I became rebellious in school and in the community. I tracked down my biological father, hoping to find a sense of home with him. Although we grew closer, he eventually was killed over drugs, and I realized my life was in shambles.

I was taken in by a family to stay in the school district; however, I was both defiant and mischievous. My life wasn't going anywhere because, after losing both of my parents, I just didn't care about anything. I got kicked out of school for stupid decisions and placed in alternative school. I was like the devil and had no cares in the world. I was coping negatively with drugs and drinking because I just wanted to escape my reality.

When I started alternative school, I realized that teachers were more one on one because it was a smaller group, so that helped me a bit. I remained close with my stepbrothers, even though it was their dad who had killed my mom. I knew it wasn't their fault; I couldn't move on with my life if I blamed them.

Tina, the mom who took me in, started helping me put everything into perspective. She brought me into a stable environment and a loving home and helped me get back on my feet and experience happiness again. Things were looking up—I finally felt like I was in a secure place where I could feel comfortable. Tina became my mentor, teaching me not to resent but to respect others and allowing me to love again. She was the best thing that ever happened to me, and I am beyond grateful for her care and support.

Melissa Ann Hopely

I asked her how I could ever repay her. She said, "Just do it for someone else." She was an angel who helped save my life.

Today I know where I am and who I am. I made it through school and am now a business manager at a home healthcare agency. I'm engaged and have a beautiful son and an apartment, which I call home. It took a while to get here, but I am grateful for the support and love of so many.

My mom's murder caused so many unexpected changes in my life that I was forced to grow up fast. I wish my mom was alive, especially so she could see my son. In some weird way, though, I think my parents were meant to die, because now I am advocating against domestic abuse. I'm sharing my story to help others who are struggling with these situations.

I'd give anything to have my mom back, but I know that now I have to provide for my family and be a loving husband and father and an advocate, so no one else has to go through what I faced. I'll be the first to admit there are times I find myself crying over it. I do my best to cope with music and also hanging with my friends and family, but this tragedy changed my life forever. I'm not embarrassed to admit I still struggle with the harsh reality of it all.

Every year I hold a vigil for my mom, but ever since her workplace was sold, I realized I wanted to do something bigger in order to help others. I organized a beef and beer to raise money and awareness to help end domestic violence and abuse. I want to donate food, clothing, and toys to families that have to start from ground zero, just as I did.

I also plan to talk to young adults in schools about the importance of speaking up in tough situations, and the fact that they are not alone, even though stuff like this does happen. Domestic violence is overlooked and covered up far too much. If I can help even one kid or one family not to be in the situation I'm in, then I know I did what I set out to do.

Through my nightmare, I learned you can't help anyone until you help yourself. You need to focus on yourself and learn ways to make good things come out of bad situations—you have that power. Sometimes we don't have complete control, but we all have a voice and need to use it. It's easy to think, "That won't happen again," but too many times it does.

Follow your own passions, be the person you want to be, and do the things you want to do in life. Don't let anything ever stop you, and remember: home doesn't always have to be a physical place—it's what's inside your heart and with the people who care about, love, and support you.

～

After hearing Steve's story, I realized how, even through such hardships, you could rebuild a home by using your heart and strength. Just one year after that horrible night back in July 2008, my dad decided he had to sell our family home. My brother, my sister, and I were sitting around the kitchen table in tears, begging him to keep the house, but we all knew our house hadn't been much of a home since the issues with my parents started. Negative energy had filled the rooms, and between all the arguing and ignoring that went on, my brother, my sister, and I tried to stay out of the house whenever possible. It felt like our home was completely broken on the inside, only surviving to the outside world by our fake smiles and the well-built walls that surrounded us.

Having to move was another transition I wasn't ready to deal with. My dad bought a three-bedroom fixer-upper because he was so good at flipping houses, but the first time I entered it, it felt cold and completely destitute. The worst part about the transition was that I was only a year out of college and couldn't afford to move out on my own, so I was forced to move in with my grandparents, who had an extra room.

In the beginning, I was basically going back and forth to my dad's, friends', and grandparents' because I wanted to feel that continuous sense of belonging and security. It seemed any time I lost it, even for a second, I could just pack my stuff and stay somewhere else for the night. I started traveling more too, because I was doing public speaking. Every time I met someone new or found myself in a new place, I felt a sense of comfort, but it was never the same comfort I had felt in the home I grew up in.

Around the same time we moved, country singer Miranda Lambert came out with her single, "The House That Built Me." I would keep replaying it over and over again, thinking about all the memories and wondering if I could ever go back to experience them again. She literally sang everything I was feeling: *"I thought if I could touch this place or feel it, this brokenness inside me might start healing. Out here it's like I'm someone else; I thought that maybe I could find myself. If I could just come in, I swear I'll leave; won't take nothing but a memory from the house that built me."*

Growing up I was lucky enough to live next to cousins on my dad's side. We borrowed eggs and butter and even took the fence down between our back yards. It added to the comfort of feeling at home because we were always surrounded by love, even if we had to escape next door to get it. I grew close with Joanna, a native of England who was my dad's cousin's wife. She introduced me to real English tea, and it was nice to be able to vent to someone and not be judged. There were times I felt exposed and misunderstood by my parents, so having that escape helped me a lot.

Over the years, we stayed close with Joanna and her family. Recently my dad, my sister, and I went to a Fourth of July party at their house. As we sat in the backyard enjoying the crowd, games, food, and music, we couldn't help but look to our left and see the fence that separated what once was one huge back yard between the two homes. That back yard held so many memories—my pet hamsters' burials, our breathtaking swim during Hurricane Floyd, the countless football games in the snow—that I wanted to go back in time to the place I had once called home.

I had the urge to let out some tears, but with everyone right there, swimming, partying, and playing games, I knew it wasn't the appropriate time. My stepmom Terri was sitting to my right, and we started reminiscing about the moments we'd spent together on Crescent Hill Drive. Ironically, Terri and her family were our neighbors for over ten years. Her home was just up the street, and I used to play with her daughter Kelly. She had also carried my little sister down the street to my mom after a bike accident.

Terri has her own story. Her youngest daughter, Kristi, was born with a very rare genetic chromosome deficiency. I used to see Kristi walking as much as she could up our street with Terri, and each time I saw her, I could tell something was different about her. I had never realized that she was a medical miracle—especially now at eighteen years old.

Terri had it much harder than most parents but never complained, and Kristi, who is now my little stepsister, brightens up many of my days. This kid needs a reality show because she not only tries to do things on her own, she also is hilarious. She comes off younger than her age, but every second spent with her is a constant reminder of how blessed I am to have these people in my life.

Everything seemed to be hitting me in the face as I thought about Terri and her daughters and how I was so blessed to have such an amazing extended family. I'm not sure if it was my old house, the fact that my family wasn't the typical American family anymore, or the feeling that I was way too far from home, but growing up I believed that every house on my block was ideal, and behind every door and window were perfect, all-American families. Maybe it was my optimism or just my defense mechanism protecting me from the harsh realities of life.

As I took a last look at where I once lived, I could see parts of my old home were falling apart. It annoyed me to know that the new owners didn't care, but ultimately I realized it was just an outward reminder of what had happened behind those walls just a few years ago. One of the greatest lessons I have learned in life is that nothing is perfect. I'm glad it's not, because being perfect and all the same doesn't allow for any opportunities to learn, grow, and experience. The more and more I thought about everything, the more blessed I felt and the easier things became. I knew being at that party wasn't so much about me coming home; it was more about visiting the place where my journey to finding my new home began.

Chapter Nineteen

Forgiveness

People forgive in many different ways. Sometimes some things take longer to forgive than others and sometimes things are never actually truly forgiven. Not forgiving can actually break families, friendships, work partnerships and always leave us with something that was never fully worked out. So what does forgiving actually do for us? Does it help us move on with our lives? Does it help us start fresh? Does it help us let go of something hurtful in our past? How can we really know when it's the right time to forgive and if the person or event deserves forgiveness?

In order for me to move on with certain things, it was so important that I forgive and let go, but never force myself to forget. Forcing myself to forget things would actually hurt my healing process and leave me no room to learn and grow from my experiences. Also, forcing myself to forget would really just hide the problem and bottle up my emotions, which usually made things worse in time. But I felt I somehow had to forgive because it seemed like every time I didn't I was held back and left with a huge unwanted burden.

There were so many things I found myself struggling to forgive. I guess I was so angry with the issues I had that I didn't even recognize the blame I put on others and myself. It was like I was forcing myself to forget instead of actually forgiving people, situations and even myself. I think forgiving was scarier because when I forgave I was admitting that the issue happened. Even though I could move on in some way, it was so uncomfortable to have to relive the experience and the feelings that went along with it. I just thought it was easier to just forget about it and in time it would just go away, but overtime I was learning that never helped.

There were a lot of times I had to forgive others in my life, but there were also many times I had to forgive myself. Forgiving myself was harder than anything else because when I was forgiving myself, I was admitting I was wrong and that was something I struggled with a lot partially because I wanted to people please and be perfect for those around me, but partially because I had had issues with self-worth that it just made me more depressed.

There were distinct situations I can honestly say that without forgiving, I couldn't have moved on. The first was with my parents for getting divorced. I was so mad at them and for some many years tried to forget it even happened with consuming myself in my work and own life. I had so much anger built up, but I knew if I didn't forgive them I couldn't ever rebuild the bond we once had and that was something I needed in my life. The second was forgiving the kid who bullied me in high school. I never directly forgave him, but in my heart and in my mind I did. It was hard having to relive the experience in my mind, but I knew I would never move on and I also knew that he didn't mean for things to go that far. I don't think everyone who bullies does. Unfortunately, those bullying or making fun of others can be struggling with things as well, but it doesn't make it right.

I hate admit, but I too did hurt my peers at times. It was usually because I needed to make myself feel better and usually it stemmed from others hurting me and then having to deal with my OCD and depression and wanting a simple quick escape. That was me trying to forget just for a second what I was truly facing in my life. I have apologized to those peers and they have forgiven me, but that doesn't mean I forgave myself. You see, as a speaker you share your story and as a bullying victim at times you talk about how you were hurt by others, but I make it a point to let the audience know that I too was guilty of hurting others and whatever the reason, it was wrong. Sharing that part of my story was always hard, because in my mind I wanted to forget those things happened, but in my heart I knew I had to relive the experiences every time I spoke to youth because it was going to help them.

I don't know what clicked, but one day I just forgave myself for everything. For the blame I put on myself for my mental health issues, the guilt I felt for continuing the cycle of bullying at times just so I could feel some sense of worth in that moment, the feelings of failure I felt for not being where I want to be career wise and most of all, the hardest thing I had to forgive was the fact that I hated myself at once and thought life wasn't worth living. I can't explain the burden that was lifted and I can't tell you that you will feel the exact same way, but forgive yourself for anything that is holding you back. Whether it's not landing your perfect career job, hurting someone, missing the game winning catch or blaming yourself for something you had no control over; whatever it is, you deserve that forgiveness.

As I got to talking to my friend Josh one day, I never realized how much he struggled to forgive himself for something he had no control over, but felt a great responsibility for. I was inspired by his strength to not only get through this life-altering situation, but finally forgive himself so he could move on with his life.

$\sim$

Meet my college friend Josh Evans; a gay rights activist

There was a lot in my life I had to forgive myself for, and it seemed like I spent my whole life fighting to ignore that realization so I could pretend everything was fine. But I knew there were things holding me back from being the real me.

During my freshman year of college, I began realizing and coming to terms with my true feelings and who I was becoming. I met someone who finally made me feel comfortable. He gave me a reason to not care what anyone else thought and to come to terms with the fact that I was gay and it was okay. He and I went through many hard times together that I didn't learn to appreciate until a few years later.

In my case, I never had to deal with bullying about being gay in high school because it wasn't something that I ever talked to anyone about. I was never sure what I really wanted back in those days, and no one had ever asked me about it. At that point, it was just something in the back of my mind.

Unfortunately, I then had to deal with it during freshman year of college. I was lucky enough to have someone going through these troubles with me, making me feel like everything would be okay. We knew that we were going to be judged and that people were going to talk about us. At first, it wasn't at all easy to face and it affected us both physically and mentally. But as we began hanging out more often and really getting to know each other, we became more comfortable, finding out about each other's pasts, coming to terms with what was going on, and realizing we weren't in this alone.

I will always remember like it was yesterday the first time we told someone what was going on between us. It was the night we told my best friend of seven years that I had feelings for another guy, someone who we both became good friends with. Word quickly spread to our entire group of friends, and next thing I knew, he didn't want to see or talk to me out of embarrassment.

I had a very hard time dealing with how everything was falling apart even quicker than it had come together. I wanted to take it all back, to just return to how my life was before I had to deal with any of the problems that went along with coming out. I contemplated leaving school and going home, back to the life I knew and away from facing reality.

It was like I wanted to forget everything that had happened and move on, but the only way I could deal with things was to face them head on and forgive myself for never allowing me to be me. After I came to terms with this, things worked themselves out between us—with a few hurdles here and there.

We ended up in an official relationship but unable to publicly express this to anyone. It was hard to be together and want to tell anyone and everyone but have to hold back. There were times when people would be at a party drinking, and somehow our names would come up in conversation, and people would begin to talk about us. We had to hear about our own roommates talking about us behind our backs just to make themselves look better with the other guys.

Not knowing who would be accepting of us and who wouldn't was harder than I ever imagined. The two of us went through freshman year together, living, learning, and becoming more comfortable with being gay.

If I had never met my first boyfriend, I'm not entirely sure how coming out to my parents would have happened. I never officially said, "Hey Mom and Dad, this is _____ and he's my boyfriend," although that may have been easier.

I remember telling my mom over the phone one day when she asked about him. The feeling of being able to say, "Yes, we are together," was absolutely amazing. To finally be happy with who I was is indescribable.

I didn't have the conversation with my dad until months later, when he asked. Either way, I was finally comfortable enough to not be ashamed of telling my family. Everything else just kind of fell into place after that: telling people the truth if they asked, and introducing him as my boyfriend to certain people.

I never felt the need to come out and say I was gay unless someone asked. Neither of us ever wanted the fact that we were gay to be an impression someone had of our personalities. After being talked about, having to deal with our families and friends, and learning the ups and downs of a relationship, we were happy with the people we were becoming.

In the long run, things happened, mistakes were made, and we grew apart, but I will be forever thankful for having him with me to experience the first phase of my life as a gay male.

In the years following, I went through things that made me feel as if there was no hope left in my life. It all started with a car accident that left me hospitalized in the first semester of my sophomore year. About four months later, I lost my best friend and roommate D'Angelo to sickle cell anemia, something that no one was expecting.

Having to cope with this loss was not easy, and the pain I felt made me feel hopeless. I had lost someone who meant so much to me, someone I looked up to, someone who was one of my first, best friends in college. I got through the pain as best I could with the help of amazing friends and family, and people like Missy. Missy was also a close friend of my roommate, so the loss was hard on us all, but she was always there to support everyone else and do what she could to make us smile.

Throughout the next year, I began developing a relationship with another person I had met at school. We became close friends and began dating, but never really talked about a relationship. I never knew the feelings he had for me until I wasn't sure where things were going and began to end what was going on.

There was a night where he was served underage at a bar and became heavily intoxicated, leading to a trip to the hospital. I received phone calls from the people at the hospital with him and drove over there, because he was asking for me. I eventually learned that his drinking that night had been an attempt to drown out his feelings toward me. I began to feel responsible and at the same time feel like I needed to be there for him; I truly did care.

From then on, our connection deepened, but we still never talked about whether or not we would be in a true relationship. That summer, we ended up living together in an apartment while I worked for school, running our new student orientation.

In our group of friends, people began to become concerned with his eating habits. We were unsure how to deal with the problem, and a conversation occurred one night where he felt he was being attacked. As his friends, we cared for his health and wanted to know what we could do for him, but he didn't understand. This was the night where we realized that he was troubled beyond an eating disorder. His rage over the conversation led to his attempting to run away, which led to jumping down a flight of stairs and gashing his head open. None of us knew what to do except try to be there for him.

The angrier he got and the more negative things that happened, the more deeply I found myself caring for his health and wellbeing. I felt like I could never leave his side, nor did I want to, because I wanted to make sure that he would get better and get through any issues he was dealing with. I never realized that my caring would lead to even worse things.

While running Immaculata's freshman student orientation, I left my phone on a table, and he got a hold of it and read text messages from a friend. The messages were nothing but a friend asking me when we could hang out, but he took this as me talking to someone behind his back. The next thing I knew, I had hundreds of people checking into orientation while I was trying to figure out where he had disappeared to.

One thing led to another, and it was determined that he had tried to take his own life.

Unsuccessful in his attempt, he would end up in the hospital with all of his friends concerned with what would happen next. I didn't know how to deal with suicide or how to help someone who was having these types of thoughts. I just wanted the best for him. While I was visiting him in the hospital, we determined that we would be together— something I was not expecting to happen. I felt like running away from the problem wouldn't help him get better, so I needed to stay.

We went on to live together again in a new apartment with my best friend. The three of us made our apartment our home together, and things began to look up. Unfortunately, things quickly went back downhill as my boyfriend stopped taking his medication and refused the help he was being offered. Our relationship turned horribly wrong, but I cared too much for him as a person to walk away and give up.

I dealt with the daily pain of not knowing what would happen next, if he would come home happy or mad. Not many people knew or

155

understood what I was going through or how I was being treated. I knew that deep inside he never wanted to hurt me or make me feel bad about myself, but something inside of him was making him this way. I wanted him to get help and get better so we could continue to be happy together.

Around Christmas, I decided that I couldn't be in a relationship with him anymore, but I didn't want him to feel as if I was giving up on him. I expressed my feelings to him in fear that I was doing the wrong thing. He was angry, upset, and didn't know how to deal with things ending. I reassured him that I was still there for him, regardless, and that I wasn't going anywhere.

Eventually, on a cold morning in February, I would experience something that has changed my life. He was missing again while I was home from school during a break. The night previous, we'd had a fight where he felt like I wasn't being honest with him, and we had ended things on a bad note. I knew, when I got the call that he was missing, that nothing good could come of it.

I told my family what was happening, and they drove me to the apartment. After we got there, I went into our bedroom and didn't see him anywhere. I walked to the closet and found him there. Sadly, he had taken his own life, leaving many people puzzled as to how it could have happened.

From that day, my personality and my entire life changed. I have never been the person I was before, and I'm not sure that I ever will return to that. Having to go through this was one of the worst things that could have ever happened in my life. For months after the incident, I felt responsible, like it was my fault and like there was more I could have done. Truthfully, he was sick and he wasn't getting the help he really needed, but I couldn't come to terms with that.

It is a hard story for me to tell, but what I realize now is that I learned more about others and myself through the experience. What I want others to realize is that they should never, ever give up on a friend who is going through something as serious as thoughts of suicide. Ask questions and find out what you can do to help, but if you feel someone is capable of hurting him or herself, seek professional help.

I would also advise anyone going through something similar to get help not only for their friend, but also for themselves. I made the mistake of not getting help for myself with everything I was experiencing.

Being gay in a world where we are looked at as different is difficult, but we all have a story. If people talk about you, just let them talk, don't let their words hurt you. You will find yourself and the people who belong in your life when the time is right. You will come across people like Missy, who will teach you that, no matter what happens, things will get better.

Good people do exist; never give up the hope of finding them. Let your story shape you, learn from your mistakes, learn from others, but most of all learn to accept yourself. We each come from somewhere different, and we each come across people in our lives who are there to help.

Take sexual orientation out of the equation, and we are all human beings. We all go through hard times, and we need to realize that we have each other. If we are able to come together and tell about our journeys and how we dealt with the pain or suffering, we will see that we should never give up.

Two things that will always be left in this world are hope and the ability to forgive. Forgiveness is vitally important because without it we can never truly move forward. It enables us to grow stronger and learn about others and ourselves.

When I got the call about Josh's boyfriend's suicide, I was shocked because I didn't see it coming. Both Josh and his boyfriend were so positive and outgoing, but that's where the term "you just never know" really comes in. I honestly had no idea that Josh was living with so much guilt for so long and putting so much blame on himself for so many different things; some he couldn't even control. Josh had to forgive himself at some point, because he would have never been able to move on with his life. After talking with him, he helped me understand that it wasn't that he would forget his boyfriend, what happened and their great times, but if he forgave himself and what happened, he could finally start living again. That's when I realized Josh was right and he helped me see that it was okay to forgive others, specific situations and myself so I too could move on with my life.

Chapter Twenty

Fear of Failure

Paulo Coelho wrote in his book *The Alchemist*, "There is only one thing that makes a dream impossible to achieve: the fear of failure." I've had a lot of fears in life, but I think the fear that haunted me the most was fear of failure. Not to say I wasn't determined and didn't take any chances ever, but I think I let myself miss out on many things because I was too afraid I'd fail or be rejected.

With each moment of each day, I'm realizing failure is a big part of life. Fear is just a false alarm that sometimes has us playing way too safe and not giving ourselves the things we most desire or deserve.

My grandmother and I had this ongoing joke: anytime I said the word "fail" or anything even close to it, I owed her a dollar. I do admit, I was saying it too much—mostly to reassure myself that failure wouldn't happen. But the more I said it, the less desire I had to try new things because my fear was so strong.

Although I never actually had to pay my grandmother anything (except a few ice cream cones here and there), I couldn't help but realize how much the fear of failure was paralyzing me. My fear wasn't allowing me to do the things I deserved and wanted to do. I knew I had to make a change; although it wouldn't be a complete cure, each step would make me stronger and help me realize that failing was a healthy part of life, allowing me to learn, grow, and not make the same mistakes as in my past.

I saw a video recently that featured public figures like Abraham Lincoln, Michael Jordan, Albert Einstein, Walt Disney, and Dr. Seuss, illustrating their failures and how without them, they never would have succeeded. As the video ended, I felt empowered—I couldn't believe these extraordinary people ever had the word failure in their vocabulary. I also realized that if they hadn't found the strength to strive again, we'd live in a much different world.

I thought of all the times I had learned from my mistakes and failures, but also all the times I missed out on opportunities and even fun because I let the fear of failure take over. Would I be in a different place today? Be further in my career? I can't even begin to answer those questions without driving myself crazy, but I can look back at all the times I did fail, looked fear in the face, experienced things I couldn't even fathom and also realize how right now, I am in the exact place I am supposed to be.

Sports were my life while I was growing up. I always tried to be the best at everything and show off in any way I could. All my worries seemed to run away when I played sports; when I made mistakes and errors, it was easy for me to get up and try again. Whether I struck out in softball, missed a free throw in basketball, or made a bad pass in soccer, even though I got frustrated, it was usually easy for me to get up and try even harder the next time.

I had a drive in me with sports, but when it came to real life, I couldn't seem to face fear. I worried about making mistakes in school, and not being the smartest or coolest. If I embarrassed myself, there was no coming back from it. It was like I was hiding the real me because I feared judgment so much that I wouldn't even take chances—like joining the school choir or plays because I was so afraid I wasn't good enough.

Although people see me as a very confident person today, I still struggle with negative thoughts and feelings about not doing well with things or being good enough. Now, however, each time I have those thoughts, I know it's a false alarm. If I don't take any steps or face challenges, my wishes and dreams will just remain false hopes instead of true possibilities.

My first real national keynote speaking engagement came on October 11, 2009, in Cotuit, Mass., at a suicide prevention film fundraiser. I was just a few months out of college, not fully trained in public speaking, and still finding little bits of self-confidence. I couldn't believe it when I got the invitation, but part of me wanted to turn it down due to fear that I wasn't good enough and there was someone better than me for the job. I almost missed out on a life-changing experience. On that day, as I looked into the crowd and realized I was in a position to inspire these strangers with my own genuine words and honest story, I knew at that moment that living in fear would get me nowhere in life.

As time went on, although the fear of failure still lingered, I started doing things I'd never imagined before. I was now speaking for the amazing organization Minding Your Mind, which graciously gave me the chance to represent it through speaking engagements in schools. Minding Your Mind also trusted me to take part in press conferences and TV interviews on its behalf. This was the boost of confidence I needed to feel as though I was ready to face my fears.

I appreciate all of those people who helped me to grow, including a dear mentor from the Chester County area named Tracy, who provided my first-ever speaker training. I won't lie, I had a bit of confidence, but there were many times when I feared making mistakes or failing. I even believed I wasn't good enough and was going after a dream that was too far out of my reach. With a lot of support, though, I pushed through my fears.

There are still times when I catch myself wondering if what I'm doing is worth it and fearing that I'll never make it. But, as my grandmother said so many times, "We all have already made it in some way." I knew this made sense, but on one fall night while I was working at a pub, I realized just how right she was.

It was 9:55 p.m. on a Saturday night, and the dining room closed at 10 p.m., so when four people in their mid-twenties walked in, I grew aggravated. I was determined to turn them away; however, something in my gut stopped me, and I let them sit down. I ordered their drinks and went over to talk to the bar regulars and relax a bit while the four people chatted away. When I went to check on them, I decided to sit down, as I sometimes do with my customers, and see what their stories were.

They asked what I did outside of the pub, and I explained how I spoke and was an advocate for certain causes. I mentioned that I recently had gone to Nashville and opened for a State Radio concert in memory of a student who lost his life to suicide. (On a side note, I almost didn't want to speak before the concert, knowing how well known State Radio was and how I had to set the tone for a rock concert, so I was hesitant to accept the offer by Minding Your Mind. But again, something in my gut told me to.)

A few seconds after I mentioned the concert in Nashville, I saw one of the girls getting teary eyed, and it seemed like she lost her breath for a second. She just looked at me said, "OMG, that concert was in memory of one of my best friends, Kyle—I can't believe this."

I couldn't believe it either. Here we were in Pennsylvania, miles and miles from Nashville, two strangers sharing tears and a moment of comfort without even expecting it. I'm not sure if it happened for a reason, but between my accepting the proposal to speak at the concert and facing my fears and allowing those four people to sit at the pub after closing time, I knew it meant something. I was a stranger in this girl's life, and because of meeting her, I gave her some sense of closure that she couldn't get otherwise. She also helped me, making me realize that if you live in fear you can't experience those amazing, unexpected things that happen in the unknown.

That night my thoughts went everywhere—I was crying, smiling, and crying more because I couldn't help but think, "Man, if I had chickened out, I wouldn't have experienced what I did that night."

After the concert and meeting Kyle's friend, I grew inspired to try some new things. That's when I decided to take up singing and writing music. I had always loved both but was always afraid I wasn't good enough.

After hearing negative comments from people who cared for me but disagreed with my decision, I almost didn't take a chance, but I actually got a gig at a local coffee house. I asked my guitarist friend Justin to perform with me. I didn't know him well before the gig—we just had a mutual friend in common—but from what I knew of him, he seemed like a rocker-type guy who feared nothing.

Ironically, though, after practicing with him for weeks before the event, I learned that he too had faced some fears, set backs and criticism. Learning this helped me realize once again that I wasn't alone and shouldn't let fear or anyone else stop me from experiencing things.

〰️

Meet Justin; my musician friend

Contrary to the stories of most musicians, I didn't start at an early age. I wasn't one of those kids you hear about whose parents bought him a guitar for Christmas at the age of four and went on to become a guitar prodigy; it kind of a happened naturally and unexpectedly.

When I was a teenager, I really wanted to be a professional wrestler. I was obsessed with it. I had a wrestling federation in my dad's back yard, often destroying things around the house, like garage doors, shed doors, trees, and various other parts of the landscape. My father kind of talked me out of it due to my lack of size and, perhaps, my destruction of his property.

I wound up going to a lot of concerts with my father during my teenage years. He would always purchase two tickets to a given rock show and drag me along (to a lesser degree, he'll still do that to this day from time to time). He never played an instrument but was always a big music enthusiast. Looking back, it may have planted a seed in me to take the path that I'm on.

In my senior year of high school, I took a mandatory intro to guitar course. I didn't really apply myself in that class (nor in any other class I had during that time period). But I did manage to learn a very simple guitar riff. I also learned "Wild Thing"—two simple riffs and songs. I remember thinking that it was cool that I knew how to actually play something on an instrument that was otherwise foreign to me.

Right around the same time period, my buddy Chris (a close friend of mine and a guitar player for seven years at the time) told me that he was writing songs. That was the coolest thing in the world to me—somebody I knew was writing his own music. I remember going to his house, and he would play me his songs. He would show me the lyrics he'd written to be sung over the music, and I would attempt to sing along. I had no idea what I was doing, but I was having a great time doing it.

Sometime shortly after my first semester of college, I bought my very first guitar—a Takamine G series acoustic for around $200 (not a great guitar, but good enough for me to learn on). I then went on to spend most of the following semester skipping class so I could mess around on the guitar. I started teaching myself how to play more and more songs— easy songs that captured my interest and boosted my confidence.

Not long after that, I wanted to play in bands and write music. I was convinced that was what I wanted to do with my life. I remember being in a band called Regolith for a short time. We recorded a demo in the singer's bedroom. We didn't have a drummer, so we used crappy drum programming for the beats to the songs. They were just awful recordings, but I was still having a blast during the process. I'm pretty sure we only had one gig as a band, some on-campus thing in the cafeteria. Nothing of significance happened with that band, but it definitely made me want to pursue music and get signed, tour, make albums—"live the life."

After roughly seven or eight years of one failed project after another, I had pretty much given up on the notion of joining or forming a good band that had the potential and the desire to go all the way. I had been in projects composed of musicians with drive but lacking talent, with talent but lacking drive, or who were destructive egomaniacs.

I moved back to Pennsylvania from Florida on the day before Christmas Eve 2008 with the singular goal of doing music my way, in the form of a solo project. I had a bunch of songs I had written over the years that had never seen the light of day, and I wanted to record them just to have a little something to show for myself. Even if it never got me signed, that was okay. I spent the next several months hard at work on my solo album. It was nearly finished in the spring of 2009 when I received a text message from my friend Adam, simply stating, "I have a proposition for you."

He then introduced me to a gentleman named Bill who to this very day is the best guitar player I have ever worked with. The three of us jammed with the idea of forming a band. I went into the jam session with mixed feelings: I had grown tired of trying to form bands that never wound up leaving the garage, and I was so close to finishing my solo album. But, I figured, what the hell? Why not? If it sucks, then I'll go back to work as a solo artist.

Turns out, not only did it not suck, it was a great jam. Adam and Bill are extremely talented at their instruments, and we all had a fun, long conversation after jamming. I left that night feeling that it was worth giving this project a shot to see if we could make a run at it.

Within the next few months, we found our singer and drummer and went on to form a band we called Kennedy Red. For the first time ever, I was in a band that played well, had drive, had fun, wrote solid music, and performed live on a regular basis. We went on to open for such bands as Days of the New and Accept (almost opened for the Misfits too, but that fell through). We recorded an EP with Grammy-nominated producer David Ivory, who worked with the Roots, Patti Labelle, Erykah Badu, and Halestorm, among others.

We had a series of conversations about whether or not we wanted to work with David Ivory. He had a very high price tag just to cut five songs. We knew the gravity of the situation. It was going to be arguably the biggest sacrifice that each and every one of us would make in our musical endeavors. It even led to some lineup changes in the band.

This was uncharted waters for me. All I'd ever known was the playing aspect of music, not the business aspect. I wasn't attracted to it because it caused some turmoil within the band and made it somewhat more of a chore or a job, rather than a passion I enjoyed. I also knew, however, that I was at a crossroads: I could do the easy thing and walk away from the band, or do the hard thing and commit to working with Dave, spend thousands of dollars that I didn't have, and take the all-in approach in an attempt to make my dream a reality. I chose the latter.

It took over a year just to pre-produce, record, mix, and master (complete) five songs. I didn't enjoy the process too much, nor did I enjoy working with the production company, but I was in it for the long haul. It was important to me to stick it out through the hard times to see if there would be a payoff in the form of a record contract.

During the process, the band became entirely too business-minded and rigid, scrutinizing every detail of the band beyond necessity—how we dressed on stage, how we moved on stage, and every guitar note, bass line, vocal melody, and drum beat. We couldn't agree on anything as a band. We had become a business; a brand, if you will. I would refer to the band privately as "the brand," taking a sarcastic jab at how rigid and stiff we all had become. It started to feel like we were unhappy housewives who had decided to stay in the marriage for the kids.

It even affected my personal life. I was perpetually flat broke—I spent every dime I had on making the album (which cost the band about $15,000 altogether). I had become immersed in credit card debt that I had trouble making minimum payments on, along with a truck payment, a student loan, an outstanding parking ticket, a dental bill of $50 that took me about nine months to pay, and normal monthly bills like phone, insurance, and rent. It got to a point where I had to choose between putting food in my mouth or gas in my truck because I didn't have enough money to do both. Without gas, I couldn't go anywhere, which meant no dating, no hanging out with friends—nothing. It was sort of like being on financial house arrest, and it affected every aspect of my life.

At the age of 28, I moved back in with my mother so that I didn't have to pay rent. I needed to pay off debt and basically crawl back to the start.

Through it all, I still forged forward for one reason: I believe in having no regrets. As strong and as beautiful and as wonderful as my parents are, they both have the commonality of never taking chances and never pursuing what they really truly wanted. They let fear of rejection and failure hold them back.

I decided at a young age that, for better or for worse, I didn't want to be like that. That is what motivated me to give up my $50,000/yr. job and move to Florida on a whim. That is what motivated me to sacrifice all of my money and a good chunk of myself for the benefit of Kennedy Red. I did not want to be the proverbial forty-year-old man sitting at a dive bar on a Tuesday, drinking beer and thinking about what might have been, if I had only persevered. I don't have to think that way because I *did* persevere. I *did* try my hardest.

I'm fine with falling short of a hard goal, as long as I gave it my best shot and didn't allow fear to stop me. It is healthy to face your fears. In fact, it can be a downright adrenaline rush to face your fears. It's important to remind yourself that if you never try, you always know what the end result is going to be: no different. If you do try, you may succeed or you may fail, but you have the satisfaction of knowing that you had the nerve to do it, which is very powerful.

I have zero regrets about what I've done. Hardship is only temporary if you make good, healthy decisions to get out of it. As of this moment, I've paid off all of the debt I got myself into; I also completed my solo album earlier this winter and have been performing live in support of it and having a blast. I'm playing music on my terms once again and for all the right reasons.

Throughout Kennedy Red's journey, I've met some great people, done some very cool things that I never thought I would ever do, and have some great stories. I am now going back to school for my psychology degree and hope to open a private practice while continuing to play music and inspiring youth to do the same. I guess if you were to learn anything from me, it would be to never let fear stop you from trying anything. Be true to yourself and your convictions. And the only true failure I see in life is to run away from life's challenges—so don't do that.

It really is amazing how we cross paths with different people for different reasons in our lives. When I sat next to Justin as he played guitar while I sang at the coffee house, I just thought he was a carefree, musician with no challenges. I especially felt that way when I learned of his recording contract with David Ivory. I never saw failure as an option for him. When I really got to know Justin and learn his story, I saw that he did struggle with failure, but what I learned about how he dealt with failure was most important. I was still struggling with not wanting to fail at all (I still do at times), but Justin's story got me thinking in other ways. It wasn't about not failing at all, but literally facing the fear of failure and taking chances (while being smart) so you could persevere in different ways and learn from when you did fail. I started seeing failure in a more positive light and realizing that everyone has failed at different times in his or her life. As Justin said, "if you never try, you always know what the end result is going to be: no different." You have the power to succeed and make many amazing things happen and not let the fear or actual existence of failure stop you. If you do happen to fail, be proud of yourself for taking the chance and learn from it so you can continue to persevere and stay resilient.

Chapter Twenty-One

Heroes

M ost of the time when we think of a hero, we picture a very in-shape man or character, fierce and brave, wearing a cape of some kind with a symbol that represents his or her strengths and super powers. But when the French Novelist Romain Rolland wrote, "A hero is a man who does what he can do," it really got me thinking.

I always felt a huge connection to anybody who would stand up for something or do the thing others wouldn't. Whether it's standing up for someone who's getting bullied or even telling the old woman in the bathroom that she is about to walk out with a long piece of toilet paper stuck to her shoe, those things, whether big or small, help people more than we can ever imagine. Each action we take toward people can stick with them, whether it was the middle finger you gave out of a split second of road rage or the rumor you spread about that girl sitting next to you in class—or the smile you shared when walking by a stranger. No one fully knows the impact we have on others because we can never know everyone's story.

So what defines a hero? Is there a guideline or specific criteria? Does someone have to be of a certain age, race, or class to be considered a hero? Does every hero gain recognition or receive an award? And if you are called a hero by someone, should it be known to the whole world?

Sadly, sometimes in life we look for reassurance. Personally, after I was called a hero a few times, I felt the need to post it on my social media pages. "Why do I have to tell everybody?" I always questioned myself. It was like I needed reassurance from others to know I was a good person doing good things for the world. Over time, I've come to realize that a true hero isn't someone who looks for or needs that recognition; it's the person who does what he or she can do in a given moment simply because it is the right thing to do.

Last year I was asked to speak at a heroes' luncheon at a high school in New Jersey. All of the sophomore class students were asked to pick a real life hero in their lives and write an essay about them, followed by an invitation to a luncheon at the school. Upon arriving, I remember looking around the room and seeing hundreds of people, all different in age and ethnicity, and realizing how being a hero didn't discriminate. I wanted to hear every story of every person in that room and learn how each of those heroes touched someone's life in some way. I knew each story would be unique in every situation and detail, but this is what I lived for: hearing about people who had made an impact on someone's life without the thought of being recognized or thanked.

This past month I was late paying my car loan. It was partly my fault for typing the wrong numbers in my online account, but it was also the bank's fault for sending the wrong information to me. After many phone calls and failed attempts, I received a call from the collections department. The guy from the bank was very rude as I was trying to explain the miscommunication about my payment. I guess with everything else going on in my life, that was the last straw, and it left me crying for over an hour. I let his bad attitude ruin much of my day.

After I composed myself, I called my car dealer with the hope of changing banks. My call was put through to a finance director named Matt. I was embarrassed but starting crying as I explained to Matt how the guy at the bank had been mean to me. I couldn't compose myself as I was talking.

After Matt had listened to me ramble and cry for over ten minutes, he said, "Melissa, please don't let your day be ruined because one guy wasn't having a good day at work. Life is too short to let that affect your whole day. There is still so much time in the day to make it a good one."

I gave one last whimper and said, "You're right. Thank you so much." I went on with my day, feeling a sense of hope and smiling at everyone I passed. Matt's one good deed changed my day for the better, and possibly the strangers' I passed as well.

I decided to call Matt back a few hours later to ask if he remembered the crying girl from that morning. Of course he did, how could he not?

I thanked Matt for being the one person who listened to me when I just needed to vent. I told him that I considered him my hero that day. I also promised I would pay it forward to someone else. I could tell immediately he was getting choked up.

The best part about that whole situation was not just Matt taking the time to listen to a complete stranger vent; it was when he told me I had made his day as well. I couldn't believe that one issue followed by one phone call could do so much good for two strangers miles and miles away from each other, leaving Matt with the realization that in my eyes, on that very day, he was a hero.

It's inevitable that things like what Matt did for me will happen every day. Some stories of heroism are hard to grasp, especially like the one about a four-year-old boy who saved a little girl from drowning and lost his own life. As horrible as it is, it makes me wonder if human beings have that hero instinct from a very young age, but sometimes choose not to take action.

After typing "child saves" and "child hero" in an Internet search engine, I couldn't believe how many pages came up of children who took heroic actions and saved the lives of others. Some died taking action while others lived to tell their stories, most of the time not even realizing they were seen as heroes. It's ironic because, as they grow up, children and teens often hear, "You are our future," but these kids are present right now and have the power to make a difference in people's lives at any given moment. That's what I found out back in high school—my life was saved by my friend Mary Beth Vogel, when she came to my room to see if I was okay, at a time when I was so lost that I was considering ending my own life.

Mary Beth and I still have a close bond today, like a little sister/big sister relationship. She was the big sister I never had, always standing up for me when people picked on me or started to cause trouble. I always admired that about her because I know it's sometimes hard to stand up for someone else due to fear of also being judged, but that never stopped her. Nowadays with our busy schedules, Mary Beth and I sometimes go months without talking, but when we see each other it's like no time has passed.

I've brought up that situation at times, reminding Mary Beth that she will always be my hero. She just says, "Miss, stop, you were there so many times for me too—and never forget that'd I do it again in a heartbeat." It's amazing that the one person who saved my life on more than one occasion was actually looking to thank me as well. The best part about it all is that, nearly ten years later, she still has the letter I wrote to her when I left the hospital back in high school.

Mary Beth and I recently started playing on the same women's soccer team. Most of our teammates know what happened back in high school, and we go on as if that awful day is just a bad memory far off in the distance. Sometimes I catch myself having flashbacks of that day when looking at or high-fiving Mary Beth. It's funny—as hard as that day was for both of us, the flashbacks aren't bad at all, but only calming and inspiring. I picture a very bright room with white walls and a light shining behind Mary Beth as she grabs my hand and helps me up.

Yes, it seems like a movie scene, and sometimes I wonder if that day even occurred. I think, "Seriously, that stuff only happens in the movies," but for Mary Beth and me, that day did happen. Although it's been almost ten years, Mary Beth has helped change my life more than she can know. She opened my eyes to life, to helping others and to realizing that I do matter and people do care about me. She also let me see that I too had the chance to be that hero for someone else and to never let fear and judgment stop me from doing the right thing. Furthermore, she helped me realize that there were other people out there making a difference and that I had the unique gift of sharing the stories of those extraordinary people with the world so I could at least help one other person and as I always say in my speeches to youth, so I too could "Be a Mary Beth" for someone else.

Here is the letter I wrote over 10 years ago to Mary Beth that she still holds today:

Dear Mary,

My girl, how are you. I'm so sorry I put you through all that, I know it was alot. You were there for me when I needed you. Thanks for telling my mom, I know how hard it was. Now I know I can count on you. Thank you again for being my big sis. Cya you soon.

Love,
Missy

~

Meet Megan; from Texas

It wasn't long ago when I was in high school. I remember walking down those hallways, knowing I was hiding something big that I didn't want anyone to know. I was afraid that if people found out they would judge and ignore me. I lived in denial for four years, because I couldn't let my parents find out that their daughter was a lesbian.

I had my fairytale when I met this girl in my sophomore year of high school. Our relationship was just like anyone else and their first love. We were head over heels in love. And what I wish people could see is that love is love, which is why, after being with this girl for over two years, I finally knew I had to tell my parents about her.

It was one of the hardest things I had ever done, and they didn't make it any easier with the way they took it. They kept saying, "It's a phase and a choice." That's when I decided to start traveling more to see my girlfriend every chance I got. Eventually I left my family and moved to Dallas to be near my girlfriend, because having a long-distance relationship was too hard, especially with limited support at home.

I faced a lot of depression and had many thoughts of wanting to give up, but my girlfriend reminded me that I had so much to live for. Sometimes I regret leaving my family because family is family, and I know they will always love you no matter what. It is definitely the most certain thing for me in life, but at that time it was hard to see.

I was judged by peers, felt like I was living a lie at times, and just didn't understand why I couldn't be me. After my girlfriend broke up with me, my aunt Mickey let me move in with her. She helped me out in a hard time and helped me get back on my feet. My parents finally came around after a very long year of struggles. Ironically enough, my mom was one of the people who helped me most after my first love and I split up, and I can't thank her enough for her unconditional love.

I learned a lot from this struggle, especially that there are many heroes around us. Between my ex-girlfriend (who is still a good friend), my mom, and my aunt, my life was saved in many ways, and I finally feel like I'm not living a lie anymore.

Life's lessons will be thrown at us left and right, no matter who you are. Just remember, everyone goes through things, so don't ever think you are alone. Never give up on yourself because you think you're different. Be who you want to be and love who you want to love. If you are struggling with coming out, or being judged, or even a break-up, you are not alone in this.

Remember, you have a purpose. True heroes are everyday people, whether they're straight, gay, bisexual, black, white, or brown—the next hero could be you. You just never know who might change your life or whose life you may change.

Megan's story helped reassure me that heroes are everyday people we meet along the journey. It also got me wondering about the many stories of heroism that went untold and how some of the people walking around as heroes had absolutely no clue. This was especially true when it came to soldiers who fought to protect our freedom.

When I first met my Aunt Judy's boyfriend, Brandon, I had no clue he had fought in Iraq. He was just a normal guy living a pretty normal life. But what I later learned was that this guy made a great sacrifice for his country and that I was in the presence of true hero, whether he wanted to believe it or not.

∼

Meet Brandon; a United States Marine

I was always interested in being a Marine, but after the twin towers came down on 9/11, I found myself more motivated to serve my country. I wanted to make it through boot camp and gain the title of Marine because I knew it would make me proud, so I signed up at seventeen, right after graduating high school.

I experienced fear in boot camp because it was strenuous and emotionally and physically draining, not to mention they kept you up for days. But I knew they were trying to prepare us for the real stuff. I stayed quiet for the first couple of weeks because I knew how intense things could get if you said or did something wrong.

I was stationed in Camp Pendleton for four years and started my tour in Iraq on August 23, 2003. It was extremely hot, but you got used to it. We had some down time when we played football, worked out, and boxed to keep ourselves busy, but writing and reading letters kept us going. We didn't have much free time, though, because we had different missions, which involved cleaning our weapons and preparing for unexpected ambushes.

Some of us handled things better than others. We had the chaplain if we needed anything, but I didn't use him much. There were times I saw the strongest, toughest guys freeze because they were mentally paralyzed. Some guys found out too much from home through letters, and sometimes it drove them crazy because there was nothing they could do. I guess finding out like that and being so far away would drive anyone nuts.

I'll never forget what happened when we experienced the biggest ambush we would face during my unit's Iraqi duration.

We had a routine mission to set up a security perimeter around a village, so we went about our normal proceedings like we had many times before. The village was filled with women and children, which unfortunately didn't mean that it was a safe place. Sometimes terrorists used women and children as decoys to trick us with their guerilla warfare.

As soon as I heard shots, I jumped into the Humvee and started driving fast. In situations like that you just didn't think. However, one of our men froze because some women and children were caught in the ambush. I busted out of the gate, not realizing there was one guy left behind. I couldn't leave him, but I didn't want to put the rest of my men in danger. I sped backwards and, as I slammed on my brakes when reaching him, he ran right past the Humvee because so many shots were being fired that he was literally running for his life. Eventually we met in the middle and sped away, but I'll never forget that day, and I know some of the guys still struggle with it today.

I served in the Marine Corps for four years. I experienced a lot in that little time. In the seven months I was in Iraq, I walked where Jesus walked, met Condoleezza Rice and actor Gary Sinise, and met brothers that I'll have forever.

The hardest part about coming home was readjusting to normal life. I remember when we got back to base from our Iraq deployment, we all ducked right after getting off the bus because of routine gunshots. There were no routine gunshots in Iraq, but we all got a laugh. We were all offered mental health services upon our return, but I declined, thinking I was completely fine. I didn't realize that even before I left for my service I may have been experiencing some issues with anxiety.

When I got out of the Marines, it was a totally different world. I was now divorced because I had been too young and stupid in my first marriage, and things changed for both of us when I was deployed. I had to get used to the new technology and the norms that were now a part of society. I learned to cope with alcohol, which wasn't great, but it was helping me at that time. I started experiencing really bad insomnia and anxiety. Socially when there were too many people around—I couldn't handle it. I was in the middle of a haircut in a barbershop one time and just got up and left because it was too small, with way too many people.

My girlfriend started noticing my issues and mentioned that I should get help and talk to someone. I was diagnosed with post-traumatic stress disorder (PTSD), which has added on to my already existing anxiety disorder. It was hard for me to be willing to get help, but I knew I was drinking too much to cope, and I knew that I couldn't live like that forever.

I definitely wouldn't change the experiences I had, but I know getting help was well worth it, and I'm still getting help today. I can't believe it's already been five years that I've been out of the service. It's amazing that some of the experiences are still affecting some of the other guys in my unit too, but getting help has helped turn my life around.

Soldiers are tough and can handle a lot, but at the same time, they are human and can struggle—not just physically but also mentally. There is nothing wrong with getting a little bit of extra help. In the long run, it can make life a lot easier to handle.

Brandon was hesitant about sharing his story mostly because he didn't see himself as a hero; just someone doing something he wanted to do. I could understand how weird it would be for your girlfriend's niece to come to you and ask to share your story, but I couldn't help but be inspired. I saw him at so many family parties and raising my little cousin and never fully knew how he saved his unit that day and how dedicated he was to serving our country. It's hard to fully understand how many heroes walk by us everyday without our knowing. But I think it's even harder for us to grasp that we too can be someone's hero whether we know it or not.

Chapter Twenty-Two

Leaving a mark on the world

Do you have to be in *Forbes Magazine* to leave a mark on the world? After graduating college, I was trying to figure out what I was supposed to do with my life. I wondered every day if money or fame would truly make me a "somebody" and help me leave my mark on this world. It's sad because sometimes my thoughts circled around the fact that I may have already missed any chance or that I would never be good enough or receive the same opportunities as others.

Part of my issue was—in a non-conceited way—I knew what I was capable of and meant to do and I knew there were others out there feeling exactly the same way. Sometimes it was like a never-ending cycle of excitement and hopelessness when you thought, "This is it!" but then didn't find the exact opportunity you expected. The cycle included questions like, "Has my time passed?" "Am I too old?" "Will my dreams ever come true?" "Why can't I have what he or she has?" and "When will I get a break?"

My other issue included my anxiety and depression producing much self-doubt and stealing precious time that I could have used to work toward truly living my dreams. It also didn't help when I saw others living "my" dreams, because it felt like I was forced to watch someone else live the life I could only dream of while my heart pounded uncontrollably.

As I thought more and more about it and sat back and moped at times (while honestly wanting to feel some sort of happiness for these people), I realized I was actually the only one wasting my own time and stopping myself from living my dreams and my life for that matter. Maybe I was afraid to fail and disappoint my family and friends, or maybe I was afraid to actually succeed and not be clear of the unknown. Regardless, with each person I met, each story I heard, and each amazing moment I experienced, I realized that it wasn't all about fame and money, and it wasn't about getting handed the things you wanted; but about working hard, making your mark on the world in your own way, learning from your decisions, and living every moment of your journey. I'm not saying I have it all figured out, but with each experience I'm learning that lesson more and more.

Mr. Wills, my high school history teacher, imprinted something in my mind that I think of often. One day, during my senior year of high school, he said this to my class: "If you want something, then go out there and get it. It's never too early or too late. If you want to be a newscaster, then start sweeping the floor at the news station and work your way up. You must start somewhere."

Almost eight years later, his words have stuck with me, but I'm finding some difficulties in truly living by his advice. I wonder how you do that, when so many people are judging you and telling you what to do and how to live? Things like, "You should get a nine to five!" "When will you move out?" "Great, you're speaking, but you still need to do some real work," "Your time has passed, you should have started this years back," or, "I don't want you to get your hopes up if your dreams don't come true."

Maybe it's what some people say, or maybe it's the thoughts in my own head, but negative thinking, pessimism, and doubt sometimes pose major issues for me, preventing me from taking any steps forward or finding the strength to move on. I get that we have to sacrifice and support ourselves, but it all becomes confusing when I see so many people not making millions, but living their dreams and experiencing happiness. Then I see others who have all the money in the world and are struggling to feel even one ounce of happiness. Is making your mark on this world about money, happiness, helping people, or working toward your ultimate dreams? With so many mixed messages, I waste too much time worrying and wondering about things I can't even foresee.

It was getting easier and clearer for me to recognize that certain people were coming into my life to teach me lessons and help me grow. Although I couldn't see the reason right away, I learned overtime to trust the fact that I would be able to overcome the issues I was facing and continue to be inspired by and learn lessons from others, especially those wanting to make a difference in the world with no expectation of getting something in return.

Melissa Ann Hopely

❧

Meet college student and advocate; Erin Casey

People make wishes every day with birthday cake, shooting stars, eyelashes you name it. Since I was a little girl and for as long as I can remember I've had just one wish: "Please just make me smaller, skinnier, thinner, lighter, just make me shrink...please." These examples may seem small when you first look at them for we're talking about make believe, wishes and abstract ideas but these wishes represent how I thought as a little girl, as early as I can remember. I thought the most important aspect of myself was my weight. It dictated my self worth, it affected my mood and it told me everything I needed to know about myself at the time. The scariest part about that situation at the time too was – I had no clue anything was wrong with those patterns. I believed it was okay. I had no reason to believe that it was those very thoughts that were wrong or bad, instead I thought it was who I was. That started around the age of 11. It was not until college that I received any real treatment for my eating disorder and other mental health issues. I sought help early into my freshman year after quickly realizing that my thoughts and behaviors were out of control.

I never realized how much my mental illness had dictated my life until beginning treatment. I mean after all, there is only so much a person can take of complete self-disgust. To be honest, as emotions surfaced for the first time, things got worse before better. I became self destructive in eating disordered behaviors, in self-injury and the like, but I persevered with treatment holding onto the hope that I could one day enjoy a life that would be happy and healthy.

During college, I was in hospitals, partial hospitalization treatments, and inpatient and residential treatment programs and more outpatient, individual, and group therapy and psychiatry appointments than I could count. I have seen more doctors, therapists, and psychiatrists than I could remember.

There were times when I felt hopeless, there were times when I felt angry, there were times when I felt misunderstood, prodded and poked. There were days when I felt like the doctors just wanted to give me more medication. Looking back today though I see that I learned something from each program, each doctor and each therapist leading me to recovery.

When I began pursing recovery I had an idea that it would come and then I could move on with my life, I would be happy, healthy, and the darkness would lift. And every single time that I felt that I failed to achieve that idea of recovery I had developed – I punished myself with more disordered behaviors.

This lead me to hopelessness, this lead me to no longer wanting to live, this lead me to believe that I was never going to get better. I thought we had tried everything. But I kept going; I kept going because of supports in my life, my faith, my family, my friends, treatment providers, roommates, friends from treatment and so on. People always told me that recovery and treatment would get easier someday. Honestly, I didn't know if I believed them until it started to happen. In combination of being exhausted from fighting with myself and my brain and a full-hearted desire to get better. I completely surrendered to my treatment providers. I gave up on what I thought my life was supposed to be. I began using the tools I had been given, and at first hating every second of it, then finding it got easier, then harder, then easier, then harder and so forth. I started keeping track of the times between behaviors and setting goals, things I could not have done before. I began recovery.

And I'm here to tell you that my original idea of recovery was wrong, completely wrong. I've learned that recovery does not mean my mental illnesses have no impact in my life and it's all a memory; it's about adaptation. It's about adapting my life so that I can function, live, and be healthy given the challenges that I have. It's always changing, always growing, and always morphing just like life.

Today when I make wishes, I don't wish to be smaller, or thinner, or shrink to any degree. Today my greatest desire is that my story and experiences with mental illness can be used to shine a light on and reduce the stigma associated with mental illness and treatment around the United States. The first fruit of this was the creation of an event called Where I Stand, which was held in Roanoke, Virginia on October 27, 2012. The purpose of the event was to raise awareness, education and funds for the treatment of eating disorders. It incorporated dance, poetry and personal stories. I organized the event and told my story publically for the first time. The response was phenomenal. I knew then I started to make my mark.

Continuing with mental health outreach, during my senior year of undergraduate work at James Madison University I became the President of our University's chapter of Active Minds. Through this, I created and oversaw an event titled "JMU Dancing with the Stars for Suicide

179

Prevention." The purpose of this event was to inspire the JMU community to become aware and active in their own mental wellbeing after all, we all have mental health.

Today, I am a college graduate and turning the "Where I Stand" program into a non-profit organization aimed at prevention and early intervention of mental illness through awareness, education and research. Our vision and hope is to create and facilitate mental health planning in K-12 public education around the United States.

To close, I want to tell you this: it is true that my mental illness led me to my passions and my goals in life. People often ask me "Was it worth it?" You will never hear me say it was worth the pain my family and I experienced, but I can tell you this: seeing the hope, awareness, the change, the difference and the mark my story has made on this world or in one individual life makes it easy to accept it.

My name is Erin Casey and I Stand for Recovery.

Erin asked me to host the "JMU Dancing with the Stars event" and I was completely honored. We had just met a year before when I spoke at a previous event at the university. I knew after our many conversations leading up to the event; she was so dedicated to making a difference at her school. I was reminded of my days in college when I held my events and could relate to the passion and her desire to help others. Whether it was letting them know they were not alone or there was help available, she just wanted to make some sort of mark on her peers' lives. That's how it was for me in college. It was about not expecting anything in return, but giving as much inspiration as I could to others. I wonder when that changed. Maybe it was the pressures of being out in the real world and having to make enough money to take care of myself or maybe it was my OCD and depression or maybe it was a combination of everything. Whatever it was, I knew after working with Erin and thinking about all those who inspired me and gave so much without wanting anything in return, I could get back to that way of thinking and I knew I was strong enough to especially with all the support I had.

I've lost my fair share of family members, friends, and acquaintances and have heard many eulogies that touched some part of my heart. The most incredible thing about a eulogy is that it's not about the money you had or the job you did, but more about who you were, what you did for others, and the mark you left on this world. It's normal after a funeral to find yourself thinking that life is too short, feeling the urge to do everything you wanted to do in your whole lifetime right away, or anxiously striving to feel a sense of being alive. But why does it take someone else's passing for us to think about actually living?

About three years ago, I was asked to speak at the funeral of my college soccer coach, Fran. The four years I played for Coach Fran were an emotional rollercoaster in many different ways. During my freshman year, the team was so bad that I actually showed up to my first practice in softball cleats, while the team was a few games into the season. I'd been invited to join the team by Karen, the captain, because of my general athletic abilities. We had a tough season, and sophomore year wasn't any better.

I was on a team that never made playoffs in the history of the school, let alone had an even statistical season between wins and losses. We were losing some games by more than eight goals, goofing off at practices, and losing any sense of anything that went along with being a team. But it seemed like something changed during my junior year. I realized that the change was happening all along, and each loss and obstacle was just a challenge making us stronger. I had no idea it was all part of Coach Fran's five-year plan and his chance to leave a mark on his players—not only on the field, but off the field as well.

During my junior year of soccer, we broke even with nine wins and nine losses. This was the first time this had ever happened to our team, and it was a huge accomplishment for the whole soccer program. But Coach Fran wasn't there at all the games because of his battle with cancer.

My senior year was the most emotional sports season of my life. I was finally on a winning team, with powerhouses in many positions and a coach who gave his life to our team. We were still having fun, especially when Coach Fran created competitions and the losers had to sing "I'm a little teapot" to every other athlete that was practicing nearby. We were competitive, but we were more of a family then we had ever been before. Sadly, part of our closeness came with the bad news that Coach Fran was sick again.

Coach Fran was frail, had trouble being in the cold weather, and often had trouble breathing. He had been stricken with leukemia years earlier and had experienced two bone marrow transplants. His body had never fully recovered and he remained weak. Because of his determination and dedication, I never really learned he was sick until one of my teammates told me, well into my sophomore year.

The thought of my soccer coach getting sick again never crossed my mind until I was walking down to practice and saw Coach Fran with a megaphone on a scooter, speeding down the path telling us to get our butts moving to practice. My teammates and I were laughing, but at the same time, I couldn't help but think how strong this man was. Instead of letting his illness stop him from doing things, he found a way to do the things he wanted to do.

Fran eventually had to be rushed to the hospital. While getting loaded into the ambulance, he looked as his wife and said, "Honey, make sure my girls practice today. We need to win this playoff game." I couldn't believe how strong and determined this man was, even though death seemed much closer than any of us wanted to believe.

Anytime I complain about something, I can't help but think of Coach Fran and just how strong we are as humans. He left a mark on my life in many ways that he would never know. Fran was a very successful businessman, but that isn't how I remember him. I see him as a coach who gave his life to his team and wife, a father figure who did his best to care for his players both on and off the field, and a man who didn't let anything stop him.

As I was speaking my final words about him to his wife, my team, and the crowd during the eulogy, I mentioned the mark he left in the lives of so many and the quote he always told us before any game: "I fight the good fight because I refuse to give in, I want to win." He left a true mark that would never fade, and neither fame nor money had anything to do with it. In my book, he won because he fought the good fight, not only for himself but for so many others as well.

After Fran's funeral, I really started thinking about what mark I wanted to leave on this world. But I also wondered if I would ever have anything to show for it. These thoughts were in my head every day, from the time I woke up. I would look around my room, realizing that I lived in a fifty-five-plus community with my grandparents. I was blessed to have a roof over my head, but seriously—at twenty-six years old, having experience with speaking nationally and internationally, appearing on TV and radio stations, and connecting with famous public figures, why did I feel like I had nothing to show for it at all and why did I feel so empty at times?

I didn't have my own place, an expensive car, a high-fashion handbag, or a credit card with a $100,000 limit. My name wasn't all over the headlines, and there weren't people itching to have me make appearances at their events and on their shows. After these ridiculous thoughts would take over my mind, followed by a buildup of anxiety and physical pain, I wondered if this was a general feeling among others, or just part of my OCD and depression.

I think my OCD and depression were a part of it, but I honestly think some of our societal values and what we see in the media today are a big part of these issues, especially for our youth. It's like we are taught to have the best clothes, cars, and electronics and always wear a fake, happy smile to try to impress those around us. Focusing on that stuff causes us to miss out on the most important things in life—like actually helping others out, being ourselves, and experiencing the things we actually want to and deserve to, not what the media or others say is right or wrong.

I always share these thoughts with my grandmother, who has left a mark on this world many times. From raising six kids and foster babies, dealing with losing her brother unexpectedly, and dealing with her own battle with breast cancer and mental health and addiction issues in her immediate family, she always knows the right thing to say, even when she is struggling as well.

When I complain about having nothing to show for my life so far, she just sighs and says, "That's sad, Melissa—nothing to show for it? Are you kidding me? How about all the young lives you've saved? How about all the strangers you have helped? How about all the hope you spread around every day, just through your words alone?"

It's always hard for me to believe or realize that I have done these things. I get so caught up in the idea of becoming great that I miss seeing the mark I've already left on this world. Every time I would appear on television, meet a public figure or celebrity at an event, sing or speak on stage, or find a new opportunity, I would get a rush of adrenaline and count on that rush to get me through my day or week.

I even noticed this after having the honor of meeting President Barack Obama on his last visit to Philadelphia for a fundraiser event in June 2012. There I was, this everyday person, shaking hands with the most important man in America. The eye contact, the smile, and the handshake gave me a bigger adrenaline rush than even my skydiving experience. I was running around yelling, "What's up, Obama, yeah, we shook hands, what, what!"

The feeling lasted for days and days. After I flaunted it on my social media pages and told anyone and everyone, the feeling completely died down. My depression and OCD then kicked back up and continued their never-ending cycle.

Two weeks after meeting President Obama, I ran into a friend of mine who couldn't stop talking about my meeting him. He was impressed and happy for me, but as we continued to talk, he seemed confused—why wasn't I still overly exuberant about my experience? Honestly, I was waiting for my next new opportunity to gain that adrenaline rush and feel that feeling I so longed for.

My grandmother had been noticing my cycle. As we got to talking one day, she told me, "After you have a speaking engagement or you experience something really cool, you then go into a state of depression if something else doesn't happen right away."

Part of me was surprised that she knew this, but part of me wanted a quick fix from her. She was always great at giving me little pep talks and making me look at situations in a different light. I knew what I was doing wasn't healthy, and I realized that I might need a little extra help. It's funny because I speak to young adults about getting help and not being afraid to deal with their emotions and struggles, but here I was taking part in this vicious cycle and being afraid to get help myself.

Why was I being such a hypocrite? I think part of it was because I had been down that road before. I was in a good place and, honestly, I think I wanted to believe that becoming well known would erase my depression, my OCD, and any and every worry or obstacle I would face. The adrenaline rush I could gain from being known was more appealing than getting help and trying to live without the constant pursuit of that rush.

I knew somehow I'd be leaving some sort of mark on people if I were actually known. Deep down I knew this wasn't right, and I was hoping to find some sign that it wasn't about any of that at all.

I started getting more bookings to speak. Even though I was experiencing the rush, I was also experiencing something else I had never really known, which was helping me see the bigger picture that I had been missing for so long. Just as Fran and my grandmother had always taught me, I was already making my mark on this world.

After speaking at a school in Pennsylvania, I received this response from the guidance counselor, and it changed my perspective immediately.

Yesterday I had a very quiet, very shy student come to see me because she has been struggling with depression, and she decided that she has had enough. She said to me, "If Melissa was able to get help, and she was brave enough to go to a hospital to get help, then so am I."

She said that she would have never known who I was, and that she would have never come to see me, if she had not seen your assembly. She is currently hospitalized, and her mom told me today that she is doing much better.

We don't know what would have happened to her if you didn't do what you do, so thank you for helping to save her life.

I was speechless and stunned. I didn't know how to react, but I did know that I couldn't give up; I had to keep working to leave a mark on this world.

Soon after this, I was asked to share my story on an NBC 10 News special called "Beyond Bullying," with news anchor Lori Wilson. Until I met her I had no idea the mark she was about to leave in our community or the care and dedication she always showed as she worked to make our community more proactive, safer, and more understanding.

∼

Meet NBC 10 News anchor; Lori Wilson

I knew I wanted to tell people's stories from a young age. I've always had the desire, ever since I was in elementary school. When I got to the age where people asked me what I wanted to do, I told them and was always met with discouragement.

I often heard, "That's a pretty competitive field, not many people get to do that. Maybe you should try something more practical." But I never had a plan B. I think when you believe in your own dreams and pursue them with passion, you never fail because your success is in being the best you can be.

I have a strong faith in God. I believe He has a purpose for putting me on television, and that is what has always kept me. Through years of moving from city to city, even getting fired, leaving homes, relationships, friends—I always knew in my heart there was a purpose for my life, and that is what I live to fulfill every day.

Over the years and through each story I tell, I realize that in life we have to be proactive. When you see something that's wrong, even if it's someone else being bullied, you have to do something. To me, if you don't do something about it, you become part of the problem because your silence helps the cycle continue.

Doing the right thing, standing up for the innocent, serving others—those are our responsibilities. Anytime we have the chance to give others love, comfort, help, encouragement, advice, or esteem, I believe we should.

This is the main reason I decided to push for a thirty-minute program on bullying at the NBC 10 News station. I pitched the idea to the producers and wanted to work as hard and diligently as I could to make this meaningful and educational.

Bullying is not a new problem, but because of social media, it's now a lot easier to do than before. I've always stuck up for the underdog, and I truly believe we are all special and created equal, but a child who is bullied doesn't feel that way. If there is anything I could do to help parents talk with their kids about bullying and let them know they don't have to suffer in silence, then that's what I wanted to do.

The bullying special was one small contribution to the collective conversation. If people are talking about bullying, then they are aware of it, looking for the signs of it, and could potentially save someone's life!

I asked Melissa to take part in the special because her story was unique and she was a pretty active and involved student, but she still got teased. I know it was a lot for her to handle. Bullying happens in a variety of ways and, yes, even athletes and popular kids get bullied. None of it is okay, and I wanted kids to know that even your so-called friends can bully you.

I had to tell Melissa's story to help give kids and parents a better understanding of what bullying can look like. Her story also had an impact. I received a lot of positive responses after the special, because people could relate and felt like they weren't alone. People also were able to see, through Melissa's story, that you can survive bullying, develop a healthy self-image, and even help others who are suffering from being bullied as well.

I wanted to let kids know, especially those getting bullied, that they mattered and still had the power to leave a positive mark on this world.

Recently, Lori volunteered to emcee Minding Your Mind's free annual mental health forum and I could sense the passion and drive she had to help the community. I was shocked to learn that soon after this event, Lori would be leaving the Philadelphia television world and head to her home state of Indiana. After seeing her last news day at Philadelphia, I grew more inspired by her. Philadelphia had become a home to her, but she now had the opportunity to go home to be with family and leave a mark on her hometown that had given her so much in years past.

The NBC Bullying Special had an overwhelming amount of positive feedback, which helped me in so many ways. I was so honored that Lori would even come to me to share my story and I wondered how she even knew that I was a speaker through Minding Your Mind. The whole experience boosted my confidence and with each moment that passed, I was seeing more and more the mark I was leaving on my community. Even though I was still struggling, I knew I had to continue my work and keep the hope that I would get through somehow.

When I was at the core of obsessing about how I could make a bigger mark on this world, I admit I was struggling tremendously. I even thought doing the interview with NBC would make me a better person. Yes, I knew I was technically helping others and so grateful, but why was there a part of me so empty that I thought I had to fill it with constantly being known as someone who every single second tried to make a difference for others? Although it was dying down, I knew it wasn't healthy and with every thought, I was literally beating down my self-worth with belief that I needed to be better and do more.

The whole time I felt like I was looking for something to fill my void and absence of self-worth, something amazing happened. His name was Rich Rice and while shopping at his work, I knew there was something about him; something that I felt could help me with my life. Maybe it was the warm welcome his eyes gave off or maybe it was his contagious smile, but after a few minutes of roaming the aisles, I soon realized we were staring at each other every chance we got. After we started talking, Rich asked me out on a date and since that day, my life has literally changed forever. I always thought I had to impress people with my work and that it was what was supposed to define me as a person, but Rich opened my eyes to seeing more to life. I learned that I could actually love someone, be loved and that I had much self-worth even without my work. Each day he continues to teach me that I have already made a mark not only on others, but on his life as well. I could write a whole other book on how we met, how we helped to save each other from the personal challenges we both faced and how we continue to support and love each other together through everything and anything. He came into my life for a reason and left a mark on me that has literally helped save my life again. I finally feel loved for just being me. Not for what I have or haven't done or *need* to do, but for just being the person I truly am and that's how it should be.

Chapter Twenty-Three

There's got to be a reason

The world is full of many things we refer to as coincidences, but the more and more experiences I live, the more and more I wonder if these amazing things were meant to be.

I've had many coincidences, but I never thought one could match up to the girl walking into the pub and knowing the student the suicide prevention concert was for. I found that I was wrong a few different times.

I heard about a volunteer opportunity for a mental health conference in Philadelphia. I immediately jumped on board. When I got there I saw an older gentleman speaking to a crowd of 100 plus. I learned the doctor was Dr. Aaron T. Beck, the founder of cognitive therapy. I couldn't believe it. This man's work actually helped save my life. Was it a coincidence that I was there?

I saw Dr. Beck taking a break over by the coffee station and I went up to him as he was jotting down notes on his notepad. I think I surprised him because the first words out of my mouth were, "Dr. Beck, I just wanted to say thank you for helping to save my life." Dr. Beck's work actually led to the use of CBT, which was the therapy that helped turn my life around. He was surprised and I could tell humbled.

We kept in touch over the years. When first meeting him, I really didn't comprehend whom I was meeting. You read about people like him in texts books, but I guess when you're in the moment it's hard to really believe what is happening. He was literally one of the most world-renowned doctors of psychology and many would kill for the chance to talk to him as I did. I know volunteering at that conference was no coincidence because I was meant to meet Dr. Beck and ultimately thank him for helping to save my life.

Soon after this, I was asked to speak at a private school around

189

the Philadelphia area. After my speeches, a teacher mentioned a friend of the family who was struggling with OCD and body dysmorphic disorder (BDD). I knew about both disorders all too well. BDD is related to OCD; a person sees himself or herself completely differently from how others see him or her. I always saw the major flaws in myself that many others didn't see (both physically and mentally), and I was about to find out how much I had in common with a guy named Nathaniel.

Nathaniel and I talked via phone, text, and social media. He had to live his life day by day, never knowing whether he would even be able to leave his house the next day. It pained me to know he was struggling so much, and I felt it was my personal responsibility to help him.

On his good day, Nathaniel came to my soccer game, and we grabbed pizza afterwards. He was handsome, smart, and athletic and a really caring soul. I enjoyed the fact that we could open up to each other, support each other, and ultimately not judge one another. I had never really connected with someone my age who was experiencing such issues with OCD, and it was comforting to know that someone else knew how it felt to struggle with the same thing.

As the weeks passed, Nathaniel and I stayed in touch but couldn't find a good day to meet. I texted him a "just thinking of you" text and heard nothing back. I knew he was working and also taking part in treatment to fight his OCD and BDD, so I didn't take it personally.

The next day I received a call from the teacher who initially had us meet. She sounded concerned and completely flustered. I called her back immediately and, as she took a deep breath and started speaking, I learned that Nathaniel had taken his own life the night before. I didn't know what to do but cry and scream and throw things across the room. I felt like it was my job to protect him and help him, and somehow I failed.

I found some people were puzzled that I was so upset by his death, because we had only seen each other once and hadn't known each other for that long. In a short time, he became a friend who I wanted to help. In the week leading up to his suicide, we had joked about my helping him out in the dating field and teaching him a little bit about dating, because his OCD and BDD had robbed him of that. We had a lot of laughs over that. He really liked one of his coworkers and I was trying to give him some tips and the confidence to ask her out. With each time we talked, I felt things were getting better, but I had no idea the internal pain he was facing.

As the months passed, my life went on, but on one particular day, I received a letter in the mail from Nathaniel's father.

I learned that he was going to take a pilgrimage called "Walking with Nathaniel" from the Philadelphia area to Boston, and I knew I somehow had to participate.

I emailed Nathaniel's dad and asked if I could walk some of the way with him. I walked only eight miles, from Bryn Mawr to Bala Cynwyd, but it was the most empowering eight-mile walk of my life.

As we walked and talked, I realized that Nathaniel and I were even more connected than I had thought. We had seen the same doctors, been in the same treatments and studies, and found ourselves in the same vicious cycle with BDD and OCD. I didn't know how to take everything. Honestly, it was draining, but as with the coincidence in Nashville, I couldn't help but cry and feel empowered to keep moving forward in my journey to help others.

Whether or not meeting Nathaniel was a coincidence, I knew I had to share his story with the world. I recently wrote a song called, "I'm Sorry I Didn't Know," because I felt others could relate to not really knowing the pain some of their friends were experiencing, but just wanting to help save them. It brought some closure to me and so did the letter Nathaniel's father wrote. I'd like to share the letter with you:

Dear Melissa,

This thank you card is long overdue. It has taken Judy, Carrie, and me some time to get our feet back on the ground. Losing Nathaniel has created a huge void in our lives. Although you did not know him for a long time, I'm sure you quickly saw how much of an amazing man he was. He had so much integrity, courage, and grace. It's simply not fair that so much beauty outside resided in tandem with so much pain and suffering inside.

We witnessed each day his hard efforts to move forward and live some kind of normal life despite his OCD and BDD. He admired your ability to do just that. Your lives coinciding was no accident. The universe wanted you to meet, at the very end of his life.

I remember how nervous he was to go to your soccer game and spend some time with you—time with a beautiful young woman—a young man's dream. He felt so inexperienced in that regard. His

191

disease robbed him of a normal adolescence. His meeting with you gave us hope that his life might be opening up and going into a more promising direction, in spite of so many overwhelming odds.

I hope you got glimpses into his beautiful spirit. As his parents, we saw daily the beauty of his soul and body. How cruel BDD is—he did not deserve it. Thank you for giving him just a few hours of your time so that he could imagine that he could maybe have a somewhat normal life; all of this at the end of his short twenty-four years. I'm grateful that Deanna suggested your name and that your lives intersected at the end.

In May Judy, Carrie, and I walked the ancient Pilgrimage route, the Camino de Santiago de Compostella in Northern Spain. Each step of the three hundred and forty miles we walked grounded in some measure of our pain and loss. Life has its unexpected surprises, and this one is huge. It's our resolve to make some sense of all this and to certainly honor as much as we can Nathaniel's gifts to us and his spirit.

Thank you for dedicating several songs to him at your concert. Thank you for loving our son.

Denis

~

Meet Nathaniel's father, Denis Asselin; a mental health advocate

Starting April 24, 2012, I began a five-hundred-mile walk from Cheyney, Pa., about thirty miles outside of Philadelphia to Boston, Mass. I walked in honor of my twenty-four-year-old son, Nathaniel, who took his own life after a thirteen-year struggle with body dysmorphic disorder (BDD) and obsessive-compulsive disorder (OCD). The route included stops at hospitals, clinics, doctors' offices, and treatment facilities that were part of Nathaniel's journey, as well as places of joy such as the Bryn Mawr Birth Center, Goshen Friends School, the Shipley School, Westtown School (where he was a student, teacher, and coach), and the Good Fellowship Ambulance and EMS unit where he often volunteered.

Nathaniel Robert Nicholson Asselin was born August 21, 1986, and left this earth on April 15, 2011. He possessed a brilliant mind and a great natural sweetness. He was so caring, and everyone was drawn to his company. Nathaniel and his sister Carrie had a special bond that transcended the five hundred and seventy miles that separated them while she was in college over the last four years of his life. They spoke frequently, and she stored up her funniest experiences and her most difficult challenges to share with him. He listened and advised well. Above all, they laughed together over the widest imaginable range of expressions, experiences, and shared memories. Their senses of humor were perfectly matched.

At Nathaniel's young age, he showed an intense curiosity about the world, exploring it eagerly. There was never a dull moment in the Asselin household. We spent many happy days at the family cabin in the New Jersey Pine Barrens, at the shore, and on camping trips out west and in Canada. He attended Goshen Friends School for three years of pre-school, and then started at Westtown School in kindergarten. For fourth and fifth grades, he attended the Shipley School where I taught, then returned to Westtown in middle school where his mother Judy was a teacher. An exceptional writer and a whiz on the computer, he concluded his formal education through independent study and home schooling for part of his sophomore year through senior year.

The anguish with body dysmorphic disorder (BDD) began at age eleven and eventually made formal schooling impossible, but regardless his learning and understanding continued to grow from his life experiences.

He always envisioned a life of service. During high school and in his early twenties, he spent many hours volunteering at Good Fellowship Ambulance Club, and spent the summer of 2010 taking an EMT class there. Neighbors could always rely on him for childcare, pet sitting, or helping out with various home and yard projects. In 2008 and again in 2010–2011, he worked as assistant director of the middle school afterschool program at Westtown School, where he was an immense favorite with the students. They describe him as "funny and kind, an inspiration—a friend as well as a teacher."

He made them laugh every day and knew how to give them his full attention, a rare gift in a busy world. An expert runner and motivator, he was revered as a coach in the middle school cross-country program last fall, and led the team to a strong season. His repartee with his coaching colleague kept the mood light even when the workouts were intense. He would often talk about his students at the dinner table at home, and it was evident that he cared about them deeply and enjoyed their company.

Over the years, his illness narrowed the limits of his world, yet he carried his burden with fortitude. That he faced each day for so many years knowing the battles ahead is a testament to his courage and strength. He knew joy and suffering to the fullest in a life lived with deliberate thoughtfulness.

When you lose someone you love to a brain disorder, how do you ever recover? Well, you don't, at least not completely. Life simply changes. The pain is so deep; the loss so profound; the void so empty. It is in this state of grief that the "Walking with Nathaniel" project was born. What could I do to make the life and death of one precious person, my son, more meaningful? What would Nathaniel want me, his dad, to do? I knew I had to move forward physically, psychologically, and spiritually, and I invented a path that I called the "Camino de Nathaniel," a modern pilgrimage route from my home in Cheyney, Pa., to Boston, Mass., the home of the International OCD Foundation. All I really had to do was to put one foot in front of the other and to connect the geographical dots of Nathaniel's life experiences. In the words of Jeff Bell, I needed to transform "adversity into advocacy." So for me, the question was never, why do this? The question was rather, how could I *not* do this?

So here was the Walking with Nathaniel project in a nutshell— 552 miles walked; 1,110,000 steps; 62 fellow walkers joined me at various time and places; 25 friends and family provided me meals and/or shelter; I met with 145 professionals in clinics and hospitals; I talked with over 250 people on back roads and city streets; and 267 people signed my pilgrim's passport.

So advocacy for me is about the power of stories when you tell them. I told Nathaniel's story over and over again as I walked this spring, hoping each time deeper listening would happen, truer understanding would emerge, and conversations about brain disorders would begin. And they did. In other words, what can the precious life of a single person teach us about being better people by who we are and by what we do? The enormity of Nathaniel's pain and suffering has got to matter.

So I now say, "Hello, My name is Denis and I'm an OCD/BDD advocacy-aholic." I can't stop telling Nathaniel's story. So few people out there know what BDD is. During my walk, I had promised myself to talk to at least five people a day about Nathaniel, and I did—to the coffee and donut cashier, the postal worker, the family in the local restaurant, the policeman, the construction worker, the waitress, the hotel clerk, and my evening hosts—to at least five persons per day. You do the math: 5 persons times 45 days equals 225 people.

In the days and years to come, we will be nourished by the memory of Nathaniel's humor, his wisdom, his noble spirit, and his abiding love for friends and family. It's time for us to get brain disorders like OCD and BDD out of the closet. Let's recognize the absolute integrity in the mental anguish of all sufferers. Let's be sure everyone knows that you don't choose to have and live these diseases. Unfortunately, they just happen.

I believe that "walking the talk" can be healing.

I believe that adversity to advocacy is a path of hope.

I believe that the power of stories can bring public awareness and dispel ignorance.

I believe that education can help reduce the stigma of OCD and BDD.

I believe that Nathaniel's story has impacted lives and continues to do so; often in ways I can't see.

I believe that I can play some part in this new awareness.

I believe that new brain research and therapies will eventually lick these disorders. So, thank you, doctors, psychiatrists, pharmacists, researchers, clinicians, therapists, social workers, sufferers, families, caregivers, and supporters for your hard work in these arenas.

The "Walk with Nathaniel" continues...

Was it just a coincidence of meeting Nathaniel and his father or was it a "meant to be?" I didn't know and frankly, I didn't care. I was beyond inspired and knew there were so many things I could take from this experience. First, it was just another realization that I wasn't alone and had to keep battling my issues so I could continue to share my story. Second, I learned the real importance to supporting and working with others who were also trying to make a difference in the world. Third, I realized that with our unique gifts and strengths we could become stronger in our fight in many different ways. Denis' idea of raising awareness may have been different than mine and different than the ideas of others, however, that didn't matter, what mattered was we met; what mattered was we were supporting each other's work; what mattered was we were working together; and what mattered most was that we couldn't ever give up the fight to stay inspired, keep the hope and continue to help others in any way we could.

Chapter Twenty-Four

Believe it or not

I found myself wondering sometimes if the things that happened in my life actually did. They say, "seeing is believing," but sometimes there are things we can't see but only feel, like hope and strength.

A lot of the positive and negative experiences in my past are hard to believe. The fact that I experienced feelings of such loneliness when I was this outgoing girl and that I even thought that life would be better for others without me here is far in the past, but it still lingers as a part of my story. I wonder sometimes, "Did that stuff really happen, or was it all in my imagination?"

Events and talk shows I've attended also have me second-guessing and having to watch video clips to actually believe these things did happen. Why is it so hard to admit things sometimes and actually be proud and okay with the things that happened in our past?

In May 2010, I was asked to speak at the fifth free annual Minding Your Mind Mental Health Forum, called "Mysteries of the Mind." This wouldn't be like any speech before, because I was actually opening the program for Cedering Fox's Word Theatre, an innovative, internationally recognized 501(c) (3) nonprofit organization dedicated to inspiring a love of language and literature by presenting live performances of contemporary short stories. It features world-renowned actors who bring to life precisely crafted stories written by the finest authors working today.

The performances were actually being given by famous actors and actresses like John Heard *(Home Alone, Between the Lines)*, Edi Gathegi *(X-Men: First Class, House, Twilight)*, Linda Cardellini *(ER, Scooby Doo! Mystery Incorporated)*, and Nicole Ansari *(Side Effects, Deadwood)*, which was great, but that made me overly excited and nervous. I wondered, "Would they see me speak? What would they think? Could I even be on the same stage with them? Why was Minding Your Mind trusting me to speak?" These questions overwhelmed me.

There was a dinner before the event, but I couldn't eat. I was too nervous about messing up or not living up to the expectations of the audience and organization. What worried me most was that my family and friends would be there—the people who saw me at my worst and sometimes thought I was overreacting and just wanted attention. What if they didn't believe my story? What if they thought it was all a lie?

I remember some of the actors, like Nicole Ansari and Edi Gathegi, coming in to grab some dinner before their performance and my speech. Seeing and talking to them actually helped me, because I knew I was in this moment and it was really happening. As we parted ways, I knew they would be in their green room preparing for their performances, so I had less worry knowing they wouldn't hear my speech.

After I gave my fifteen-minute testimonial to a room of over five hundred people, got my first standing ovation, and looked out in the crowd, I saw not only my family, friends, and strangers clapping, but also some of the actors. These were famous, world-renowned actors clapping for me. I couldn't believe it, but after talking with Nicole Ansari after the performance and hearing her insightful words, stories, and experiences, I knew it was real and that it was okay to relive the moments in time and to use those moments for other purposes.

I also learned that even actors and public figures faced some anxiety issues, which was something I couldn't fathom before.

~

Meet actress; Nicole Ansari

When Cedering Fox, the founder of Word Theatre, asked me to be one of the actors performing in "Mysteries of the Mind," an event in Philadelphia to benefit the mental health organization "Minding Your Mind," I immediately said yes. Word Theatre always allows you to deliver rare and insightful pieces of poetry, prose, and autobiography for a good cause. Cedering handpicks the literature with a keen sense of taste and urgency, as if to save the world from being dumbed down, by bringing back poetry into our lives.

At this particular event, a young speaker, Melissa Ann Hopely, was so riveting that we actors were drawn out into the audience to watch her. Edi Gathegi, John Heard, and I were hanging out backstage in the green room when Melissa's voice came through the intercom, and we stopped our conversation in its tracks.

In her speech, she talked passionately about how she had overcome her own mental health issues and how, by sharing her battle publicly, she has eliminated the stigma she felt around her challenges. Unfortunately, some people get stuck in the shame they feel about having compromised mental health and withdraw into isolation, going deeper into depressions and disorders, and drowning their sorrow in negative coping like alcohol, drugs, and silence. Melissa wouldn't do that. She is a great example of a young person who has dealt with her mental health issues and stepped out from the shadows and into the light to share her story and try to help others by encouraging them to speak their truth. Her mission is to help people feel less stigmatized and understand that they are not alone. Melissa's speech not only choked me up, but did the same to most people in that room.

When Melissa asked me if I would contribute a piece for her book, I sat down and thought about what to write. This felt like opening Pandora's Box, as every thought and insight and question led to another point of view, another approach. I have never been diagnosed with anything, but I do know about anxiety. This profession of mine is more of a vocation if you stay with it for over a decade, and I have been in acting since I was just eleven. I ask myself, "What is this curious desire to inhabit another character's body, mind, and soul and to think and act from her or his perspective?" Surely not every actor's life is that miserable that they have to flee from it! Yet there is a great freedom in getting out of your claustrophobic world of self, and into the darkened place of a strange character; to explore every nook and cranny, to swallow, to illuminate, understand, and ultimately wholly embody a character.

When I prepare for a role, I do research on every level to get a sense of the inner and outer world of the character and every so often a button is pressed that takes me into a personal memory that mirrors the character's choices, behavior, feelings, and actions. Sometimes it's a simple body movement. That's what happened to me this year when I prepared to play Michelle, a criminally insane asylum patient in the movie *Side Effects,* directed by Steven Soderbergh.

The research for this character led me through more and more doors and as I went through them, the fine line between sanity and insanity revealed itself to me. As I was working on Michelle, I discovered that there were many moments in which I walked the thin tightrope between both worlds. As I got myself into Michelle's state, I found that I assumed a patterned way of walking in a square that my body remembered from when I was seventeen years old and was suddenly stuck and paralyzed by inexplicable fear.

I relived all these sensations: the walls seemed to be coming closer as dark clouds descended from above. My breath became shallow and panic rose in my chest, going up into my throat. My fingers spread out, as if my fingertips could feel what my mind couldn't understand, trying to grasp what I couldn't. Feelings of utter fear shot to the surface of my skin, except there was no reasonable origination of the feeling. Thousands of thoughts came into my mind at the same time, but none were of any use to me. Paralyzed by fear, my feet walked in square patterns, over and over again, like an elephant that had lost her mind from being locked up in a cage too small for her raw spirit and body. Right foot back and to the side, left foot back…

What triggered this condition? I do not know. All I knew was that I was trapped, with tears running down my cheeks and a voice that let out a wailing sound. In my loneliness, I fell to pieces, as soon I shut the door to the outside world and to any witness of my brief madness. I could hold it together when people were around, and I guess that made me semi-sane. I did the only thing I have found to help me in those moments and that is to pick up a play and read it aloud. The Greek Tragedies seemed big enough in their archaic nature to mirror my own raw emotions and I found myself closest to the characters that talk to the gods. They made my own talking and wailing to God seem almost normal and therefore ok. As Antigone proclaims:

Look at me, my native citizens
as I go on my final journey
as I gaze upon the sunlight one last time, which I'll never see
again—for Hades, who brings all people to their final sleep, leads
me on, while I'm still living, down the shores of Acheron.

Proclaiming these words calmed me down, my breath deepened, and I felt like I knew how to behave because I wasn't myself anymore. I had a script that told me what to feel, what to say and what to do.

I used to be so overcome with fear about how to act in this world that I even carried my scripts around with me for comfort, and when stressed out, I would recite them. Acting made life fun and more manageable for me. It helped me positively cope through things. For me, performing used to be more than just expressing myself, being recognized, trying to change the world, and touching people's emotions, it was a necessity to use my emotions for my own Catharsis as well as for the benefit of others to find themselves in the character or at the very least to entertain them.

Acting made me explore my own fears and hopes in a passionate and intensified way. But acting also had me over the edge at times, and that depended on the character and the approach I used to give them life. It takes great skill and practice to get into the skin of a character on the one hand, and on the other, to develop enough detachment to get out of it and save your sanity.

I have seen many colleagues unable to do that, who ultimately go into a form of madness, alcohol and drug use, and even suicide. Acting out fears, hopes, and dreams that are partly my own is a great form of expression, but that doesn't mean the fears go away, sometimes they multiply.

In my career, I have suffered a lot from anxiety and stage fright. Before I knew any better, I would stuff myself with food, or drink too much coffee, or find any distraction so I would not feel the anxiety rise before I had to go on stage or in front of the camera. The fear was always that people would judge me and I would fail them and myself. I would either feel like a million bucks or like a cockroach.

The thing that saved my life dramatically in terms of respite, peace, and keeping somewhat sane (although that depends on the individual interpretation) was learning about yoga and meditation. I was very fortunate to be exposed to it while I was still in my teens, and its study has deepened over the years and has led me to teaching others.

I first became aware of how shallow my natural breath was through the Alexander technique and the Feldenkreis Method, which was taught at Drama school. Through the application of these techniques and later on through Yoga and Pranayama, the science of breath, I learned how to deepen my everyday breath pattern and recognize whenever I would hold my breath or breathe shallowly. This happens to me in stressful situations and sometimes in social settings. The fear of not fitting in is a major anxiety, and I know I am not alone with that one. The theater, home of many different people and lost souls, made me feel less extreme and less different and, combined with yoga, I found myself on a quest to reunite with myself.

Yoga and Meditation invited Grace into my life, which entered just at that moment of seemingly unfathomable darkness. It is said that the bird of liberation glides on two wings: self- effort and grace. It can show up as the hand extended to us to help us crawl out of the cave of isolation and communicate with the world around us with a renewed sense of hope. Yoga brings flexibility to your physical body and mind, Meditation puts you in touch with your own depth, Breath control changes your glandular secretion and can literally change your state of being in seconds through specific Pranayama (breathing techniques). All these efforts lead you naturally to the study of the Self and will reveal to you the beauty that resides within you.

I found some coping mechanisms to be so helpful when experiencing anxiety. Breathing is so important. Deepen your breath. It sounds like a no-brainer to most, but it is something that we all forget to do. Also, observing my body and focusing on my muscles for any form of tension helps. I also recognize my thinking. When I catch myself in any negative thoughts like, "I am stupid," I turn it around and think, "I am smart." This can seem really weird at the beginning, and if you have to fake feeling smart, fake it! My great acting teacher and coach Susan Batson used to say, "Fake it till you make it."

Unfortunately, we don't get taught these things in school. I believe that learning how to train our mind should be a major subject in education. Why wait until we are so riddled with fears and disorders to "re-train" our mind? We need to learn how to take responsibility for our state of being and, to do that, we have to go deep within our inherent wisdom, which meditation can do with practice and patience. The mind is just as important as the body, and we have to start a normal conversation about it.

As Mahatma Gandhi put it so beautifully, "Be the change you want to see in the world." You have that power and strength from within to do that; sometimes you just need some useful tools to help you through, and that's what yoga does for me.

∼

Nicole said it right, "Be the change you want to see in the world." I've heard that from time to time and I think it's sometimes hard for us to believe we are actually making a difference. Sometimes it's nice to have the reassurance of others, especially mentors and that is what Nicole has become to me. I learned breathing tips from her in times of high-anxiety moments, but I also learned the importance of continuing to be myself and literally take in every amazing moment. But her testimonial doesn't do justice because I was learning things from Nicole even when she didn't know. Her Facebook posts have her traveling, taking part in many different yoga events, connecting with amazing people and spreading words of wisdom for others. It's sometimes hard to believe that I've met so many amazing and inspiring people like Nicole and the people you met in my book. It's also hard to believe I experienced so much at such a young age. However, to be filled with inspiration from others stories and be able to share my story to help at least one person, that's one of the greatest gifts I have been given. Whether you want to believe it or not, things have happened and will continue to happen in your life and you will continue to meet people everyday. The things and people may be unexpected and more extraordinary than you could imagine, but it's up to you to live out the moments, instead of saying, "This could never happen to me," because anything is possible.

Chapter Twenty-Five

Say what you need to say

We all have things we want to say, things we regret saying, and things we regret not saying, and it's important that we use our voices to stand up for others and ourselves. It's really important to say what you mean and mean what you say, but for goodness sake please don't be mean with what you say; you never know what it can do. The world is too fragile and in need of all the positive energy it can get.

In the past, I had a lot issues with saying the wrong thing and never the right thing at the right time, mostly so I could just be noticed. Thankfully, today that's a different story most of the time. I decided to use this chapter as my "tell you all the things I want to say with no regrets hopefully at the right time" kind of chapter.

The Power of One: I think sometimes one specific thing has the power to change everything more than we want to believe, especially when that one thing is very negative. Whether it's the last text you send while driving or the decision to bully someone else to make yourself feel better, those things all have the power to change things in many ways.

My question is, "Why waste any of your power on the negative?" Seriously, think about it: what if the last thing you said to someone was, "I hate you!" and they died that same day, and you had no way of taking it back?

Yes, we say "That won't happen" so nonchalantly, but seriously, how can we really know? You want to believe the person (whether you were close to them or not) knew deep down you didn't mean it, because unfortunately it's normal to get angry and take things out on people. But if life is so unpredictable and we fear death, knowing it can come at any time, why do we waste even two seconds of our lives making both our life and someone else's so miserable at times?

Don't forget just how much power we all have, but also how

much regret we can find. One thing can change everything and affect not only us, but other innocent people as well. Unfortunately, things can go wrong and we may not have full control, but we still have the power to change things for the better. We have a great power both as an individual and together. If we unite, we can make positive changes in this world one person, one act, and one good deed at a time.

> *I can see it in your eyes that there is trouble inside*
> *I don't know why but I figured I'd stop by*
> *To see if you were okay before I got on my way*
> *I can sense it friend that you think the pain won't end*
> *But together, tackling fear, we will get through my dear*

Jealousy: After speaking to a group of students at a school outside of Philadelphia, a girl approached me looking very sad and uncomfortable. She explained that she had never felt pretty and was jealous of what the popular girls looked like and the lives they had. She felt self-conscious because people would say mean things about her.

It took me back to high school, when I was the girl trying to be everything for everyone and losing sight of who I was, and becoming so jealous of the popular crowd. Sometimes we waste too much time being jealous of the life and things others have, and sometimes we even find ourselves spreading rumors about others when we don't actually know the whole truth. We don't truly know what other people go through or how their lives really are.

I admit there were times I joined in on spreading rumors and picking on others as part of the vicious cycle of someone making fun of me. I thought if I made fun of someone else, it would make me feel better. I knew it was wrong and, during most of my high school career, I worked on ending that cycle, even though the personal issues I faced didn't stop. I always wanted to have good comebacks and now, thinking about it, there is one that makes me laugh, but is dead on if someone is saying something bad about you: "Can you give me a second so I can grab a pen and paper to take notes, because I didn't know you were an expert on my life, and I'm learning so much I didn't know."

Even today, I admit that I still struggle at times with being jealous of others. It's not that I'm not happy for them or myself, but sometimes it's frustrating when you work hard, know you have the ability, and aren't given the same chances or get the same breaks. I think it's a natural thing to feel jealous, but it shouldn't stop you from being you and doing the things you want to do, whether or not you think someone else is doing them already.

I'm just finding that in general the more we dwell, compare, and complain, the more we miss out on making our lives the way we want. Live your life, no one else's. I know it's easier said than done, but the more you envy and try for someone else's life, the more you miss out on the beauty in front of you—and you may miss opportunities that are knocking on your door.

Remember, if you personally don't take steps or do something different, then things won't change. You were born an original, so don't ever live your life to die as a copy of someone else's life.

I said all of this to the girl I spoke to, the one who thought she wasn't pretty or good enough. I knew it wasn't going to change the way she thought right then, but hopefully letting her know I'd been there and sometimes still found myself there would give her some hope.

By the end of the day, after doing five more speeches to over two hundred students, I passed that same girl in the hallway. I remembered her tears as she had spoken privately to me that morning. She did something that had me in tears. I mentioned that I sometimes write positive things on my wrist to help me when I'm down and also empower myself to make it through the hard times. As she showed me "beautiful" written on her hand, I started to tear up. I realized on this day, through her strength, she was able to take a step, fight the jealous thoughts she had, and not try to be a copy at that moment, but just her own, beautiful self—inside and out.

Judging: It's so natural for people to judge others. Sometimes you get thoughts that aren't nice, and it's easy to get upset with yourself for even allowing them to cross your mind. In my opinion, yes, even having the thoughts in the first place isn't great, but it's what you do with those thoughts that matters most.

Experts say that ninety-three percent of communication is given by nonverbal cues. Sometimes we make faces and gestures at people, both intentionally and unintentionally, that can affect others more than we truly intend. Be aware of your actions and mannerisms around others. Also, spreading rumors, posting things online, and joining in with the negative remarks and actions of the crowd toward another person isn't right either. It's really important to watch not only what you say about others, but also your mannerisms. Remember: roses have thorns, but that just means thorns have roses too, so don't be too quick to judge.

What happens if the thoughts do stay in your head, but you now have a negative first impression of someone, and that impression causes you to make a judgment? The issue I have is that we all have bad moments and things that affect us. Unfortunately, we sometimes take things out on others, or others see us acting out in a bad, mean, or negative way. This may cause people to gain first impressions of others that they hold on to.

I remember when I was twelve years old and my softball team was collecting donations outside of a convenience store to help support our trip to represent Pennsylvania in the softball nationals in Florida. A memory of one man has stuck with me till this day. Here we were, innocent twelve years olds in our softball uniforms asking for donations from complete strangers with the risk of being turned down. As I asked for a donation from this man, he looked over, gave me a mean face, shrugged his shoulders, made a grunting noise, and walked into the store.

I remember hearing one of the parents say, "What a mean person, what crawled up his sleeve?" I was nervous to have to see him again, but as he walked out of the store, he reached out and put something in my bucket. I thanked him and, as he drove away, I realized he had just donated $20 to my team.

I ran over to the parent who had made the negative comment and explained what had happened; he looked surprised. I remember wondering why the man was so mean initially and what had changed him. I would never know the reasons, but I did know one thing that stuck with me: judging someone by a first impression isn't always accurate, and fighting fire with fire doesn't work either. I could have stepped on the guy's foot or kicked him for being so mean (hey, I was a kid), but instead I just tried to smile and let him know I wouldn't hold it against him.

Later in my life, there was another story that stuck with me. I met an amazing girl named Audra McLaughlin who sang her inspiring anti-bullying song "Breaking Through" at a youth event called "MyFest". After hearing the song I was struck by the empowering message and even worked with a Philly film contact to try to produce a music video for the song but it was never finished. Recently, Audra auditioned for NBC's "The Voice" and had all four chairs turn to her powerful rendition of John Prine's "Angel from Montgomery." She is now being mentored by American Country Singer Blake Shelton on "Team Blake." However, her beautiful performance wasn't what hit me most, it was the story behind her will and fight to improve her musical talents and follow her dreams over the years.

I had always wondered if there was a story behind Audra's song "Breaking Through." The words of the song read:

> *You're walking down the hallway*
> *And all you hear is whispering*
> *As everyone stops to stare*
> *Nobody comes to rescue you now*
> *Building walls between us*
> *Will anyone ever break through*
> *The vicious cycle they have put us through*
> *But you have something they don't*
> *And you have something the world wishes they could have*
> *If you would just stand up*
> *And let go of everyone on your shoulders*
> *You would finally break through the walls that have been*
> *surrounding you*

Audra went on to tell me that she was bullied in elementary school because she was put in separate small classes, which were considered the "stupid classes." She talked about just wanting to fit in, but wasn't popular enough for anyone to want to be her friend in school especially being in those classes. She mentioned a couple of girls she used to hang out with who she thought were her best friends. The issue was the girls were also friends with some of the popular kids and when they were in school they would act like they weren't friends with Audra and that she didn't exist. This really upset me that this talented, beautiful girl had to go through this just because she needed a bit more guidance in her studies. Audra mentioned that over the years music became her escape from everything. She said she tried other things like sports, but music was her best positive coping method. She started focusing on music and song writing and saw others experiencing issues with fitting in and being bullied just as she did and that's when she became inspired to write her song, "Breaking Through."

I was so inspired by Audra's will and self-confidence to not only share her story but share a message with the world that it is not okay to bully and judge others for being different and to let people going through anything know that they were not alone. Now, Audra is on "The Voice" sharing her beautiful gift of music with the world and inspiring others to be themselves, follow their dreams and never give up. I am so proud and inspired by her.

Hopefully the next time you come across a situation like this, you'll give someone another chance and hold back your judgment until you see the bigger picture.

So keep judging a book by its cover
And not hearing the words from down under
Maybe you should read in between the lines
Because you'll be sure to uncover more than meets the eye
Yea more than you'll see
Yea more than you'll find
And instead of judging try being kind
Because sometimes our world is so harsh and blind
And we miss out on stuff that's one of a kind

With myself, not by myself: I've heard people mention the trouble they have with going out to a movie or restaurant by themselves. I think it's completely normal, although I used to be afraid to go anywhere alone, mostly because I was afraid to be judged and see someone I knew while I was alone.

Over time, it's gotten a lot easier for me. I love sitting at a coffee shop looking around, taking in the scenery, or grabbing a bite to eat at a restaurant on my break from speaking. Some of my inspiration came from friends who could so easily do it, but a lot of it came from my becoming comfortable in my own skin. There will always be some negative thoughts that you have about yourself—like thinking that you look terrible in a certain outfit or that your hair looks like a bird's nest—but ultimately, if you are comfortable with yourself, things can get much easier.

It took me a while to get to this point, and with each step, I learned to love my flaws and express my personality through the things I loved. Also, once I started really being myself, I was able to find the best friends that loved me for me and not who I was trying to be. I also found the love of my life who loves me for me and continues to help my self-love grow each and every day. People feed off of confidence and the expression you give of yourself. Even when you're by yourself, it's amazing the people you can meet. Don't be afraid to smile at someone when you're sitting or walking alone. Don't be afraid to see your favorite movie and laugh out loud with no one next to you. And don't be afraid to wear that bright outfit you were too nervous to wear.

I took a leap of faith when staying in LA for four more days after my speaking engagement. I was nervous because I didn't know many people, but I was excited for the adventure and my newfound freedom, now that I was feeling comfortable in my own skin.

My first night alone was scary in a gross, scary hotel in downtown LA, which isn't the best of places. But during my speaking engagement, I met an amazing girl named Allison, who said she knew right away we would be friends because of my personality and the impression I gave her. I felt the same way about her. I wasn't alone at any point after the second day of my trip. I not only was able to stay at Allison's apartment, but we became great friends and still are to this day.

Allison also was able to take much from that trip. You heard her story earlier, where she mentioned it was the first time in a while she had felt alive and like herself. We both took a leap of faith, fearing judgment, but because we both stayed true to ourselves when first meeting, we built a great friendship that we still have today.

Although I enjoyed my mini-adventure of being alone for that first day, it was amazing what being myself did for the rest of my trip. I later learned from a good friend, "When you're out alone, you're not by yourself, you're *with* yourself, and you're pretty awesome, so enjoy those times."

It all makes sense to me. Enjoy being yourself just with you and the place you desire to go every now and then, but remember people can sense you genuinely being you, and that can lead to many amazing, unexpected things! Also keep in mind that life gets busy: don't forget to make time for yourself and the ones you love, look up at the clouds, breathe in air, say thank you, dance in the middle of an open field, wear crazy colors together, shake your *bootay*, ask to sit next to someone at a restaurant—whatever you want, just make sure you live a little and be yourself.

Fear of failure: To this day, I'm learning that living in the fear of failure won't get me anywhere. I'm still afraid to make mistakes and disappoint people that I feel expect a lot out of me. It's a back-and-forth battle because I'm trying to live life minute by minute, but when I hear comments like, "OMG, you're going to be famous someday," it seems to trigger that fear of failure, which actually stops me from taking steps toward my dreams and the things I want to do.

Don't get me wrong, it's an amazing compliment. But after hearing the complete opposite from others—like, "When are you going to get a real job?"—it becomes very confusing.

I'm sure many people have felt this way and wanted to think of the perfect comeback. Mine at the moment is thinking, "There will always be people who say you can't, and that's when you turn around and say 'watch me.' Then you just go and do it with the utmost respect."

I can remember reading a quote from George Bernard Shaw, who said, "A life spent making mistakes is not only more honorable, but more useful than a life spent not doing anything." I also remember reading something similar from Randy Pausch's book, *The Last Lecture*. He mentioned that he would rather hire someone who had made mistakes and failed than someone who did not try, because he felt the person who failed had more experience.

After thinking for a bit, I realized that if Albert Einstein hadn't failed with his theories and tried again; if Dr. Seuss hadn't been turned down by more than twenty publishers and courageously submitted his work to one more; and if Michael Jordan hadn't got cut from his high school basketball team and worked even harder to get into the NBA, then our world wouldn't be as it is today.

The fear of something will always be there, whether it's the fear of failure or something else, but fear is a false alarm that we listen to way too often. Don't ever be afraid to make mistakes. You have the great possibility to learn and grow from them more than you can even imagine, and the storybook of your life isn't fully written yet.

Many people have asked me questions like, "Where do you draw the line?" and "When do you stop?"

I hate hearing those things. My initial thought is, "Worry about your own life." But then I realize people are truly looking out for my well-being, and I can respect that. Here's the thing: I know there is much more that I haven't experienced, especially since I'm only twenty-six, but sometimes I wish I could know what the future holds. Until I met my boyfriend Rich, I was in pursuit of something that would make me feel completely alive and purposeful all the time. It was like I was missing a piece of me and needed to fill it somehow. Meeting Rich has literally saved me and helped fill that void. What I'm learning is that the more and more I experience through my journey, the more I am realizing it's not all about that big "it," but about everything in between.

Many things will happen within your life, and success isn't measured by money and one huge thing, but by the journey. With each up and down, you become stronger in some way and find some hope somewhere. You also meet and connect with different people who can bring new opportunities and joys into your life. Sometimes they may even save you just as Mary Beth and Rich have saved my life on different occasions.

Just think, I had no singing or writing experience in 2010; now in 2011, 2012, and 2013, I have met talented musicians who have helped me find a voice and inspired me to write my first three songs, "HopeStrong," "Spread the Love" and "Love is the Answer." I also just recorded a music video for "HopeStrong" that shares the important messages of stepping up for others and not bullying. Amazingly, some youth I spoke to took part in the project, which made it such a humbling experience.

Yes, I still experience fear; yes, I am scared of failing at times. But the positive experiences I've had and the people I've met in the process have helped me become stronger than fear itself, so I refuse to give up.

I think my musician friend Matt Santry sums this up in his song "I Just Blinked."

I just blinked, now it's gone 64 and I'm still going strong
I'm grateful for all I have, but I spent all my youth on worry and someday just never came
So get up and live like you wanted to, like you wanted to see, like you wanted to dance, like you wanted to go, like you wanted to be

That storybook ending: I was feeling stuck for far too long. Having no hope that things would change for the better. I'm not sure if it was the issues in my family, the struggles with my work or my OCD and depression or many things combined, but I can confidently say that through meeting and being inspired by people all the time, I knew somehow things would be the way they were supposed to be and turn out better than okay. It's funny—people say I inspire them, but I'm finding that I'm inspired by many amazing people each and every day.

As cliché as it sounds, the truth is that with every step, whether forward, back, left, or right, we are led in some direction, and although it may not be the direction we want, what happens during that right or wrong turn will allow us to experience something that becomes a part of our overall journey.

It is my hope that we can all somehow see our sacrifices as different turns in our journeys, our mistakes as potential lessons learned, our pursuing as determination for creating a reality that we believe in, and our regrets as different decisions that we made at one point in time that we have the chance to make better.

We all truly do live and learn through life, whether we see it directly or not. People have asked me many times, "If you could, would you live without OCD and depression?" I always hesitate to answer because, yes, I do wish sometimes (okay, more than sometimes) that I didn't have to deal with those issues, but then I remember that living without OCD and depression wouldn't guarantee life would be easier, just different.

Even through my overburdening obsessions and compulsions and feeling the physical ramifications of anxiety and depression at times, I am honestly blessed, proud, and grateful for the life I have. I won't say things are perfect, because I still battle OCD and depression, and my family dynamic is still rebuilding itself. But I am reassured by the fact that no family, no person, no problem is ever alone in their battles; we all go through "a something."

I've found that every story in the world is different, but also that each person within his or her own story has worth and some sense of hope. I hope you won't feel defined by one thing that has happened or feel there is no hope left for the change you desperately want. I also am not going to sugar coat everything and say that your life will be perfect after reading this book and that you will find yourself inspired by everything, every second of every day.

What I do hope is that you take a step back, look around, and realize that everything you think you know or is found isn't, everything you think is can change, but living in fear will leave you missing out on so much. I hope you know that your own story is important in this world, so don't let anyone ever take that away from you and don't be embarrassed to share it anyway you want to.

I'm finding it really hard to write an ending for this book for a few reasons. For one, I keep meeting people who share their inspiring stories with me, and I am so moved that I want to put each one of them in

213

this book. Second, I have wanted this book to be finished for so long now and I was afraid to miss putting in something crucial. With that worry, I can honestly see why it took so long because things are falling into place in the right moment. I think it is all happening at the exact time it's supposed to. Meeting the love of my life Rich is the number one example, but another perfect example has to do with my little brother Kenny. He is just 23 and now into his second month of recovery from addiction through many failed rehab tries, many family fights, many times we didn't know where he was or if he was alive and many times we couldn't even trust him. Before I couldn't even mention his struggle and it wasn't due to embarrassment, but I do admit I was so angry and sad because it is my little brother and I couldn't save him. Kenny is now working very hard to stay healthy and in recovery. He looks better than I've seen him in years. He was just diagnosed with Depression and is now finding positive coping, taking his needed steps and taking one day at a time. In some time, Kenny wants to share his story letting youth know that addiction doesn't just affect the one addicted, but affects those around him or her and makes you miss out on so much of life. I lost my brother for sometime and I am glad to have him back and even more hopeful that one day through his hard work he will stand next to me on stage and share his story with youth letting them know there is hope and that recovery is possible. Aside from this, the final reason and I think the biggest reason I can't find an ending to my book is that with each event that passes in life, I'm realizing that there is no perfect fairytale ending that we sometimes strive for, but amazing moments that happen throughout our lives.

If you did ask me to pick my fairytale ending, I couldn't do it in complete confidence, because I know I don't want to miss out on all the other parts of my life. But if I had to pick one, maybe it would be me on a beach in the fall, with happy tears streaming down my face as wild horses run past me into the sunset. The only sounds would be the crashing of the waves and the galloping of the horses' hooves as they pounded the white, glistening sand. I would be staring in amazement, remembering every face of every person I'd ever spoken to and the sense of hope and strength in each one. And Rich, the love of my life, would be right by my side, holding my hand and supporting me like he always does.

In movies the fairy tale ending as we see it is directly followed by credits with no evidence of the ups and downs the characters would face after the *fairytale moment*, so it's impossible to say this is my definite fairy tale ending. But I already know that parts of my fairytale have shown themselves through the many amazing experiences I've had and the many inspiring people I have met along my way.

We all should all let ourselves dream of our own fairytale ending, because the truth is, we can have at least some of those things in our lives. It may not be all the time or forever or at the very end, but your dreams and wants are possible at many different times in your life.

One of the main lessons I've learned is that you can't appreciate the good without the bad, the happy without the sad. My wish is that you are able to find that time in your life to appreciate the good around you and live it like a fairytale dream, but also that you will stop making excuses that halt your progress, as I did when I began to write this book. There is no guarantee for a tomorrow; the more we wait, live in fear or push back dreams or the things we want, the stronger regret becomes, and the less opportunity and hope we give ourselves to experience happiness and live our dreams, whatever they may be.

Life can be difficult, and there are many times we may question why horrible things happen, especially after something so amazing does happen. Just remember that you are not alone in anything you go through and that it is okay to ask for help. Life is filled with ups and down, beauties and beasts, but it's your journey, your life, so never lose sight of your dreams, your uniqueness and gifts, your power to help others. Always remember that you can never be replicated, you are never alone, and hope is stronger than fear.

Also, don't forget to acknowledge and thank that passing stranger or person who held a door for you or smiled as you passed. You never know, maybe that's just one of those inspiring people you are supposed to meet in your life.

My grandmother always says, "The rainbows of life follow the storm" and I try everyday to live by those wise words. And knowing that and the fact that I have the support of my family and friends makes everything a lot easier and my journey clearer.

So to me there is no real ending, I just see it as the amazing journey of life to be continued...

Stay #hopestrong and always remember #Umatter.

Photo Album

*Melissa and her boyfriend Rich, volunteering at the non-profit
organization Minding Your Mind awareness event.
(www.mindingyourmind.org)*

Melissa speaking at youth day - Pennsylvania Capital in Harrisburg, PA.

Childhood friends, Melissa and Mary Beth at their 7th and 8th grade dance. In high school, Mary Beth became Melissa's hero and helped her get through one of the toughest times in her life.

Students taking Melissa's motto #hopestrong and inspiring other students to see that their story matters, and to take a stand against bullying.

Check out Melissa's anti-bullying music video for her song "HopeStrong" and purchase #hopestrong bracelets at www.melissahopely.com.

Melissa and Philadelphia Mayor Michael A. Nutter

"Hopestrong" motto and music video

Kristen East, Mariel Hemingway, Melissa Ann Hopely

Photo courtesy of: Aimee Marie Photography
www.aimeemariephotography.com

About Melissa Ann Hopely

Melissa Ann Hopely is a well-accomplished international motivational speaker and mental health, anti-bullying and suicide prevention advocate. She has been speaking for four years reaching over 50,000 audience members who consisted of children, young adults, teens, adults and senior citizens in more than 10 states, 20 cities and two countries. She has been a featured speaker in Philadelphia and the surrounding Philadelphia area, NJ, NYC, CO, KS, San Francisco and Los Angeles, CA, NYC, Rochester, NY, MA, VA, and Toronto, Canada. Melissa speaks with Minding Your Mind's Free Mental Health Speaking Program and Neon Entertainment and is on the board of the Philadelphia Chapter of the American Foundation for Suicide Prevention (AFSP). She has been recognized for her advocacy work with numerous awards including the honorable mention Jerry Greenspan Student Voice of Mental Health Award given by the Jed Foundation of America at a gala in June 2009 in New York City along with an advocacy award in Chester County, PA.

Melissa has appeared on several local radio and television programs including 99.5 WJBR's Sunday Morning Show, the CW Philly's Speak Up and NBC 10's *Beyond Bullying* Special. She was also a featured extra as Mark Wahlberg's science student in M. Night Shyamalan's film, *The Happening* and is involved with numerous national mental health and anti-bullying organizations, which have given her the chance to host and attend many events where she has worked with celebrities and public figures such as Brittany Snow, Joey Pantoliano, Ron Howard, Glenn Close, Nicole Ansari and Mariel Hemingway.

Melissa recently completed the role of Whitney in the suicide prevention and anti-bullying play, "When the Smoked Cleared" and is now working with the writer of the play, Shenille Latrice on the "Peace in the City" Tour for the organization iChoose2live. Currently, Melissa is working on original music that embody her powerful messages of hope, the fact that we all matter, have a story and are never alone. Melissa just finished recording an anti-bullying music video to her first single, "HopeStrong." The word #hopestrong has become a positive motto that is quickly spreading and encouraging her ever growing youth following.

For more information, please visit:

www.melissahopely.com
www.teamhopestrong.com
www.mindingyourmind.org

Resources and Help

Mental Health and Suicide Prevention

Minding Your Mind: www.mindingyourmind.org

American Foundation for Suicide Prevention: www.afsp.org

The Jed Foundation: www.jedfoundation.org

Active Minds: www.activeminds.org

NAMI: www.nami.org

You Matter, Don't Quit: www.facebook.com/youmatterdontquit

Walking With Nathaniel: www.walkingwithnathaniel.org

International OCD Foundation: www.ocfoundation.org

National Suicide Prevention Lifeline: 1-800-273-TALK (8255) www.suicidepreventionlifeline.org

Bring Change 2 Mind: www.bringchange2mind.org

No Kidding Me Too: www.nkm2.org

Bullying

The Trevor Project: www.thetrevorproject.org

Stand for the Silent: www.standforthesilent.org

iChoose2Live: www.ichoose2live.com

Stop Bullying: www.stopbullying.gov

The National Center for Bullying Prevention: www.pacer.org/bullying

CPSIA information can be obtained
at www.ICGtesting.com
Printed in the USA
LVOW12s0014090617
537491LV00001B/87/P